This Is Living

Lynn Redgrave
This Is Living

A DUTTON BOOK

DUTTON

Published by the Penguin Group
Penguin Books USA Inc., 375 Hudson Street, New York, New York 10014, U.S.A.
Penguin Books Ltd, 27 Wrights Lane, London W8 5TZ, England
Penguin Books Australia Ltd, Ringwood, Victoria, Australia
Penguin Books Canada Ltd, 2801 John Street, Markham, Ontario, Canada L3R 1B4
Penguin Books (N.Z.) Ltd, 182–190 Wairau Road, Auckland 10, New Zealand

Penguin Books Ltd, Registered Offices:
Harmondsworth, Middlesex, England

First published by Dutton, an imprint of New American Library,
a division of Penguin Books USA Inc.
Distributed in Canada by McClelland & Stewart Inc.

First Printing, May, 1991
10 9 8 7 6 5 4 3 2 1

REGISTERED TRADEMARK—MARCA REGISTRADA

Library of Congress Cataloging-in-Publication Data
Redgrave, Lynn, 1943–
    This is living / by Lynn Redgrave.
        p.   cm.
    ISBN 0-525-24987-7
    1. Low-calorie diet diet—Recipes. 2. Redgrave, Lynn, 1943—
Health.   I. Title.
RM222.2.R434   1991
613.2'092—dc20   90-23706
[B]   CIP

Printed in the United States of America
Set in New Baskerville

Designed by Steven N. Stathakis

For John

*Who has opened my eyes to myself,
has been a part of every good
thing that has ever happened
to me, and has loved me
through fat and through thin*

Contents

Acknowledgments

Writing this, my first book, has been a fascinating learning experience for me. I want to acknowledge the help and support of the following people and organizations.

First, Foodways National, the H.J. Heinz Company, and DDB Needham Worldwide Advertising Agency, for embracing the notion of the title of this book. Thanks to Jerry Herrick, who was then President of Foodways in Boise, Idaho, for having the audacity to report to his company that the crazy lady he had just met playing Sister Mary Ignatius on stage in Hollywood might make an acceptable spokesperson. He and Kathy, his wife, have become our good friends.

Special thanks to Barbara Warmflash of Weight Watchers International for her expert advice and guidance, as well as for her assistance in coordinating the many facets of preparing this book for publication. Thanks also to the staff of the Publications Management Department and the Program Development Department, and of course to the entire staff of Weight Watchers International in Jericho, New York, who let me into their kitchens and generously gave me their time.

Special thanks to Mel Berger, my literary agent, who initially ploughed his way through my hopeless handwriting and thought this might be a book worth reading, and then to my editor, Matt Sartwell, who patiently brought me through to its completion.

Thanks to Dr. Roslyn B. Alfin-Slater of the UCLA School of Public Health and to Dr. Judith Ashley, who helped develop my attitude toward nutrition.

A number of friends and colleagues generously shared their weight-loss stories with me, so my grateful thanks to Dom De Luise, Richard Simmons, Florine Mark, Richard Karron, Al Goldstein, David Graden, Sandra Ryden, Peggy Hall, and Emily Benham. Thanks to Jean Louis Rodrigue for his expertise on the Alexander Technique, and to Serena Ponter for the tips on Massage Therapy.

Thanks to Marion Finkler, who did some of the early word processing while I was "treading the boards" on Broadway, and then to Lori de Los Santos and Nicolette Hannah, who continued the process in California.

A number of photographers on both sides of the Atlantic generously gave me carte blanche to reproduce their work, so my thanks go to Martha Swope, Henry Grossman, Lewis Moreley, Araldo di Crollalanza, and Michael Crawford. Also to my friend Zoë Dominic in London, for digging out a nostalgic array of her 1965 National Theatre *Love for Love* photographs so that I could choose the one of myself and Laurence Olivier.

Thanks to my parents, Michael and Rachel Redgrave, who by each writing their own autobiographies, *In My Mind's Eye* and *Life Among the Redgraves,* when well into their seventies inspired me to think I could try a little sooner. Thanks to my son, Benjamin Clark, and my daughters, Kelly and Annabel Clark, for being proud of me!

Lastly, and most importantly, my loving thanks to my husband, John Clark, who encouraged, inspired, provoked, cajoled, pushed, and just plain "made me do it." As my editor and collaborator, he got up at ungodly times of the night to put my new material into the computer and magically transformed my longhand scrawl into a new printout for the morning.

Topanga Canyon, California

Foreword

As an actor, I go from character to character. At first they stand apart, alone and aloof, strangers in my life, without form, like ghosts. But after a while, I find I am able to see them, how they dress and walk and talk. I begin to uncover their strengths and weaknesses, and slowly they materialize as ideals. Yet our individual presences must merge, their image must become one with me. That is my job, what I am paid to do. It is also my passion.

The successful achievement of this union is by no means a foregone conclusion, but if I have worked hard, and if I am lucky, I can make it happen.

At last my day comes, my actor's supreme moment. When I can begin to think and breathe as that person, I know I have broken through. Let the curtain rise!

Like just about everybody, I've spent much of my real life going through a similar process, struggling to bring the me that I so much want to be together with the me I had settled for. This struggle can be a trip along a rocky road, for it's a part of the challenge that something always goes wrong. The details of our stories are different. In my case, I had become trapped in a compulsive addiction to food. Me and my ideal were kept apart by a power that I only half jokingly used to call my "Fat Ogre." Fat Ogre had come to stand for a force that messed up my life, and I thought I'd have to wrestle with it forever.

But I won my fight, and with the help of Weight Watchers banished my ogre to oblivion.

In my commercials I say, *"This Is Living."* For me, that statement seems to say it all. It says that we can be freed from our past, from whatever it is that's holding us back, so that we can feel good about ourselves, and be able to behold a wonderful future for the rest of our lives.

My Story

Prologue

September 1983. Two a.m. and I can't sleep. That flight from California always throws my system off.

I'm making tea in the kitchen at my mother's cottage. Wilks Water, her special love, her folly, lies nestled in a gentle fold of a serene little Hampshire village not an hour's drive from London. This used to be her idyllic weekend escape, but now both Mum and Dad live here full-time. Mum's hopefully asleep on her side of the cottage, Dad's certainly asleep on his. He won't waken; he's taken his Parkinson's disease pills and we won't see him now till nine in the morning. I take my cup of tea, in the hope that it will calm my mind, into the dining room, once the scene of lively family gatherings. Except now it is littered with papers, piles of books, and photographs, the research for the manuscript of Dad's final book, In My Mind's Eye, *finished at last thanks to the efforts of my brother, Corin.*

I look at a picture of us all together as a family, a publicity shot dated 1947. Dad is dressed in actorishly casual clothes, holding the elegant hand of Vanessa, who's in ballet dress

3

and standing en pointe *on one leg. They're in the fore-ground, and farther back, sitting on the steps of our stately riverside home in Chiswick, are Corin, Mother, and me. Everyone is smiling, but not me. My face is round and glum, arms wrapped around my dog.*

I pick through a stack of papers and sit down by what is left of last night's fire. I read a letter or two and feel a little guilty. More photos, Mum and Dad in happier times. Dad in his many disguises—kings and common men, heroes, villains. Lear and Shylock. Hamlet, Uncle Harry.

Memories.

I shouldn't be looking, and yet this is my history, this is where I come from. This, I guess, made me what I am today. I allow myself a small laugh.

Here are his diaries, and I look up a few entries.

His feelings, his fears, and his friendships are chronicled in a neat hand. Achievements and failures. A drinking problem.

The clock in the living room chimes quietly, ting . . . ting . . . ting. Three o'clock.

One last snap as a spark flies from the grate.

Here. His journal for 1943—that's the year of my birth!

Apprehensively, I turn to my day, March 8th. A long, long entry. Last night's air raid. A day at rehearsal. A good performance in the play, it was Turgenev's A Month in the Country *at the St. James's. Who came around to see him afterward. An appointment at the Garrick Club.*

But no birth. No Lynn.

The house is silent. I feel overwhelmed and sad. Suddenly my mind is clear, as I choose to leap back down the lanes of my memory, events falling patternless like autumn leaves.

1

Childhood

'm the third and last child in a family of actors. My grandparents on my father's side were actors, my grandmother's father too. Wonderful, colorful characters. Fortunatus Augustine Scudemore, Daisy Scudemore, Roy Redgrave (his billing, "The Dramatic Cock o' the North"). My father, Michael, was already a shining star by the time I was born. Brilliant, volatile, dashing, sensitive, selfish, erratic, intellectually superior, and intensely shy. He had outstanding good looks, the embodiment of the leading man. Plus a blazing talent for transformation that allowed him to be both matinee idol and character actor. He rose rapidly to the top, along with his peers Laurence Olivier, John Gielgud, Ralph Richardson, and Alec Guinness, and became an international celebrity with his first film, Hitchcock's 1938 *The Lady Vanishes.*

He was also bisexual, in an era when such a revelation could not only ruin a career, but put you behind bars. He married a well-known actress, Rachel Kempson, and begat three children, Vanessa, Corin, and me, in that order.

Our mother was and is an exquisitely beautiful woman, but possesses none of the vanity that so often accompanies great beauty. I think she has always been quite disbelieving of this attribute. A loving mother, she did her best to keep our lives simple and structured, to be a safe haven in the midst of often stormy seas.

We had a privileged upbringing. When I was three years old we moved to a big old mansion of a house in London by the Thames. We had a sprawling, seemingly endless garden behind, a cook, a chauffeur, a gardener, a secretary, and a blessed round, bow-legged Norfolk Nanny. My sister and brother were articulate, healthy, opinionated, and outgoing. In contrast, I was desperately shy, constantly sickly, and anemic. At least I had my beloved Nanny, my imagination, and my dog.

I'm awake early this morning. Bronchitis again. I can see across Nanny's bed, but only as far as the window, which is misted up. Nanny's bustling about. She's keeping the kettle on the boil so it will fill the room with steam. Then I'll have to sit under a great big towel. Then she'll make me a glass of hot black-currant Ribena to soothe my throat. It'll be lonely today because I won't be allowed out of bed, and with Corin and Vanessa at school and Mummy and Daddy away on tour, the house will be empty, except for Birdie the cook and Nanny. Nanny will buy me a comic book this afternoon, perhaps read me a story. She doesn't read as well as Mummy, but it's better than silence. Birdie won't climb all those stairs to see me, she'll be down in the basement kitchen, and when it's lunchtime they'll haul my food up on the dumbwaiter to the nursery below. Then Nanny will bring it up the extra flight of stairs to me.

She brings an enamel washbowl in from the bathroom next door and washes me as I lie in bed. I'm always so weak when I get sick. I brush my teeth and spit out the foam and rinse my mouth. After shaking the thermometer she puts it under my tongue, and looks worried. Tut tut tut, she says when she looks at it. Now she brushes my hair, that feels so nice, don't go. But she does. Downstairs now, having her breakfast. I won't call. So quiet . . . just the gentle popping of the gas fire.

Yesterday was Sunday, and I had fun. Vanessa and Corin were home, and they spent time with me. I love Vanessa. She's tall and beautiful and kind. She makes up games and pictures and stories just for me. I was frightened last night because it was dark and I was in bed, and I'm not supposed to get out once I've been tucked in, but I heard those scrapey noises again. Vanessa heard me crying and came into my room and told me the noises were from the mouse family who live behind the wall. They're having a big ball, she said, and they're all dressed in their finery and they have their own orchestra and a mouse-sized banquet table. I promised her I'll never be frightened of scrapey noises again.

Corin's very friendly with Vanessa, but not with me. He says I'm a crybaby. That's because last week he taught me how to climb to the top of the big brick wall between our garden and Doctor Mary's, but he wouldn't show me how to get down again. I cried and Nanny came out and got cross with Corin and then he got really mad at me.

They're going to play the Important game again tonight. That's where Vanessa is President of the United States and Corin is Prime Minister of England and they make me the Royal Dog. But I'll be too sick.

Every summer we took our holidays at Bexhill-on-Sea, in the county of Sussex, always in smelling distance of the ocean. It would be a rented semidetached or rooms in a certain large, ornately Victorian hotel one or two blocks from the front.

I was four, maybe five—which year was it? A day stands out. Nanny had wheeled me back from the beach in my stroller, for Daddy was coming. He was arriving any minute, quick have your bath. I didn't remember Daddy very well—he'd been away in America for nearly a year. I liked Nanny and Mummy, but men were scary. And unfamiliar.

Nanny helps me out of my bath onto the slippery cork mat which stands on green shiny lino. The bath is old-fashioned, and stands on huge claw feet. She wraps me in a big towel. "Rub a dub dub, three men in a tub, The butcher, the baker, the candlestick maker, They went to sea in a rotten potato." Into my nightie—into my dressing gown—hair brushed, slip-

pers on. Down to meet Daddy, the stranger from America.
There he is sitting on a chair and I can't see the sur-
roundings well, but with him is a tall good-looking man, and
Daddy says, "I've got a present for you." I open it. It's slip-
pers—beautiful yellow slippers with little bear heads on the
front. I put them on and they fit, and I think, oh, Daddy,
thank you, thank you, they are the most beautiful slippers I
ever saw and I love them and I love you, and I hug him. But
the person in the nightie and the dressing gown and the glum
face just stands there and says nothing, and Daddy says, "Do
you like them?" and the glum one says, "Of course," in a cross
voice. I leave the room in disgrace. Later, Nanny is hugging
me as I cry and cry.

I was constantly surprised at how a long clear sentence in my
head would come out bluntly in a flat voice, perhaps two words.
The image of what I was feeling always seemed to be changing.
I knew even then that the me that others saw and my inner self
had not met, and all the frowning and concentrating in the
world couldn't bring the two together.

The little girl who didn't really remember her Daddy but
somewhere deep inside longed to see him and hug him and
love him had been sabotaged by the glum ungrateful one who
only dressed, looked, and sounded like me.

I was really saying thank you to him, Nanny, and he didn't
understand.

My father must have found me maddening.

When I was a child, successful motherhood meant chubby babies. Round pink cheeks, pinchable knees, and dimpled elbows
were a sign that you were, despite hardships, a good mother. I
must have been an affront, contracting all the childhood diseases
that are now preventable, including chickenpox, whooping
cough, mumps, and even, according to Doctor Mary next door,
a mild brush with polio. Recurrent bouts of bronchitis alternated
with mild attacks of pneumonia, and always I seemed to have
a cold. Of course, much of our 1940s cuisine consisted of powdered eggs, boiled-to-within-an-inch-of-its-life cabbage, prunes,
lumpy custard, and rabbit. (Boiled, minced, pie-d, stewed, ham-
burgered, meatballed, sandwiched—to this day, I cannot eat

rabbit.) Yet by the time I was three—it was post-World War II Britain with home-grown food and fresh vegetables. So why were we fed the blandest, dullest, most unappetizing excuse for a healthy diet ever invented? English food!

Into this humdrum regimen of dullness peeked welcome interludes of pure joy—the most insidious being sweets. English candy for some reason is the tastiest in the world, I think most people would agree. Luckily, the frequency of these mouth-watering orgies was automatically limited, for sweets were considered a luxury, and were severely rationed. Then one day word came—SWEETS OFF RATION STARTING NEXT WEEK. Vanessa, Corin, and I set about earning money, saving our allowance, selling anything saleable so that on the great day we'd have enough money to buy a sugar mountain. We were delirious with anticipation. After all, we had been almost completely deprived of them for what was then our entire lives. The first visit to the store of endless delights was of course on opening day. A long line of kids and adults had already formed when we got there. Mrs. Boswick, the postmaster's wife, measured out the treasure. Most sweets were sold by the pound then, not prepackaged, and I can still remember and taste that first big buy: eight ounces of lemon sherbet powder, six barley sugar canes, six Cadbury chocolate flakes, fourteen chocolate-covered marshmallows, nine sugar mice, and two pounds of Bassett's Liquorice Allsorts. We carried home our shopping basket filled with little white paper bags, climbed the mulberry tree at the bottom of our garden—and pigged out.

As with many other British families at that time, our one-egg-per-person-per-week ration was augmented by a clutch of fecund chickens who, when their productive abilities had expired, were relegated to the stew pot, destined to nourish small, starved bodies. They occupied a big hen house under Nanny's rule, and every so often it would be time for one of these hapless creatures to be terminated. At least, dinner would not consist of rabbit that night. . . .

Vanessa, Corin, and I are trudging the last mile of our daily trip home from school when suddenly, wafting its way through blossoms and rose gardens along the road lining the river, the most electrifying aroma greets us. Three finely tuned noses identify the source. Chicken! Quick! Through the black painted door in the high wall of our front garden—along the path to the house, and up the stairs to the nursery. The big wooden table is laid, and Nanny welcomes us with warm hugs. Worzel Gummidge is on the radio and soon we're at the table, hands washed, napkins tucked in.

But an awful silence descends. We're stunned by guilt.

In our greed and excitement we forgot to think. Chicken, but who? Which one? Emma, Pom Pom, the old white and black one we never named? Our heads are bowed in a silent prayer of sorrow and regret, and only then do we tuck in to the best of meals.

It should come as no surprise to find that the nine-year-old owner of those thoughts was beginning to develop another persona; a rather fat one, and a rather ugly one.

I was becoming more and more aware of this false me on the outside that other people noticed, contrasting with the person inside that I knew much better.

As time went on, the outer me, quite beyond my control, got into the clutches of a strange power, another force which I wholly invented, and to which I gave the name "Fat Ogre." I could blame it for everything that went wrong, especially for all the destructive things I did to my body (a bit like saying "The Devil made me do it"). I may not have loved my appearance, but I found I could just love to hate this apparition!

Fat Ogre was at first a small, insistent voice inside my head, a demonic little Jimminy Cricket who controlled my thoughts.

ME: I'm full. I don't want any more!

F.O.: It's creamy and chocolaty, look at these nuts. . . .

ME: I've just lost eight pounds, I can't, I can't. . . .

F.O.: Just touch it, that's all. . . . Pick it up!

ME: Mm-mm. Munch-yummie. . . .

F.O.: Well done.

ME: Well, I blew it now!

The Sweet Binge was not the only culprit in the saga of fat—if England had lousy cooked food back then, it did have one triumphant product. *Milk!* The lush green pastures of England to this day feed the cows that yield the thickest, creamiest liquid of any country in the world. Nectar that brings forth cream and butter and cheese. Tasty and fortifying, rich in calcium, and guaranteed to fatten the skinniest child.

At Cousin Lucy's farm "Whitegate," in Bromyard, Herefordshire, we learned how to milk Lucy's one and only cow, Ada. We learned how to skim the cream in the cool slate-floored dairy house, and then to churn it into the richest yellow butter for a nonstop trip to the kitchen table and its final destination, between fresh toasted scones and lashings of strawberry jam.

A two-week trip came every spring and sometimes summer too. Lucy Kempson was my mother's father's cousin—related to the Wedgwoods, of best bone-china fame. She was in her seventies. I always felt great affection for her, even though she secretly reminded me of Alice's Ugly Duchess. Not many knew that she had been one of the first women to attend Oxford University. Now she was in retirement, and people vaguely referred to her as "that Blue Stocking."

During the early wartime bombing, Vanessa and Corin had been evacuated to live full-time at Bromyard. Dad and Mum were often touring in a play then, but at least they knew the children would be safe. So coming to Bromyard became part of my life too.

Nanny would always take us, and we'd always go on the train, an interminable journey with stops at tiny stations with unforgettable names. Tewkesbury, Ripple, Earl's Croombe, Severn Stoke, Wittington, and finally Worcester Shrub Hill, where we'd get off. Lucy's faithful gardener, William, would meet us in the impeccably chaste Austin, load up, and then there'd be more miles of winding country lanes, through the villages of Broadwas, Doddenham, Knightsford Bridge (where Worcestershire meets Herefordshire), and at last Bromyard. Up the hill, through the gates, and finally a lurching stop in front of a large, sprawling house.

Lucy would be there to greet us—usually dressed in pale blue and lace knitted twin set. "Hello Ducky, hello Ducky," outstretched arms.

"Can we have the same rooms, Cousin Lucy?"

"Yes yes, up you go. Hello, Nanny."

"Hello, Madam," Nanny would say, hanging on to her dignity while throwing a disapproving glance at William, who'd been doing his best at the wheel.

William also looked after the chickens, a mixed bag, and of course Ada, the cow. Every few years she'd be replaced by a new one, but Ada was always her name.

Up the big wooden staircase, stopping only to stroke the Siamese cat and drop off Vanessa at the end of the corridor and Corin in the room with the piano, then Nanny and I would continue up yet another staircase to the little attic room which we shared at the top of the stairs.

Oh goody—the blue tin is by my bed, and that means biscuits for the morning. Open it quick—yes, digestives and Custard Creams.

Yippee, tomorrow we'll have breakfast in the dining room—and then we can go out the French windows and down the steps past the bullrush pond, and through the kitchen garden, and over the stile to the barn, and up the wooden ladder to the hayloft. Jump in the clover, open the hayloft door—and there will be Ada!

Oh, Nanny, tonight Vee's doing a play in the living room using lots of Lucy's old dressy-up outfits—ostrich feather fans and black velvet evening dresses. And tomorrow I can help at Bredenbury school stables, 'cos school's out and the ponies will be free. Then I can ride down to Bromyard and see Dr. Lewis and his family. Sarah is my age and Lucy says she's had polio too. And we've got to have tea at Dumbleton Cottage with Great Aunt Joan. Oh please, hurry up tomorrow!

Next morning, breakfast would be announced by Frances the cook, banging the big brass gong in the hall. Frances personified English country cooking at its best. Her specialty, butterfly cakes—little cupcakes with their tops cut into wings set in frosting. She'd preserve into bottles rows and rows of pears, plums, and damsons, which were grown on the property and were kept in the air-raid shelter, a concrete bunker such as were built for many homes in those days, and noted for their cold damp atmosphere and great possibilities for children's hideyholes. Out of bed we'd tumble, dressing gowns, slippers, and then, peering through pebble glasses, there'd be Lucy, in yet another twin set, this time with her pearls, waiting to hurry us in to breakfast. "Come along, Ducky," she'd say to me. "Sit down, don't let it get cold." Seated next to her, I'd soon be happily tucking into my porridge, awash in dark brown-sugared cream. Then fried eggs, crisp-edged whites surrounding rich yellow yolks (from chickens who had never been shut in cages). Thick-cut English bacon done to a curled turn. Then damson jam generously spread on whole wheat toast.

"Eat up. I know you can't get breakfast like this at home."

Later, after a morning's hard play, a quick run down rolling hills to the river for a minnow-catching, tummy-stuffing picnic lunch, topped off with fresh-picked White Hart cherries.

Eventually Lucy died and left the property to Mum and her brother Nick. Uncle Nicky and his family moved in, and of course we still visited, but it wasn't the same.

Back in London, I'd dream of Lucy and Frances and William and Ada and country food. . . .

Queen's Gate School, and by fourth grade my eating habits had become pretty awful. In retrospect, one could say that this course of behavior was inevitable, for the food was really repulsive. Typically, gray mystery meat, ground up and swimming in grease, accompanied by overcooked green cabbage which smelled of basement kitchens and dish rags. Most of the other vegetables were from cans: peas, carrots, or beans. Huge bulk cans, their contents kept warm in vats and reheated and served again and again till they were gone.

Pudding was always "something and custard," with the custard too hastily prepared, full of disgustingly gooey lumps. The "something" was always the most dreaded part of the meal to me. Prunes in syrup. Or for a special treat, figs in syrup. The smell made me gag. I loathed all forms of dried fruits. And then—most loathsome of all—the once-weekly horror "Spotted Dick." Yes, that was its name. A large gray-white roll of steamed suety pudding filled with dates. Suet pudding, by the way, is an age-old favorite in Britain. A steamed sponge mixture made from flour, water, and shredded suet, which comes from the fat that surrounds beef or lamb kidneys. It's used in many flavorful ways, and my English-born husband still craves it. I learned to sneak the dates from my portion of pudding into a hanky and to slide the figs and prunes under the bread plate. Of course I'd still be hungry, so I'd fill up on slices of white bread and margarine, sprinkled with sugar.

After school, and on the way home, I'd regularly make a stop at the sweet shop and buy a couple of ounces of Cadbury's chocolate buttons. And so began a habit that took years to lose, eating while walking.

Every Tuesday, Nanny would take her one night off a week to attend the local "Whist Drive." She'd been playing for many years, and her prizes were stored away in the bedroom drawer for the day she would retire to a little cottage up in Norfolk, a gift from Mum and Dad. Fine linens, silver flatwear, coffee sets, candlesticks, all wrapped in layers of white tissue paper.

Every Tuesday, left alone, I'd go to bed early with the radio and a big tin of cookies. My idea of heaven. Tuesday night at seven o'clock was also "Journey Into Space," and if properly timed, the program and a whole tin of Scottish shortbread would finish together on the hour.

More and more I resorted to secret eating, enjoying forbidden extras when no one was around to tell me I shouldn't. Then I would be too full at proper mealtime to eat more than the tastiest morsels, perhaps only a crunchy roast potato or a piece of crispy chicken skin.

Since all of our meals were served in the nursery, my in-between snacking and consequent lack of appetite went largely unnoticed.

Except after church on Sundays. . . .

The dark polished dining room table is enormous, and it's all laid out with the silver and the Wedgwood. Daddy's down at the far end with his back to the window and Mummy's at the opposite end and please don't let me have to sit at the corner next to Daddy.

"Mummy."

My tiny whispering voice sounds huge and echoey. Try to say it quieter.

"Mummy, can I sit next to you please?"

And Mummy says, "Yes darling, of course you can," as she always does, so I breathe a sigh of relief and try to disappear into the Regency striped satin seat cushions.

Vanessa and Corin are on either side of Daddy, and Nanny's opposite me. Daddy's talking about Charles Dickens and keeps getting up to fetch books from the library and read little bits out loud, and I feel full even though I've barely touched my food because I've been nibbling all morning and a mouthful of roast beef is going round and round in my mouth getting tougher and grayer and I can't swallow it. Keep reading, Daddy, don't notice me, please. But he does.

"What's the matter with Lynn?"

"She's had enough, Mikey."

"You've eaten nothing, Lynny. Finish your plate."

Oh, Daddy, I can't, I'm full and fat and warm and blotchy, go back to Charles Dickens, don't look at me again so I can turn to Mummy and whisper:

"Do I have to finish it, Mummy?"

And Mummy puts her finger to her lips, shushing me to be quiet, and then when no one is looking clears my plate away.

Each year I grew a little taller, a little chubbier, and a little lonelier. I was always the tallest in the class, something I hated. Vanessa and Corin were tall too, but they wore their height grandly and gracefully, it seemed to me. I tried to stay unnoticed, and as a result developed quite appalling posture, an offense, I knew, to my perfectionist father. I remember awful incidents where he'd run his hands over my missing waistline before trying to make my by-now rigid shoulders drop from their fixed position up by my ears, and he wasn't against staging these little performances in front of his friends either. Then I'd yell in anguish and run to my bedroom and lock the door.

I had few friends at school and reached out gratefully to the "support system" adults at home. Joan Hirst, our family's secretary and savior through the up and down years, was always a warm and lovingly supportive friend to me (and I cherish this relationship, which has continued to this day).

Joan was married to Geoff Hirst, who was a violinist performing on cruise ships, which meant he had to be away from home often for months at a time. I know his absence left her feeling very lonely and when I felt lonely too I always knew I could run into the dining room where each day Joan would be tap tapping away on her typewriter taking care of my father's business affairs.

With her I felt at ease, comfortable enough to talk about anything together.

My godmother, Edith Hargraves, was another good friend to me. Edith had first met my father in 1936, working for him as his dresser and then his secretary. She had become an avid supporter of the arts, and it was with her that I was first exposed to ballet, and the operas of Gilbert and Sullivan. She was and is (for at this point of writing she is in her ninety-sixth year) a fairy godmother to me. "I've tickets for Margot Fonteyn in *Sleeping Beauty* at the Royal Opera House on Saturday," she'd say. "And of course we'll have dinner at the Strand Palace Hotel." Sometimes we'd go to the Savoy Theatre to see the D'Oyly Carte Company perform *The Pirates of Penzance* or *Iolanthe* or *The Mikado*. Edith was determined that her one and only godchild should benefit from her own artistic passion. She never married and still lives alone, but continues to go to the theater and ballet regularly, taking her friends along with her.

With only these adult friends but few peers, it was probably inevitable that I should come to concentrate on my one and only real friend, Rosalinda. She was the most beautiful chestnut pony, a gift from my fairy godmother. I came to live for riding. I trained and trained, and I'd go to horse shows in the summer and fox hunts in the winter, inseparable, never happier than with her. I was sure that I was going to be an Olympic show jumper. As an equestrian, being a Redgrave didn't get in the way—it wasn't a horse world name, and I was already sick of the effect my name had on people.

STRANGER: What's your name?
ME: Lynn.
STRANGER: (showing extreme disinterest) Lynn what?
ME: (mumbling) Redgrave.
STRANGER: (suddenly animated and turned on) Oh, how wonderful.

I hated the hypocrisy, the second-hand fame, but in the narrow focus of the show ring or hunting field I could be my own person. Any success I had on Rosalinda was mine and hers alone, not attributable to my family. Furthermore, on horseback I felt at one with my horse, a desirable state for the budding champion, but as myself on solid ground, the struggle remained.

A small progress was made when I was about thirteen. The event was miniscule, the effect quite extraordinary. A great friend of the family, Doris Langley Moore, came to tea—we happened to be in the country staying at Wilks Water for the weekend. Nobody else was around, so I dutifully brought a loaded tray into the living room, and sat next to her. I could smell some exotic and antique perfume and wondered whether and how I should start a conversation.

Six lumps of sugar had just gone into my tea and I was about to sneak a seventh when Doris said, "I gave up smoking by postponement."

I watched her carefully, the words hanging in the air. Doris was the sort of person who, while I was in awe of her, was exciting to meet. An eccentric but worldly woman, she had written several novels, was known for her rare costume collection, and had even borne an unusual daughter she had named Pandora. She never talked down to me, and I felt she must know everything; I mean, who else in 1955 had a daughter called Pandora?

"I postponed having a cigarette until lunchtime. Then I'd say to myself—I've postponed this long, I'll wait now till tea and that will be my treat. At teatime, why not wait till after dinner? and so on. I was smoking three packs a day. Now I don't smoke at all. We can all change ourselves if we want to."

"Maybe I could diet that way," I said. "Postpone eating."

"Good idea," said Doris, stirring her tea.

She looked at me, that clear steady look of hers.

"I can read palms," she said. "I'll read yours."

I held out my right hand, fascinated.

"That's odd—you've one straight line across the center of your palm. Let me see the left. Now your left hand is what you are born with and your right hand is what you make of your life." She perused my hands, while I waited breathlessly for the verdict—a glimpse into my future.

"That life line tells me you are changing your destiny. And your career. You were meant to do one thing and be a certain sort of person and live a reasonable but not over-long life. But your right changes—you even live longer than you were meant to."

I was thrilled—suddenly I felt special and important. "How many children will I have?" She touched the wrinkles beneath my little finger.

"Two."

Well, I was going to have at least six I was always sure, and live on a farm, and ride horses forever.

"There is a third line, but it's not definite enough. Wouldn't count on more than two."

I felt silly believing it, and almost wished Doris had never started this hand reading. Being a different person and changing my life sounded scary.

For the next two days I walked uneasily around the cottage. Then, venturing into the field just outside the garden I suddenly found myself striding boldly forward through high, wet grass. A new image of myself was forming. Tall, beautiful, and . . . lithe. Isn't that the word they use for tall people of thirteen? I was going to have a new destiny, and now I was going to move it along. But from what to what, though? I came to the old Basingstoke Canal, which meandered beyond the field, marsh marigolds choking its edges. I leaned dangerously over, and made the water reflect my face. A serious look. Much concentration. A conscious effort of will was all it took. The round-faced, solemn kid in dirty old cord trousers with hunched shoulders stared back, and I rejected it.

A thought began to take shape in my mind, a revolutionary thought. It took all the mile or so back to the cottage, quickening my pace with every step. My mind was made up as I burst through the front door. Change direction, change my destiny, Doris was right.

I would be an actress.

It was easy.

ABOVE: My grandparents, Margaret "Daisy" Scudmore and Roy Redgrave. (COLLECTION OF THE AUTHOR) BELOW: My parents, Michael Redgrave and Rachel Kempson, on stage in *The School for Scandal* in London, 1937. (© HOUSTON ROGERS, 1937)

Mum with Corin, me, and Vanessa in 1943. (PORTRAIT BY MARCUS ADAMS; USED BY KIND PERMISSION OF GILBERT ADAMS)

Story time on Nanny's knee, 1946. Left to right: Vanessa, me, and Corin. (© PICTORAL PRESS, LONDON)

My family in 1952: Vanessa, Rachel, Michael, me, and Corin. (© PICTORAL PRESS, LONDON)

This is Wilks Water and here I am on a visit with Mum in 1984. (PHOTOS BY JOHN CLARK)

ABOVE: Our family in London, 1962. (PHOTO BY REG LANCASTER. © EXPRESS NEWSPAPERS, LONDON) BELOW: Here's the irrepressible cast of *Billy Liar* from 1962: Nan Marriot Watson, Frank Pettit, Eileen Dale, Trevor Bannister, and, of course, me. (USED BY KIND PERMISSION OF LEWIS MORLEY)

CLOCKWISE, FROM UPPER LEFT: I played Miss Prue opposite Laurence Olivier's Tattle in *Love for Love* at the National Theatre of Great Britain in 1965. (USED BY KIND PERMISSION OF ZOE DOMINIC, LONDON) Working with Noel Coward on *Pretty Polly* in 1966 was an unforgettable experience. (© 1966 ABC TELEVISION U.K.) Here I am with Ruth Gordon in George Bernard Shaw's *Mrs. Warren's Profession* during a 1976 run at Lincoln Center. (PHOTO BY SY FRIEDMAN) "The rain in Spain..." Eliza Doolittle at the ball, in BBC TV's 1973 production. (© BBC)

TOP: My *Georgy Girl* co-stars were Alan Bates and James Mason. (© 1966 COLUMBIA PICTURES INDUSTRIES, INC. COURTESY OF COLUMBIA PICTURES) ABOVE: On Broadway in 1974, with George Rose in *My Fat Friend*. (© 1974 MARTHA SWOPE) OPPOSITE PAGE, CLOCKWISE FROM UPPER LEFT: This 1965 portrait is an all-time favorite of mine. (USED BY KIND PERMISSION OF ZOE DOMINIC, LONDON) I was Kattrin in Bertold Brecht's *Mother Courage,* produced by the National Theatre of Great Britain in 1966. (PHOTO BY JOHN TIMBERS) March 17, 1967. (© 1967 TIME, INC.)

TIME
THE WEEKLY NEWSMAGAZINE

LYNN
& VANESSA
REDGRAVE

The stage still beckons. In 1990 I was Madame Ranevskaya in Chekov's *The Cherry Orchard* at the La Jolla Playhouse, with Mark Harelik and William Ball. (PHOTO BY KIND PERMISSION OF MICHA LANGER) And in 1985, Lonsdale's 1920's comedy *Aren't We All* with Rex Harrison and Jeremy Brett. (© 1985 MARTHA SWOPE)

2

Growing Up

F ifteen was a crucial year for me.

We had been spending the summer at Stratford-upon-Avon. Mum and Dad were performing with The Shakespeare Memorial Company, later to be renamed The Royal Shakespeare Company.

If being a Redgrave child had its problems, the big plus was our exposure to great theater. From our earliest years we saw every play, so that Shakespeare had become part of our lives, and by the summer of 1958, I had seen all but three of his entire works. The Bard's language can be intimidating, but he remains for me my favorite playwright. And I know this is because of my father, who would patiently explain the plot of *King Lear* (or *Hamlet* or *A Midsummer Night's Dream*) over a morning and then we'd excitedly trot off to the theater and watch him, one of Shakespeare's greatest interpreters, perform it.

Several generations of actors, stage dynasties on both sides of the family tree, found their consummation in my father's artistry.

In the boxes of faded letters and playbills in Dad's office were the shadows of Ellsworthys, Scudemores, and Redgraves, our ancestors. Not all were famous in their day, but among the better known was Cornelius Redgrave, a tobacconist in eighteenth-century Drury Lane. According to Dad's research, he functioned as a "theatrical racketeer." Then there was Fortunatus Augustine Scudemore, who was my great grandfather, a prolific author of Victorian melodrama. He had a daughter, Daisy, later known as Margaret. She began her stage career at fourteen in the chorus of a provincial pantomime. When she was twenty-two, she came into my family by marrying George Ellsworthy Redgrave (Roy), who had already been on the stage for twenty years. He made his North London debut in 1899, and by 1902 appeared at Sadlers Wells Theatre, topping the bill with the outrageous title "Roy Redgrave—Dramatic Cock o' the North."

Dad was born on March 20, 1908, in theatrical digs over a newspaper shop in Bristol where his mother was on tour. She was alone, it seemed, for Roy had already left for Australia. Margaret, with her baby still in her arms, went after Roy, who was by now on the road with a theatrical troupe bound for Melbourne. It was there that my father was baptized. Two years later, in Sydney, Dad made his debut, carried on stage by Roy.

But life was hard, and Roy's fortunes were erratic. Perhaps he'd been in too many melodramas. Anyway, he began to find consolation in drink and in women, and after three years chasing him across Australia, my grandmother gave up, packed her bags, and took baby Michael back to England. They never saw Roy Redgrave again, and indeed, although they did hear of his death in 1922, Dad told us he had no idea where his father was buried.

I loved these stories of my forebears, and would listen for hours, open-mouthed with wonder.

When I was little, if that night's play was going to be violent or frightening, my mother would tell me the secrets of the onstage effects. In *King Lear*, for example, where she played his mean daughter Regan, she had to have the Earl of Gloucester's eyes put out, and then hold them triumphantly in her hand. Realizing the traumatizing effect this might have on a small child, she showed me the eyes that were really only peeled grapes, and the pocket where she would hide the vial of fake blood. I was still unable to really talk to my father, but by the age of fifteen, I could and did listen. When he would start to expound on the business of acting, I was spellbound.

Watching my father act was always an emotional experience. Then I could suspend disbelief completely, for this wasn't the father I was so afraid of. He seemed to actually enter the body of King Lear and Richard II and Shylock and Hotspur and Hamlet and Antony.

Going backstage to see him after the performance, I was really going to see the character and hoped I might become part of the imaginary world I had just seen.

> *Through the pass door next to the stage—the smell of painted scenery, dust, sweaty tights—Enobarbus is on the phone, Cleopatra's messenger is smoking a cigarette.*
>
> *"Please, where is Antony?" Up the stairs to the dressing room—" 'Scuse me!" (that's Octavius Caesar pushing past us now). There's a brass plaque which says* MICHAEL RED-GRAVE. *My heart beats. Knock on the door, the door opens, there he is. Antony, towering above me, his wig off, but his made-up face still with Antony's features. He's wearing a silk paisley bathrobe. I hug this Dad-Antony, but cannot speak aloud my thoughts.*
>
> > *I dreamt there was an Emperor Antony*
> > *O, such another sleep*
> > *That I might see*
> > *But such another man!*

I'd traveled to Stratford one particular summer by train, as usual with Rosalinda. We'd done this many times before because I'd often spent school holidays at a riding camp in Warwickshire, and could arrange for a horse box to be joined to the cross-country train. It had a half door so that the horse's head could lean over into the passenger compartment. Immense fun. Rosalinda munching hay from her hay net prepared by me, me munching sandwiches made by my Nanny, the train rattling along, and all seemed right with the world. At Leamington Spa, our compartment would be uncoupled and shunted into a siding so that the train could continue on its way. Off we'd get, and I'd saddle up and ride her the two or three remaining hours to Stratford-upon-Avon.

Mum had arranged for me to keep my horse at a nearby stable which belonged to Bay Lane, a famous show jumper. His father was also his trainer, and the plan was that he would take me in hand and teach me what it would take to really become a world-class show jumper like his son. He took me to horse shows and three-day events. In the equestrian world I was definitely on my way. And yet . . .

At night I was over at the theater. The repertoire that season included the *Hamlet* of my father, *Romeo and Juliet* with my mother as Lady Capulet, *Much Ado About Nothing* with both of them, and the play that triggered the change in my life, *Twelfth Night*.

Twelfth Night. I saw it seventeen times. From a good seat up front, from the side, the balcony, standing at the back and standing in the wings. Of course, I fell in love with the play, but most of all I fell in love with the Viola of Dorothy Tutin.

Peter Hall's production was set in a golden and autumnal Illyria at the time of Charles the Second, and this Viola was breathtakingly beautiful, captivatingly funny, and head over heels in love.

Shakespeare's immaculate play of mistaken identity transformed me. I thought if I could only step into that magic world for a few hours a day, become someone else, take on her looks, her voice, her thoughts, her passions, then I could not only become a great actress, I could also escape from me, the me that I couldn't abide. I could be a butterfly, emerging from my caterpillar's cocoon.

But could I act? The insane thing was, I had no way of knowing. I'd been in two plays, at school. The first time, at the age of seven, I played a shepherd in a nativity piece, with painted beard and mustache. A bit later, I played Theseus, the duke, in *A Midsummer Night's Dream*.

I rather timidly told Mum of my newly formed ambition, wondering what she would say. No one ever expected me to be an actress, even though Vanessa had finished her drama training at Central the year before and Corin was acting with a group at Cambridge University. Mum must have been amazed, but didn't show it. I remember her lying on the drawing-room sofa with a slice of cucumber covering each eye.

"Well, how much do you *want* to be an actress?" she asked. There was a long wait for an answer, for I didn't know what she meant.

"I mean, if Dad and I said we won't let you do this, and we won't pay for your training, and we disown you, would you go ahead anyway?"

I now thought this was a really stupid question, I mean, they wouldn't do that, would they?

Mum sat up, removing the cucumber slices.

"Because if you can't honestly say that if you couldn't have your way you'd jump off a bridge into the river, then you have no business being an actress."

Of course I told her no problem, of course, and all that, but I deliberated about it a lot. I knew she was right, I'd been around actors long enough to know that it could be a rotten and heartless profession. My father always said he didn't even put talent near the top of the list. Thick skin, toughness, resilience, and the capacity for hard work were more important in his view.

For the next several weeks I'd wake up in the morning and say to myself, "Is it the theater or is it the river?" and I had to remind myself that this was all a little premature, for I was still at school, although with only one year to go.

But in actual fact, what was to be my final year ended abruptly halfway through the spring term of 1959, the culmination of a two-week correspondence between the headmistress and my father. In my half-term report card she declared, most unfairly I thought, "Does not pull her weight."

It's true that my weight problem was not getting any better, although I had been seriously experimenting with diets, but the double-entendre was not lost on me, and I complained to my father that I'd been very much doing my best by staying behind to tidy up after concerts, organizing school dances, painting classrooms, etc., etc., and etc.

I think it was now, for the very first time, that I asked for his help, and unstintingly and loyally he came through.

He used strong words when he wrote to the headmistress

in defense of his daughter, and she wrote back to say that if he was that dissatisfied with the school maybe he should take me away.

At just sixteen, I gratefully left Queen's Gate School for Young Ladies midway through my school year, leaving me with an entire half year to fill before September, prior to starting my new life at drama school.

What to do to fill in the time? Given my well-established interest in food, becoming a good cook seemed an excellent idea. The Regent Street Polytechnic had a perfect program. "The Short Housewives Course" took three months, at the end of which I would be qualified to cater dinner parties. A guaranteed money-maker to squeeze in between my acting jobs. About twenty strangely assorted students assembled for the start of our first session. Most of my fellow would-be cooks were housewives, some short, some tall, but mostly from Nigeria. Their husbands all seemed to be exchange professors visiting at British universities who wanted their wives to cook in the Western style. We were divided into pairs, the morning sessions being devoted to the consideration of a typical three-course British meal, the afternoons specializing in desserts, cakes, and sweets. All of which had to be sampled and analyzed, for we had to taste both the disasters and the triumphs in order to learn.

The heat in the kitchen was overpowering, ten ovens blasting away during the hottest summer in thirty years, and of course there was no air conditioning.

My partner, pregnant and in full African tribal costume, took up a great deal of room. I was several years her junior, but she was very sweet to me, always daydreaming about her expected child.

"God willing he will be a lawyer," she'd murmur, patting her tummy while allowing the Hollandaise to curdle.

Between us we'd stir up Appetizing Soups and Hors d'Oeuvres, Wholesome Meat or Fish Entrées (with potatoes and fresh vegetables), and Delicious Desserts. Then we'd eat the lot for lunch.

We learned to keep a chicken breast frugally basted by neatly laying the paper wrappers from store-bought butter over it while cooking. We Van Dyked hard-boiled eggs, giving the whites little frills like the collars of the Dutch masters. We made radishes into roses, pounded spices for curry, and desperately attempted the perfect flaky pastry (dip your hands into iced water while trying not to let the butter melt in the sweltering heat). We made excellent shortbread—butter, flour, and sugar—English pork pies (hot water pastry around sausage meat with a hard-boiled egg in the center). Yorkshire pudding (keep the water cold and the fat piping hot), and above all, we ate. Everything.

I'd get home exhausted. Hot and sticky, but full and happy. And my mother would say, "You poor darling, you've worked so hard. I've got a beautiful dinner ready when you've had your bath."

Of course, there were occasions when it was absolutely necessary to look well groomed and fit. Meaning, no food for at least a week. One of those came in the middle of my cooking course in 1959, a very special day off to attend the royal bestowing of my father's knighthood.

As the exciting event drew near, we children began to kid mother, curtsying and calling out "your ladyship" to get her used to it. (Father was never given to quite this kind of teasing; we'd leave him alone.)

Knighthood is a very great honor in England, given for exceptional work; in Dad's case, for his services to the theater. His Hamlet the year before at Stratford, and its subsequent presentation in Moscow, was final proof that at fifty years of age he had become one of the theatrical greats. Olivier, Gielgud, Richardson, and Guinness had all received their knighthoods, and now it was his turn.

Vanessa was in a play up at Stratford at the time and couldn't come to Buckingham Palace, but Corin and I, and Mum and Dad, proudly set forth in the family Rolls-Royce, driven by Dad's chauffeur. Mother and I wore hats and new silk dresses, Corin a newly pressed suit, and Dad a top hat, morning suit, and tails. The investiture was to take place in the Throne Room and was that day to be presided over by Queen Elizabeth, the Queen Mother.

The place was packed, for there were many honors to be given, and everybody had brought their families along. It was important that when the Queen Mother arrived there would be no unnecessary disturbances, so costumed and coiffed footmen were kept busy ushering hordes of small children to the rest rooms. Above us on a balcony, suitably ancient musicians sat at the ready. They wore white lace ruffles and red and gold knee-breeches, and little white wigs. The leading violinist, wearing his wig at a very strange angle, held his bow to the strings so that he could start playing immediately the ceremony began. His job was to drown out any comments the Queen Mother might wish to make as she lowered the ceremonial sword onto the shoulders of the kneeling knight, for royal etiquette dictates that the public shall not hear the private murmurs of a member of the royal family.

I had expected a little Mozart, or perhaps some Handel or Bach, music suited to the joyous yet solemn nature of the proceedings, but as my father knelt before Her Majesty to become Sir Michael Redgrave C.B.E., a strangely familiar air broke free.

"Oh-oh-oh-OH-klahoma!"

Our eyes filled with tears, our shoulders shook, and we held hands, trying in vain to conceal the choking depths of our mirth and profound emotion.

3

An Actor's Life for Me

I went up to Stratford to soak up some inspiration for my upcoming drama school auditions. Vanessa was a member of the company and staying with her was heaven for me.

She always rented a studio room from Denne Gilkes, the resident voice teacher whose house dated from Elizabethan times. Her windows opened out onto a little walled garden which enclosed an old and gnarled apple tree, a mass of tangled weeds and flowers, and some well-worn deck chairs. After ten in the morning, actors would either be vocalizing with Denne in her cat-filled lower parlor, or wandering about outside practicing iambic pentameters at the tops of their voices.

Vanessa and I would have breakfast together at the scrubbed pine kitchen table. Tea in mugs, a boiled egg, strawberries, and thick buttered toast. When she went off to rehearsal, I'd get out my Shakespeare and start learning soliloquies for my upcoming drama school auditions.

The first school I auditioned for turned me down. The

principal, who knew my mother, wrote, "At the moment we do not see any sign of talent." I fell apart for several days, for it hadn't occurred to me that I might be rejected. Not to let it get me down, I immediately applied for my next choice, The Central School of Speech and Drama, which was where Vanessa had trained, and to my great relief I was accepted.

There was, however, an initial and major stumbling block.

Making my first appearance in tights and leotard, in the school's North London rehearsal room, the movement teacher sized me up. Sway back, overweight, slightly twisted spine, and one shoulder higher than the other. "Never be able to train you till the body's freed," she said, and with that sent me off to see Gwyneth Thurburn, the principal.

Most fortunately for me, she was a firm believer in the Alexander Technique, the gentle hands-on method of realigning the body and reeducating the mind. Instead of taking the movement class each day, I went to see Dr. Wilfred Barlow, a specialist in rheumatic diseases and director of the Alexander Institute.

For three months, half an hour a day, five days a week, Dr. Barlow or one of his teachers worked to straighten me out. As my unusual curves and compensating sways were unlearned, I grew literally even taller and finally reached the point when I could properly benefit from all of the training available at Central. The chronic pain I had experienced went away, and as my ribcage and back were freed, my breathing and voice improved too.

There followed two and a half intense years of training in the art of acting, during which time I thankfully realized the rightness of my decision, and discovered for the first time the joy of shared enthusiasm. They primed our bodies and senses and voices and emotions with the one great goal that we all kept firmly in mind, that in the end we would be employable.

In that, I was one of the lucky ones. Before my course ended, I heard of a chance to try out for a professional job, a production of *A Midsummer Night's Dream* at the Royal Court Theatre in London. Jocelyn Herbert, the designer of the show and an old friend of the family, had suggested I would be right for Helena, the taller of the "lovers" in the play. I was only nineteen, but this was to be a very young and untried cast. I was terribly excited and brazenly went straight to the principal at Central and asked for permission to audition. She absolutely refused. I tried to explain to her that I just wanted the experience of auditioning, obviously I wouldn't get the part, but still she said no.

I thought about it and talked to my mother. Her attitude was give it a go, what have you got to lose, rejection could be a useful experience.

So I played hookey, went to the audition, and, amazingly, got the job. Now I was in a terrible quandary. I had either to turn it down and keep quiet about it, or quit school almost right away.

I asked everybody I knew what I should do, but it didn't help. In the fashion of a true Pisces, I kept changing my mind, depending on whose advice it was. So I decided to ask my father for his further support. I knew I really wanted the part, and I knew I could rely on him. He was in New York appearing on Broadway in *The Complaisant Lover,* so I phoned him. I didn't relish this, for if he found it hard to talk to anyone in person, he was even worse on the phone. However, I knew he'd say it was a good idea—after all, he was a working actor, and a job is a job, and he always told us that work breeds work.

"No," he said, sounding so far away that his voice seemed to be coming to me from the bottom of the Atlantic.

"What?" I yelled.

"You mustn't do it. You should finish your training."

I felt myself getting childishly hot, tearful, and angry! Hanging up the phone, I called the director and accepted. In retrospect, I think that marked the true beginning of my independence.

I said good-bye to my friends at Central. They mostly wished me well and were a little envious, too.

Rehearsals began—oh God, how thrilling, I was a working actress. On pay day my little brown envelope contained eight pounds, to be raised to the giant sum of thirteen pounds ten shillings once performances began.

Tony Richardson was the director, who by a strange coincidence later became my brother-in-law. He had a wildly free and improvisational directorial style.

"Good, good my darling, now why don't you come center stage and do something absolutely marvelous."

My fellow cast members were almost all very new and inexperienced. Among them were Rita Tushingham, David Warner, Nichol Williamson, Ronnie Barker, Colin Blakely, Robert Lang, and Samantha Eggar. Opening night came—and went.

Caryl Brahms, the critic for *Plays and Players,* wrote "Tony Richardson . . . has given us a Dream which is different—badly spoken, badly acted, badly lit, and badly set," and that was the good review.

We soldiered on, playing to poor houses, slowly improving. And there were always the fun stories to keep our spirits up.

First Fairy was played by a rather tedious child actress from the famous Corona School of the Stage going by the name of Gillian. Somewhat conceited, she lorded it over her fellow fairies, who had only one line compared to her two long ones. Well, Tony insisted that the character of First Fairy should be able to fly. This might have been all right, except that the Royal Court stage is quite tiny with almost no wing space.

Kirby's Flying Ballet, the London equivalent of the Flying Foys in America, had been responsible for flying Peter Pan and others for years now, and so one of their burly cockney technicians was put in charge of flying Gillian from the wooden green and brown forest mound center stage (we had a very simple set) to the wings stage right. Gillian was supposed to run on to greet Puck, a huge wire hawser attached to her back, in readiness for her airborne exit. As the end of the scene was reached, Gillian, her voice squeaking her speeches like a rusty door hinge, would take a running jump onto the top of the hillock, land with an unfairylike thud, and then be hoisted jerkily aloft and swung offstage. The technician, hidden behind a canvas tree, was supposed to catch her, but more often than not we'd hear—

Splat, thud, *"Eek!"*

"Oops—sorry luv."

As luck would have it, other jobs followed in fairly rapid succession, experience building upon the foundation of the training I had acquired at Central. Six weeks in Scotland at the Dundee Rep, playing a very young and rather shaky Portia in *The Merchant of Venice,* and a dotty flapper in the farce *Rookery Nook.* And my adventures in the culinary arts were widening too. Rooming with a young doctor and his wife, I learned to love venison pie, brown gravy, and haggis with mashed potatoes and swedes. Scottish shortbread for tea, and floury brown bread rolls ("baps") for breakfast.

Next a tour around England in a comedy called *Billy Liar.* Barbara was my character, very prim and proper, chubby, and always eating an orange. It was a funny part with lots of laughs, and I could certainly justify my weight by telling myself that Barbara *had* to be chubby, it said so in the script, and after several weeks, I was certainly improving in that department. Then one day I got the chance to nip down to London to audition for a West End play, *The Tulip Tree,* starring Celia Johnson, the exquisite actress who had become a star in David Lean's delicate movie of thwarted love, *Brief Encounter.* I would be trying out for the part of her daughter, a young ballet student. The part would be mine, but we all know that ballet students are thin, so I was told to do something about it.

I went for a six-week course to Doctor G., well-known for his patented diet with the pretty pills, and sure enough the pounds dropped away. But to digress for a moment, there was an interesting side effect, peculiar only to our profession, probably. It seemed to me that the laughs I'd been getting as Barbara had stopped coming. As I continued the tour, losing weight as promised, I managed to convince myself that the disappearing pounds contained the essence of Barbara's comedy. "One laugh for each pound," I figured. Of course I'm not saying this necessarily proves anything (except that actors are very neurotic), but by the time the tour reached its final week it seemed to me that I played my entire part to dead silence. But it did seem worthwhile when I got to act with Celia Johnson in the West End.

The characters who played the characters in *Billy Liar,* that first road show of mine, will always stay in my memory. It was among them that I truly felt a sense of belonging, of "company," of that special loyalty shared by professional actors. A motley and a lovely lot, they're worth meeting as an example of what can be found backstage in the British theater, so let me tell you a bit about them. First there was Nan Marriot Watson, who played Gran. I adored her, and I must confess I was the one who gave her the name "Marathon" Watson, a sort of British Bea Arthur who could talk longer and louder than anyone I knew. She was married to an impoverished inventor. "Oh God darling," she'd say, "he's done it again. Off to the patent office this morning, but it's hopeless, it'll never sell!" The latest invention, she told me one night after the show in Glasgow where we'd retired to our favorite eating pub, were rubber Wellington boots with tiny bellows in the heels. As you walked, they supposedly blew cool air onto your sweaty feet. Then there was Frank Pettit, known to us all as Frankenstein Pettit. His character, Billy's Dad, had to say "bloody" as a description of almost everything. But Frank could never remember how many "bloodies" there were in the script, and inserted them before and after almost everything he said, for example, "I bloody well told that bloody idiot—bloody hell! It's about bloody time. . . ." This still being the age of stage censorship—in the U.K. at least—we were reported to the cops in Glasgow. Two hefty sergeants were sent in to watch the play and count the bloodies, armed with a tally sheet granting us a generous 23 per performance. Frank had got it up to 157, and the producers were fined five pounds. Frankenstein got away with a caution. Eileen Dale's big claim to fame was that she used to be a wall-of-death motorcycle rider, usually at some of the smaller amusement parks found by the seaside. One day, she fell off and injured herself, which was why she took up a supposedly gentler pursuit (acting) and spoke out of the corner of her mouth. If she was talking facing stage left, you couldn't see her lips moving. Trevor Bannister played the leading role of Billy Liar. He'd understudied Albert Finney for three years in London before it went on the road, and now had his big chance. He knew everyone else's lines too, and he'd developed the unfortunate habit of silently saying my lines for me, without realizing it I'm sure. But you could read his lips— most offputting. Then finally, a memorable occasion, silence was not enough. Thus, Billy: "Hello, Barbara" (then in a whisper) "hello, pet." Me: "Hello, Pet." Billy: (loudly) "Can I come in?" Me: "Can I come in?" I might add that he only did it to me once!

For as long as a part required me to be thin I could find the necessary discipline to keep the weight off, but a great many of the roles I played in my early years were best played at my chubbier weight.

Tony Richardson found me a small part in his hit film *Tom Jones,* my first film by the way, and in it I played a generously built barmaid who flees from Albert Finney shrieking "Rape! Rape!" Baba in *Girl with Green Eyes* (with Peter Finch and Rita Tushingham) came next, and again, I was expected to be well covered. Like the chicken and egg theory, I don't know whether I was chubby to fit the part, or if the part was chubby to fit me. I do know that I was constantly trying to get casting directors to think of me as thin and attractive, and to this end, when I was out looking for work, I would make every attempt to lose the weight I'd kept for my last role.

Fat Ogre was by now my steady companion, and often appeared chameleon-like in the guise of my adoring mother.

We're clearing the dishes after a great dinner. Mum made roast lamb and really crunchy roast potatoes, Summer Pudding with red and black currants in syrup seeping through white bread crusts smothered in Jersey cream—thick and yellow. Dad likes to finish with cheese. "Makes the wine sing," he always says.

I've got to work tomorrow, record a Shakespeare play. But I've been on a diet. It's been great, lost about twelve pounds, so all through dinner I just nibble. "No, thanks, Mum, really, I'm on a diet."

I'm in the kitchen now with my laden tray.

"You serve the coffee, Mum, I'll do this."

A crunchy potato is in my mouth—doesn't count if no one sees you do it. Tree falling in the forest . . . same idea.

Wrap the remains of the lamb in foil—oops, there's a nice little piece of skin. A serving spoon is still stuck in the Summer Pudding. Just one mouthful, put the cream jug in the fridge. What the hell am I doing? Into the dining room. Dad's finished his cheese and has gone with the others to sit down in front of the fire in the living room.

I can't hear them now. Fat Ogre is with me. I can't think. He blocks out reason, blocks out sound. His heavy breathing obliterates my voice in my head that's telling me, "You've got to work tomorrow. . . . You don't need this food. . . . You've lost twelve pounds, don't blow it now."

"Good night, Mum. Good night, Dad. Good night, everybody."

They'll be going to bed soon. Mum comes back into the kitchen. "Good night, darling, sleep well." I hug her. She doesn't notice the crumbs in my hand. I just slipped six Custard Cream cookies into my pocket.

Fat Ogre and I climb the stairs. We lie down. Soon it's all quiet down below. My pulse is running fast as we tiptoe downstairs.

This can't be happening.

Sssh, not so loud.

We open the larder door.

We open the fridge door.

We open pockets and wrappings, and eat.

I'm in bed now. Fat Ogre has left. I feel sick and angry.

I did it.

This is the worst night of my life.

Tall, elegant mother has great cheekbones and was always effortlessly slim. Never having had to lose weight she would watch my weight gains with a mixture of sympathy and distress and ignorance. She'd load my plate with all my favorite food, "You work *so* hard you might faint if you don't eat," and then, five minutes later, suggest that actresses ought to be slim. Everything she knew about nutrition came from half-truths shrouded in myths, old wives' tales that most of her generation still harbor. From her came my beliefs, which I held onto for years, that:

Lean red meat could be eaten in any quantity.

Cheese isn't fattening because there is so much calcium in it.

Toasted bread loses its calories.

A lemon soufflé is the lightest of desserts, "Just air, egg whites, lemons, dear. . . . Oh, and two pints of heavy cream and a pound of sugar."

Even now when Granny Rachel comes to stay with us in California, her breakfast ideas begin modestly and then expand. I ask her what she would like each morning. "I don't want much, just a cup of tea—well a pot actually with lemon—or milk—and sugar. Just a piece of toast—well two, and butter, just a scrape, and marmalade—oh and orange juice, and do you have a grapefruit—just half now and brown sugar—and I'd better have a boiled egg. . . ."

As I eat my slice of toast with peanut butter or boiled egg with half a muffin, no butter, thankful that I no longer see Fat Ogre looking back, Mum says, "Oh dear, you're having nothing—you are so good. I shouldn't be eating all this—by the way do you have any All Bran? Tomorrow I won't have breakfast at all." She seems to know nothing about calories or fats or protein or carbohydrates. Needless to say, this has taken its toll on the svelte mother of my memory.

The work-breeds-work theory held, and because of my brief scene with Albert Finney in *Tom Jones* I was spotted by Bill Gaskill, one of the directors of the National Theatre of Great Britain, which was just being formed, and invited to audition. Oh my God, if only . . . could I? A permanent company, no more pounding the pavements and knocking on doors, at least not for a long while. It was in September of 1963 that I became part of what was then surely the greatest acting company in the world. Some names: Laurence Olivier, Maggie Smith, Colin Blakely, Derek Jacobi, Peter O'Toole, Albert Finney, Celia Johnson, Edith Evans, Joan Plowright, Tom Courtenay. And directors like Franco Zefferelli, Noel Coward, John Dexter, William Gaskill, Lindsay Anderson, and Peter Wood.

Six or seven plays would be in the repertoire at once, which meant rehearsals in the morning, a show at night, and perhaps a matinee in the afternoon. You could be sure of a costume or wig fitting too, and if you had any spare time there were workshops for voice and movement and fencing. It meant that I had the chance to create many different characters, and keep more than one of them in action at any given time. What excitement! What a trap! Can you guess what happened?

The day came when I was asked to play two totally contrasting roles. Rose in *The Recruiting Officer* is a lusty and well-fed eighteenth-century country girl. Barblin in *Andorra*, a chilling story of anti-Semitism, is a starved freedom fighter, driven to madness. Well, the way the schedule was planned, I got to play Rose on Tuesday and Barblin on Saturday. Fat for comedy, thin for tragedy! Not just a cliché, and I happily rose to the challenge! I found I could gain or lose about ten pounds between performances, utilizing alternate programs of starving and stuffing. It was easy, and anyway, I reasoned, I was only doing my job in the cause of art.

I shared a dressing room with three skinny girls who had quickly become my best friends, perhaps because we had something very much in common. Food. The only difference was when I ate what they ate, I got fatter and they didn't.

Louise and Carrie and Janet and I took a wonderful vacation together between seasons. The four of us set off for Majorca on an economy flight from London's Heathrow.

Why is it that the mirrors you look into on vacation show you an image different from the one at home? Is it the sun, your tan, or perhaps the sensuousness of exotic places that make it not possible to notice that you are *getting huge*?

We romped around that beautiful Spanish island, consuming vast amounts of paella washed down with Spanish wine from our own bottles, which we replenished from the barrel at the village store. Huge quantities of fresh bread and butter went the same way. For variation, we dipped the white floury slices into olive oil and crushed garlic and made ourselves a big fry-up. Louise and Carrie, thin as models, loved me and loved my appetite. "Here, Lynny, you finish it!" "Lynny will eat it!" "Have another, Lynny, you're on holiday!" Janet, who could gain weight but not as fast as me, tried to help, but her remonstrations were fuel to Fat Ogre breathing over my shoulder.

One day as we lay sunbathing on a promontory overlooking an unbelievably blue ocean, a man's voice called to us from his boat. "Come for a ride," he said in English. Mad young fools that we were, we said yes and swam out to him. Giggling, we clambered aboard his small sailing rig. He was tanned and Spanish, elegant, older than all of us by a good twenty years. He offered us sodas from his cooler and asked if we'd like to come for an all-day sail the next day. He'd bring food and wine and we could swim and sunbathe. It all seemed exciting and a little risqué, but we told each other there was safety in numbers. Four to one. . . .

We needn't have worried, he was a perfect gentleman (darn it), and brought the most wonderful picnic.

I felt attractive and almost glamorous, leaning against the cabin door in my bikini. No mirrors to tell me the truth. We lounged, the four of us, laughing, a little tipsy; tanned, English adventurers in the bloom of youth.

And then he said, "What do you eat, Lynny, that you are so plump and your friends so slim?"

I wanted to die. I felt reduced again to childhood. Fat Ogre wrapped its arms about me. "You're mine," it said.

In store for me on my return from Majorca was a major treat, in fact a theatrical highlight to last a lifetime: a chance to not only work in a Noel Coward play, but to be directed by the author himself. After some years during which his plays had fallen into disfavor, pushed aside as lightweight and dated, he was enjoying his renaissance.

The play was a 1920s farce, *Hay Fever,* and the plot revolved around one chaotic weekend in the house of an eccentric and flamboyant actress and her children, when four bewildered guests come to stay. The ensemble would include Dame Edith Evans as the mother, Judith Bliss; Maggie Smith as the vampish guest, Myra, while Derek Jacobi would be the son, Simon, and I would play the shy and gauche flapper, Jackie, another of the house guests.

Noel sent word from his home in Switzerland that he expected us all to be word perfect before rehearsals began. Many actors hate this, preferring to learn lines along with the moves which they don't yet have.

My character, Jackie, has been invited down to the country by Judith's husband, but when she arrives she is completely ignored.

In reading through the script, I thought I'd like to try giving her a lisp, for I felt it might add to her vulnerability in an amusing way. I couldn't wait to try it out at the first read-through.

We assembled at the rehearsal hall to read through the entire play for the director and Laurence Olivier, who as artistic administrator always attended first days. It was only later that I heard that Coward took Olivier aside and said, "That little Redgrave girl is very clever, but does she have a speech impediment?"

"Sir" (as we called Larry) assured "Dad" (as we called Noel) that I didn't, and Noel allowed me to keep the lisp.

He was wonderful to me. I'd been afraid that he'd be rigid and old-fashioned, ordering the precise line readings he wanted. But no—he encouraged me to try anything, any bit of business that I could think of. If it was in character and made him laugh, I could keep it in. It was through him and his enthusiasm, encouragement, and wit that I really learned for the first time how to use rehearsals properly, and why it's a good idea to get the lines out of the way beforehand. Before that, I had invariably been too timid and embarrassed to properly experiment, finding that only in performance could I let go. And of course that's a little late!

There is a brief scene at the beginning of the third act when Jackie, having had the most miserable weekend, comes downstairs on the morning of her departure, tries to eat breakfast, and bursts into tears. She is all alone on the stage. "You're a very clever little girl," said Noel, wagging his forefinger at me, "I'll give you till tomorrow to invent something for Jackie to do during those first two minutes. If you make me laugh, you can keep it in." My extra weight gained in Majorca helped the scene. I clomped down the stairs mumbling to myself, tried to adjust my clothes in case anyone should be watching, and gradually built up to the tearful collapse. Noel laughed. I grew ten feet tall!

But not everyone was enjoying Noel as I was. Dame Edith was having a terrible time. She was seventy-six years old and although she'd played the role before on television, she was having a problem learning her lines, and found it most upsetting that the rest of us knew ours.

Dame Edith had had the most magnificent career in the theater. She'd played Rosalind in *As You Like It* with my father back in 1936 and it was public knowledge that she had fallen madly in love with him. I think she found young women threatening, for she treated me and Maggie and the other actresses with extreme distrust.

We all bent over backward to make her feel comfortable, to let her know how much we admired her, that we were with her not against her, but the slightest thing and she'd be thrown. It all came to a head at one of the final rehearsals in the hall, when we had a different couch because the usual one had gone to be reupholstered, the understudy was rehearsing for Maggie who had a dental appointment, and I was trying to break in my costume shoes which were squeaking. Edith floundered about with her lines that last day and to cover her very real fright, decided to blame the unexpected changes. "I can't work like this, Noel!" she declaimed, her famous voice swooping through every note in a two-octave range. "The little Smith gel isn't here, I haven't got my sofa, and the little Redgrave gel keeps stamping her feet."

Noel forged ahead, outstretched finger bobbing away. "Now Edith darling, you are behaving just like a nervous horse, shying at everything you see. Come on, everyone, offer Edith some carrots and sugar." Dame Edith was not amused.

We set off by train for Manchester, where the play was to open for its tryout.

Edith traveled with a friend, actress Gwen Ffrangcon Davies, obviously still terribly thrown by Noel's "nervous horse" remark and the youthful confidence of the rest of the company. They sat together in their compartment discussing the play, the actors, the set, the opening night, flowered hats bobbing and gloved hands gesticulating. By the time we arrived at our destination the two of them had worked themselves into a frenzy of nerves. On disembarking, they were seen arm in arm stomping off in the direction of the Christian Science Reading Room. We were supposed to have a small invited audience at that evening's dress rehearsal and then would open for the critics the following day.

Everyone was anxious, but Edith arrived at the theater tearful and desperately insecure. She asked that the audience first be sent home and we then staggered through a very uneven run-through.

Because Noel was concerned about Edith's age and health, he had early on asked Maggie Smith if she would learn all of Edith's part. Maggie was much too young for it, but if God forbid Edith missed a performance, then at least the audience would still have a recognizable name in the lead. And so at midnight, after Edith had gone home, we began another run-through, this time with Maggie. Just in case.

Monday I awoke early, excited and nervous. Nervous for myself but also because of Dame Edith. I felt awful for her, and hoped she'd had a good night's rest.

I got a phone call from the stage manager. Dame Edith was hysterical, saying she couldn't go on and that she was going back to London. Noel was talking to her and Sir Laurence had been sent for. We seemed headed for disaster.

Eventually it was time to go to the theater, where Noel was waiting. "Everything's all right," he said. "Edith will play tonight."

We heaved a huge sigh of relief. "How did you persuade her?" we asked.

"I took a bit of a gamble. When she told me this morning she had to go back to London I said to her, that's perfectly all right, Edith, because we rehearsed Maggie Smith last night, and she's going to be absolutely brilliant." So Dame Edith, great actress that she was, was out of that bed and down at the theater within five minutes, where she rose to the occasion magnificently.

Lines continued to be a problem for her though, not helped by the fact that back in London, *Hay Fever* played only once or twice a week. So a prompter was placed strategically behind the scenery to bail her out if necessary, which gave birth to one of the more glorious of show business anecdotes.

It was during a matinee, the big parlor-game scene with everyone onstage, and suddenly there was an awful silence. Edith's turn to speak, and one of those rare theatrical moments where it was impossible for another character to pick up the line for her. The nervous young prompter whispered the line.

Silence.

Again—whisper whisper whisper.

"Speak up, dear," said Edith loudly. He did.

"I know the line," she said indignantly, "but whose is it?"

The audience loved it and gave her a big round of applause.

I stayed in touch with "Dad" up until his final illness and death in 1973, and always he treated me with enormous generosity. He attended the opening of my first starring role in the West End, Michael Frayn's first play, *The Two of Us,* in 1970. A huge bouquet of flowers had arrived in my dressing room just before curtain time. I ripped open the card and then nearly fainted. Noel was out front!

The card said, "Please speak clearly and with great beauty."

4

The Fat Ogre Takes Over

So here I was, twenty-one years old, earning my own living, and doing pretty well too. I had left my parents' home, had my own little apartment, a car, and a growing reputation as an actress. I was also spending more and more time with Fat Ogre.

With so much wrongheaded dieting at home, I turned my attention to books and magazines, hungry for information that I could put to immediate use. Some were reasonably sensible, some just silly. They all seemed to work—at first I would drop pounds and pounds, but none of them told me how to maintain myself at my new weight. I fell rapidly into the Yo-yo Syndrome. Start a diet, lose weight, feel deprived, and then eat more than ever. I felt unwell much of the time. Bloated after a binge, lighthearted after a fast. Disgusted with myself, I tried to find reasons to blame other people for my hopeless state.

I tried the "Grapefruit and Egg" diet. The first day you can eat half a dozen eggs and at least two grapefruit and at the end of the week after another dozen eggs you're allowed a little chicken and fruit salad. No bread, no fat, no vegetables, no milk. The whole world takes on a yellow tinge.

Then there was the "Eat Fat, Get Thin" diet. On this you could eat almost unlimited butter and cream (shades of Cousin Lucy!). "The Drinking Man's Diet," "The Banana Diet," "The Fruit Juice Diet," and "The Fish and Chips Diet."

I went the medical route too, as we are taught to do, and tried certain doctors who today would probably lose their licenses. One such person gave me a daily fix, with a needle, of some unidentified drug while I dutifully consumed four ounces of ox tongue, two apples, and one serving of a green vegetable. He never checked my medical background, never even took my blood pressure. But I'd step on the scale and see between 2 and 3 pounds dropping off and think I was doing great. Trouble was, after ten days or so, very dizzy but definitely thin, I would have to give up—and before long even my carefully watched caloric intake would start to put the pounds back on.

Doctor G. was another doctor, he's the one I went to during the tour of *Billy Liar*. I was recommended to him by my father, who claimed good results having successfully followed Dr. G.'s regime. This one allowed you regular food, including plenty of meat, provided you took with it a handful of strange but colorful pills. He never explained what they were for, and since this was the early sixties no one, least of all me, questioned the wisdom of a doctor.

Of course, Fat Ogre never left me.

I had long noticed that the thin me and the projected fat me, which I had by now named "Fat Ogre," had two distinct personalities, and I realize now that I actually put both of them to use.

The thin me was the person buried inside the fat one, desperate for freedom, desperate to experience life. She was sensitive, witty, dramatic, confident, sexy, and afraid. Oddly, the thin me seemed to have the greater obsession with food, and could barely get through the day without eating.

I felt at the time that the fat me was my worst enemy, but highly exploitable. The fat me was puppy-dog funny. The fat me could clown and joke, even be acceptably grotesque. And, of course, the fat me could eat anything she wanted, without any feelings of guilt. And perhaps, and this was foremost, the fat me was my guard and protection. On the other hand, the fat me didn't have boyfriends, because what if she got thin and still no one was attracted to her? Yes, the fat me was also afraid. So Fat Ogre was the protection the thin me required. My parent, I guess the psychologists would say.

I'd empty my refrigerator of all fattening foods. When I'd open the fridge door on my late return home from a performance, a lonely green Granny Smith apple would peer balefully back at me.

Sometimes I'd get really desperate—having just lost 8 pounds in a week all I could think of was *food*. Any food. Not just candy, for while I did have a fairly sweet tooth, nuts, potato chips, cheese, and buttered toast were even more tempting.

I found that just one bite of anything finished any semblance of self-censorship. "Well, I've ruined my diet with this packet of nuts, I'd better eat some chocolate to make things really bad. I'll start a new diet Monday." Back to all the old tricks.

At that time I lived around the corner from Victoria Station, and at night this was a most unsavory place. A somewhat updated Dickensian environment, it seemed to me. Panhandlers, "meths" drinkers, pickpockets, pimps, drug addicts, dope pushers, and gangs. Not a very safe place to walk alone at night.

But you know how it can be—you try to sleep and all you can think is *I want food. Fattening food. I want it now.*

> *"But I've just lost eight pounds."*
> *Fat Ogre pops its head up beside me.*
> *"Don't be silly," says this traitorous imposter. "Just one bar of chocolate from the candy machine in Victoria Station. Prove to yourself you can buy just one, eat it, and go to bed."*
> *"I don't want to break my diet," I say climbing out of bed to find my purse, quickly counting out the change for the machines. "Besides, I'm afraid to go to Victoria Station." I'm dressed now, running down the five flights of stairs from my apartment.*
> *Fat Ogre starts a slow chant, "Cadbury's Chocolate."*
> *Left Right, Left Right.*
> *"Potato Chips, Potato Chips."*
> *Left Right, Left Right.*

"Aero Bars, Aero Bars."
Left Right, Left Right.
    It's cold. A damp foggy night in London Town. I dodge
two tramps, a pimp, an enraged prostitute, and a barely
teenage pickpocket.
    Into the station, heart pounding, I hear a voice. Go
home! *It's mine. But Fat Ogre has the change already*
counted out: shillings, pennies, sixpences, florins. Clink,
clink, clink. Out come the chocolate bars, chips, nuts. Quick
into the purse. Turn for home. Open one wrapper as I walk—
no voices now. Mmm—delicious. Eat quickly. Doesn't seem
so much that way. Up the five flights, key in the door, close
it. Finish the feast. Brush your teeth, don't look in the mirror,
you'll face yourself in the morning.

Of course there were the good days, times when the world
seemed to tell me I was in control. My career was still on track.
I went with the National Theatre Company on their historic
trip to Russia and Germany, and played Miss Prue opposite
Olivier's Tattle in the restoration comedy *Love for Love.* Moscow
and West Berlin also saw his towering performance as the Moor
in *Othello,* and the Brighouse comedy *Hobson's Choice* rounded
out our offering.

I was by now totally involved in theater. Lived it and
breathed it. I had a weight problem—and so what? When the
time came for me to play some of the great roles, I would be
able to lose it. Easy. When the big break came my way, everyone
would be able to see what was *really* inside me.

I envisaged my life continuing forever at the National. I
could, I thought, quite happily look forward to passing quietly
away after or perhaps during the matinee of some Chekhov
play. After all, I had only just signed a three-year contract, one
of the first company members to be offered one. I so loved that
life.

One day a call came for me to have a meeting with Olivier,
who was also, remember, the boss. What could he want to tell
me? A new role? Another tour of Europe? I was apprehensive
and excited, for a private meeting with "Sir" was not an everyday
occurrence.

I dressed smartly for the meeting. My usual early 1960s

mask of makeup to hide my puddingy face. Dark contouring looking like bruises, pearly white highlight on my cheekbones. Pale lipstick, heavy black eyeliner, and false eyelashes. Oh God, do I remember those eyelashes! Sir Laurence sat me down and offered me a drink. A strange sign, I thought. Nervously, I accepted a tomato juice.

"Baby," he began, his eyes rolling to the ceiling in a strange parody of himself, "we really don't have any parts for you next season."

Gulp.

"You just don't have enough experience under your belt, and quite honestly I can't foresee the day when any director is going to give you a leading role."

I felt hot and puffy and helpless and sad and angry. Tears started plopping out of my eyes into the juice.

"But Sir. . . ." I tried to speak. I hated myself for crying. I hated the fact that my sobs made me totally inarticulate. There was so much I could tell him if only I could stop this stupid crying.

"You are *brilliant*, baby," Sir interrupted, rolling the *r* and snapping the *t* as only he knew how, "but you are our flopsy bunny actress." Something looking like a dead cockroach was floating in my drink. It was one of my false eyelashes.

"You can go on playing *Much Ado*, maybe you could do Phoebe in *As You Like It*, but it might be better for you to leave."

I retrieved my eyelash, mumbled, gulped again, and left the room. All I could think of was "Flopsy Bunny." I cried all the way to my car, all the way home. Leaving! Leaving my wonderful company, leaving my friends, leaving my dressing room, leaving my world. . . .

I finished out that season. Just small roles, and sadly the day came to pack up my things. Was this going to be my destiny as an actor, my true state, unemployment?

The summer stretched ahead.

At about this time, my sister had been offered the title role in a film to be called *Georgy Girl*. Based on a novel by Margaret Forster, it was the story of a large and lumpy girl, living in what was then called "Swinging London." Georgy was envious of her slim and beautiful roommate, who was having a heavy relationship with a handsome but roguish lover. Georgy's parents worked as cook and butler for a lecherous but rich businessman who had his eye on Georgy. Yes, a sex-filled love triangle with four corners.

There was some talk that I might be offered the tiny part of Peg, the neighbor.

I was reading in bed in my apartment one evening, ready to turn out the light, when the phone rang. It was Otto Plaschkes, the producer. "I know it's late, but could you come over right away to my place. I have to discuss something with you."

In his living room he gave me a cup of coffee, and then said, "I don't quite know how to tell you this." I thought he was going to tell me that they weren't going to give me the part of Peg after all, though it seemed unnecessary to lug me out of bed for that piece of news. I now knew all about rejection.

"We've just had word that Vanessa hates the script and has dropped out of the movie. After your audition, the director told me he thought we'd hired the wrong sister for Georgy."

My heart missed a beat.

"He feels you should play it. I'm not as sure about it as he is, but with shooting due to start in ten days, no other ideas have appeared, so I'm offering you the role."

Sleep didn't come at all that night. I felt elated and yet terrified, very uncomfortable about Vanessa's involvement. She certainly was right for this role, at least for the sexy part, although I had secretly wondered about how she was going to look ungainly and lumpy.

I called her in Rome to find out what was going on and what her feelings were. Perhaps what I really needed was permission and approval. "I think the script is a load of old rubbish," she said. "I threw it in the Tiber. But for God's sake, if you want to do it, do it. I wish you great success." Whoopee!

There was much to do before shooting began. Ten days. Costumes to fit, songs to be recorded, meetings with Silvio Narizzano, the director. "For goodness sake don't diet," he said. "Georgy has to be big and awkward. Go and enjoy yourself between now and next week. Eat."

I was in heaven. I had a starring role in a movie, I was

going to play opposite James Mason and Alan Bates and Charlotte Rampling, and I had a license to *eat.*

The work was wonderful. Twelve weeks of all-consuming passion. I couldn't wait for that drive to the set each dark wintry morning. The long hours made me very hungry and I ate nonstop, no guilt and no self-hatred. I was *following orders*!

Sometimes I'd have to do press interviews during the lunch break. Of course it hurt to find newspaper articles headlined "Ugly Duckling of the Redgrave Family." But I told myself that I was a serious actress, this was all part of the job, and besides, they only called me that because I did the interviews dressed in my baggy Georgy sweater.

While I felt strongly that Georgy and I were very different, there were scenes that I could empathize with completely. Georgy's awkwardness with her body and her sexuality were very much mine too. When I was overweight, the touch of a man's hands on that extra roll of fat on my waist was almost unbearable, since it would give me a feeling of such self-loathing that romance always seemed out of the question. Did it come from those growing years, embraced by my father who would hold me by the waist to check if I'd gained?

On about the third day of filming we shot the scene at the big party where Georgy, dressed in a tight sequined gown, is offered a contract by her guardian. Would she consent to being his mistress? He locks his study door and, as the dance music blares in the background, kisses Georgy. She, disgusted and yet curiosity getting the better of her, responds with some passion. The thought of performing this scene terrified me. Kissing an actor you don't know is always a bit difficult, but James Mason? I was, to put it mildly, petrified.

Of course, my sensations were appropriate for Georgy too. There's a saying for actors who complain that they are experiencing unwanted feelings just before being called upon to act, and that is an impatient, *"Use it!"* Find a way! It almost always works. And James just naturally behaved like an expert ballroom dancer with a novice so that in the end, she looked like a champion too.

I think during that three weeks I became a little infatuated with James. I know I cried when he finished his part and had to leave.

Looking back, it's really amazing that *Georgy Girl* got made at all. People remember the film now as a rather commercial and bittersweet comedy, but the story actually had a very dark almost sick side to it, and upon reading the script, the British Board of Film Censors gave it an emphatic X rating. Think about it.

In the story, Georgy's roommate is pregnant and is rushed to the hospital in labor, but she doesn't want the baby, and she doesn't want Alan Bates! But shy and ungainly Georgy is secretly in love with him, and gladly offers herself as lover and mother to his child. He, though, can't handle any of this and quietly disappears, so that the child welfare authorities take steps to put the baby up for adoption. It then occurs to Georgy that her father's boss with the lascivious designs could be put to good use. She marries him! And so the film ends touchingly on the church steps, her husband/guardian in one arm and the baby in the other. . . .

Shooting was delayed several times; it seemed that "the money" was afraid of the story so that the financing was always very shaky. But eventually it got underway, corners being cut in the interests of economy, and partly for this reason Columbia Pictures shot it in black and white.

But when it was completed, no one seemed to know what to do with it. Alan and I were invited to view a rough cut, even though the music and sound effects weren't yet on the track.

In the darkened screening room, along with Silvio, the producers, and some executives from Columbia, we watched.

At the end no one said anything. Silence. Not "well done" or "thank you" or any small politeness. I was in shock. Just seeing myself on the screen at all was strange and frightening, but the total lack of reaction?

Alan took me to a little restaurant in Soho. We ordered huge plates of Spaghetti alla Bolognese and a bottle of Chianti. "Look," he said, "we had fun. We worked hard, we enjoyed working together, all of us. That's what counts. You can't win them all." I sat playing with my food. "Well, maybe it'll be better when it's completely finished and had its final cut, and the music's on," he added helpfully.

We drank a toast, I dropped a tear, we hugged, and we parted.

Now that the film was over, I was prepared for a period of "resting," which in the parlance of the actor simply means a lot of anxious calls to your agent. I knew not to expect too much until the film came out, so it seemed like a good idea to get rid of the excess pounds. But how? Left alone, I was enjoying my eating rights to the limit, and I knew I'd need some sort of supervision.

Mother had a good idea, suggesting a fat farm where I could literally starve off Georgy's weight gain. I made plans to go there with my old friend Rita Tushingham, for we both knew we'd need moral support and lots of gossip to keep us incarcerated and foodless for a week. I even fasted for two days before we went, dropping five pounds, and in the tortured week that followed dropped another thirteen.

The facility was set in a rather beautiful manor house in the country about an hour south of London. In the mornings we'd be awakened with a glass of hot water with lemon in it. Lunch after the third day was half a grapefruit. Tea was black only. Dinner another half grapefruit. In between were saunas, steambaths, and consultations with the doctors. Exercise was optional. If you felt up to it, there was an Olympic-size swimming pool and several tennis courts, but the only time we made a move toward them, we felt so weak we collapsed in a giggling mass on the footpath. So we substituted massages—much more acceptable.

It was hard to sleep properly, for our bodies couldn't adjust to the shock. The main topic of conversation around the building was *food*, a subject that permeated everything we thought and did. We'd brought mountains of reading material, but being alternately light-headed and headachy, the telly was easier to focus on. It was then that I noticed that when you're on a diet, all TV shows seem to contain food scenes. The news announcers bark headlines about a robbery at a *bakery*! A cache of illegal arms has been found in a *chocolate factory*! Soap powder, automobile, and floor polish ads disappear, and on come *food commercials*, sizzling sausages, crackling bacon, melting chocolate, creamy cakes! And the soap operas all seem to have long *eating* scenes. Even as you virtuously starve yourself into stunning giddiness, the world continues to be against you.

I awoke each morning anxious to get on the scale, and the

elation I felt at each dropped pound served to get me through the rest of another endless day. One of our fellow inmates was Vidal Sassoon. Vidal didn't really need to lose any weight and was there primarily for the rest, and maybe to get some indoor sun. He was allowed to eat a salad once a day and, joy of joys, an orange with his grapefruit, but thankfully he got to eat his extras in a different dining room, along with the other eaters so that their eating wouldn't upset the noneaters. Conversation with him was always fun and helped keep us going.

Not everyone lost weight. We ran into a youngish couple at the sauna early on, and I began to notice that as Rita and I shrank, they got bigger. One day they confided in us. "We can't stand it," they said. "We drive to the pub every day. Last night, we had roast turkey, french fries, and beer. We're going for lunch now, want to join us?" Feeling quite saintly, we politely declined.

A couple of months later, several pounds regained, and Georgy the actress and *Georgy Girl* the film were both ready for what was to come. It was entered in the Berlin Film Festival of 1966. The British Board of Film Censors decided it wasn't quite as immoral as they thought at first reading and decided to give it an "A" (meaning that anyone over sixteen could see it). Columbia rustled up some money, and it was decided that I was in good enough shape to go over and help promote it.

The cinema is huge. A gigantic screen. I watch the film amid a packed, highly appreciative audience. I look at lumpy Georgy up there trying so hard to be loved. "That's not me. It's a character."

A film festival official taps me on the shoulder, ready for my onstage appearance, it's the last few minutes of the movie. I'm escorted backstage to stand hidden by the edge of the curtain next to the huge screen. Georgy is about to be married, but from my angle, she's distorted, twisted, massive. The baby is thrust through the limo window past a startled James Mason into Georgy's arms. The Seekers' theme song, "Georgy Girl," starts to play. The final credits are rolling, the audience wildly applauding, even whistling. Hey there, Georgy Girl! *I've got to step out there in a moment. . . .*

It's a hit. They love it. I look at Georgy's huge sweet smiling face. "It's me," I think. And for the first time I see myself as others see me. Not the Lynn I would like to be, the Lynn I know is inside me, but an overweight, ungainly, funny creature. The film is a hit, but I feel a little sick.

Marriage and Motherhood

s it happened, my "resting" period ended abruptly at that moment. I was offered a TV play in England in which I played the trendy and eccentric owner of an antiques store. *What's Wrong with Humpty Dumpty?* was its title. The actor who played my assistant in this comedy was English-born, over on a working visit from America, and his name was John Clark. I remember this particularly, because a while later I married him. And he's still my husband.

Then came the lure of Broadway, to star with Geraldine Page and Michael Crawford in Peter Shaffer's *Black Comedy*. But first, Columbia wanted me to travel to New York to help promote *Georgy Girl*, now ready for release.

Flopsy Bunny . . .
Flopsy Bunny . . .

> *Hey there, Georgy Girl . . .*
> *I'll show them. I'll change. I'll arrive in New York thin.*
> *People there will accept me that way. And so will the director;*
> *I don't have to be plump for this part.*

My trip to New York, my first sight of this amazing city, fulfilled my every expectation, and more. I was indulged and petted and groomed, and adored. The film opened to great reviews, and the New York Film Critics were nice enough to give me their Best Actress Award. Or was I about to become the favorite flavor for that year? I don't know, but I began to worry when Rex Reed, in his *New York Daily News* one-on-one interview, described me as a "marshmallow on toothpicks." Unfair I felt, but accurate, I'm sure. Back in London, I went shopping for clothes for Broadway—and looking in shop mirrors I saw a different person. Long legs poking out from beneath a mini-skirt, and above it a thin body.

I remembered Doris Langley Moore and her cigarette postponement. I hadn't tried that technique; surely I could make it work with food. Of course, not completely, I'd have to eat something. But what if I kept postponing till early evening?

So that's what I did. It was hell. I'd tantalize myself with the thought of a thin me arriving in America. No more Flopsy Bunnies. About six in the evening I'd eat some spinach and a small steak or piece of chicken. Sometimes an apple, too. Black coffee till I was tired of it.

The play was a hit, so nuts to Rex Reed! *Georgy Girl* got me an Oscar nomination, and that led to a *Time* magazine cover. And I didn't even feel uncomfortable when compared to my sister, for she got her own Oscar nomination for *Morgan* and we made the *Time* cover together.

I felt on top of the world.

And capping it all, I was in love.

After the TV play in London where I met my husband-to-be, he had returned to his home in New York to appear in a cult off-Broadway production of *MacBird*. And it was during the rehearsals for *Black Comedy* that our friendship blossomed, and we were married after a head-spinning courtship on April 2 of that year 1967.

During those incredible months my postponement diet

worked beautifully, for I was too busy, too happy, and too excited to find it difficult.

*It's Saturday, April 1, 1967, and it's not April Fool's Day
for me. It's the eve of my wedding day. I've two shows today,
and just before the matinee, Mum and Dad and Greta, my
about-to-be mother-in-law, arrive from England. They met
for the first time on the plane and today will be the first time
that I will meet Greta, and John will meet Mum and Dad. I
remember how Mum told me before I left for New York, "I
know you'll meet an American and marry him while you are
there." But I had laughed and assured her that there was no
way I would be married before I was thirty. Last month I
turned twenty-four and Mum's amazing prediction is about
to come true.*

John races uptown after his Macbird *matinee, picks me
up at my stage door, and it's off to the Algonquin Hotel to
have the great meeting of the in-laws!*

*There's champagne and a cold buffet and Mum and
Dad and Greta and John and I hug and talk excitedly about
tomorrow, about the plays we are in, about their plane ride.
I love Greta immediately. We've spoken on the phone several
times, but now that we meet, I instantly take to her warmth
and from across the room see her striking Danish features
echoed in John's face. He's talking a mile a minute with Mum
and Dad, and laughing and smiling at the sheer happiness
of it all.*

*Back to our respective theaters for the evening perfor-
mance. It will be John's last, tonight. His company knows he's
leaving but don't know that it's because he's getting married.
We've been trying to keep tomorrow a secret because with the
Oscars only a week away and all the hype that surrounds
them, the press have been tailing me day and night. We want
tomorrow to be our day, not a media event.*

*At the Ethel Barrymore Theatre we've a typically rowdy
sold-out Saturday night crowd. Our stage manager, Bob
Borod, calls places for* Black Comedy. *"On stage please,
Mr. Crawford and (pause pause) The Bride . . ."*

On my way to the wings for my first entrance, Gerry Page

and Michael and the rest of the company blow me good luck kisses for my last performance as an unmarried woman.

After the show I'm too excited to sleep properly and wake at dawn with my heart thumping and face pink with excitement. I'm getting married today.

My pretty white mini wedding dress from Henri Bendel is ready in its garment bag. I take it out for another look and run my fingers lightly across the white silk and organza skirt and embroidered bodice. I'm getting married today.

The ceremony is being held at the house of our old family friend, film director Sidney Lumet, on Lexington Avenue. The women gather upstairs in the master bedroom to dress the bride for her special day, just as they've done for generation after generation. Vanessa, just flown in from Hollywood, has joined us, and Gail Lumet, and my little nieces Natasha and Joely keep running into the room to see their auntie's pretty dress.

I've hardly eaten a thing for days, too excited. And anyway, I'm determined to be a thin bride.

Tears are welling up inside me. I'm so happy. "Oh Mum, I can't stop crying and it's messing up my makeup." I feel I'm going to burst. I fix my hair and place the ribboned comb with daisies hanging from it in the back. Vanessa fastens my dress, Mum gives me my shoes, Greta a little pair of earrings. Tiny sapphires and a pearl from Denmark.

It's almost two o'clock and I hear male voices and laughter downstairs. Dad, Sidney, and John are talking to Mr. Nathanson, the minister who is going to do the honors.

The scent of gardenias hangs in the air. Vanessa gives me a bouquet of white freesias, rosebuds, and daisies and I walk downstairs on Dad's arm, the tears brimming to the edge of my eyelids, threatening to spill out like a waterfall. I'm getting married today.

We walk into the living room and there's John in a dark blue wedding suit in front of the fireplace whose mantel and mirror are surrounded by garland upon garland of gardenias. It's exactly 2 p.m. and Mr. Nathanson begins his speech. He's taken a lot of trouble to tailor it for the two young actors standing before him, full of personal touches and theatrical references.

The whole room is awash with emotion, as it was bound to be with our family. Vanessa's mascara is running in long streaks out from under her John Lennon-style dark glasses and four-year-old Tasha whispers, "I'm being very quiet, Mummy, aren't I." Baby Jenny Lumet, only six weeks old, decides that if everyone is crying she might as well join in and with a wail is whisked out of the room by her nanny.

The ceremony isn't long and soon we are exchanging the ribbed gold rings we'd bought at Tiffany's last week. (That had been a dotty experience. In an effort to keep our secret under wraps I decided to hit Tiffany's in disguise. Jet black wig from a tacky Broadway costume store, purple headscarf, and thick Brooklyn accent. "Oh look Honeee, ain't this ring kiooot?" Flushed with success at both our ring buying and my brilliant performance, we'd gone to meet a friend for lunch. As I entered the restaurant, where I intended to remove the wig in the ladies room, the maitre d' said, "Nice to have you with us, Miss Redgrave," and I realized my elaborate disguise was a flop.)

"You may kiss the bride," and suddenly, after all the emotional buildup, I am Mrs. Clark. Married woman. Very happy woman.

Our guests arrive and Michael Crawford, a budding professional photographer, takes our wedding pictures on assignment for Life *magazine. The cake has been half eaten by the ravenous hordes, but we pose with it anyway.*

After a wedding feast at Luchows on Union Square, where we are serenaded on piano and violin with the refrains of "Georgy Girl" and Noel Coward, John and I escape for one night of honeymooning at the Plaza Hotel. In the elevator on our way to the honeymoon suite, a woman says, "Aren't you Lynn Redgrave?" "Not anymore," we reply in unison.

John and I returned to live in London. I had a new movie to shoot there now, *Smashing Time*, in which I'd be paired in a kind of female Laurel and Hardy comedy duo with Rita Tushingham. (Guess which one I was. Right!) Luckily for me, John welcomed the idea of quitting the United States, which had become his adopted country, to return to live in England. The reasons will become clear if I tell you a little about him. He had left England many years before. He'd been a British child star, famous in the title role of the popular BBC radio and stage show *Just William* in the late forties, and before that even, had begun his career as comedy support to the late British comedian Will Hay on the stage of the Victoria Palace during the waning days of the Second World War. Claiming the right to a normal childhood, he'd run off to join the Merchant Navy as an anonymous cadet officer when he was seventeen. With the Silver Line, he'd circled the globe a few times, and arrived back in Britain after an absence of four years deciding to quit that life and resume his profession of actor. However, he found to his horror that the army was waiting for him to serve out two years of the National Service, so he emigrated to the only English-speaking country that didn't impose this dreaded duty on its young men, Canada. In Toronto, he was able to find a niche in his former career, and soon became successful as host of his own weekly television show on CBC Network, *Junior Magazine*. After five years, and anxious to return to his first love, the theater, he moved on to New York in the early sixties which is, sort of, where I found him. Faced with a decision to make regarding where we would live, he was curious to find out what it would feel like back in his homeland, and besides, he still had family in Britain.

So it was, after attending the Oscar ceremonies with my sister and mother (oh yes, Elizabeth Taylor won for *Who's Afraid of Virginia Woolf?*), we flew back to live in a little terrace house in Barnes, London, by Hammersmith Bridge.

We decided that we wanted a family right away. I'd always wanted babies. John had been married in Canada and had a little boy born in New York named Jonathan who had been sneaked off back to Canada by his mother, where she kept him hidden. He was only four, and John had great difficulty handling the fact that his ex-wife was denying him any possibility of forming a father/son relationship.

Filming *Smashing Time* made another weight gain necessary, and this time I really felt things would be different and that I could handle it. But then I had thoughts of getting pregnant. And there was a very good location caterer on the set. Also, I was cooking up a storm for my new husband. Well, you surely can guess the rest. . . .

John and I love food. And I love to cook, and was proud

to show off my Cordon Bleu expertise gained at the Polytechnic. An awesome combination of circumstances. Soon I came to turn down work for the purpose of getting pregnant. It was what we both wanted with all our hearts. I looked for signs that something was "happening," any signs.

I'd heard much about people getting cravings for strange foods when they got pregnant and so I'd justify every hunger pang by thinking maybe this was it. Cheesecake became a big obsession. I remember going with John to the movies one night in Soho. My period was one day late, so I felt a rush of cheesecake fever, and we raced from bakery to bakery till we found some, not easy in late-night London.

I found out that I was not yet pregnant, but my doctor warned me that I should be particularly careful with my weight. So there I was, the irresistible force of my Fat Ogre meeting the immovable object of me.

I discovered an amazingly easy way out. I started throwing up.

Disgusting as the thought was, it beat looking at myself growing back into the old Lynn. Not very often to begin with, just when I'd gone over the edge. . . .

But it seemed like the perfect solution. I thought I was probably the only person in the world who did this. Nobody was writing about bulimia in those days, and it certainly wasn't something to tell anybody.

John knew what I was doing and because he was sympathetic to my need to stay slim, felt it was the lesser of two evils. He would laugh and say no big deal, that's what the Romans did.

My flirtation with this potentially hazardous method of weight control was temporarily halted when I eventually did learn I was pregnant.

We were in New York, having returned from a belated honeymoon in St. Thomas, when I got the result of my umpteenth pregnancy test. Positive at last! Hooray!

We were ecstatically happy, and returned home to England in splendid style. Due largely to my husband's love for ships and the sea, we booked passage on what was to be the last transatlantic voyage of the *Queen Mary*. And of course every night there was a festive ball of some kind. The food, the best on the Atlantic, was better than ever, all stops pulled out for the Queen's retirement to Long Beach, California.

For me it was a reprieve from pressure. Fat Ogre retired from sight and my pregnancy allowed me to feel that I could—should—eat for two. We discussed plans for a home birth. It was going to be *our* baby, and so we resolved to learn all we could to take advantage of home birth facilities and procedures, which are still, happily, available in the British Isles.

At home in London I went out immediately to buy maternity clothes and literally ate my way into them.

I wanted everyone to see I was pregnant, and for the first time in my life it seemed I was able to eat heartily in company without feeling that people were watching me. I was pregnant, I was married, I was healthy, so I was allowed. . . .

In my sixth month my doctor began telling me that I should cut down on food, as I had already gained thirty pounds. I was able to slow up a little, but by the time I went into labor, I was fifty pounds up. My legs had swelled, and I found it almost impossible to get into a comfortable position at night. I deeply regretted the early months of indulgence.

That first labor of mine lasted over thirty hours of exhausting excitement. It started out in the morning at home in bed, a fully planned home birth, but despite strong contractions nothing was happening properly, so my cautious doctor and midwife reluctantly shipped me off to Queen Charlotte's Maternity Hospital in the London borough of Hammersmith. Hospitals!

They give me gas and air to breathe, and when the tank runs out they swear it hasn't.

They try to sabotage my Lamaze training. "Don't do that silly breathing. Take some nice deep breaths and just relax!"

"Relax? Are you out of your effing wits?"

John's huffing and puffing, willing me to stay with my training. "You can do it. Blow two three four. . . ."

"Oh God, look at the time," moans a nurse. "If she doesn't deliver in fifteen minutes I'm going to breakfast."

Around 11:15 a.m. I'm examined for the hundredth time by a doctor who tells me that they're going to take some blood from my emerging baby's head to test whether or not he's in distress. Not getting enough oxygen or whatever.

"Don't hurt the baby. Don't hurt the baby."

They insert the needle, then look stern. "We are going to put you out with a general anesthetic and get him out with forceps."

Another needle, this time into my hand.

"Please let John stay. Please."

"Sorry."

The baby's dead, I'm sure.

Fade to black.

When my eyes opened, two nurses were washing me, blood everywhere. I opened a dry, woolly mouth, and the new mother's anxious and predictable cliché popped out.

"Is the baby all right?"

"He's gorgeous. A little boy eight pounds, eleven ounces. Your husband's seen him. He's a bit bruised and swollen from the forceps, but that'll go down in a day or two."

We named him Benjamin and he was gorgeous. Black and blue, but strong and healthy and ours.

The next two days at Queen Charlotte's were still a nightmare of bureaucracy and rules. The hospital started its day at noon, and as my delivery was completed sixteen minutes before noon, I almost immediately became a second-day mother. That meant I should be capable of hobbling down to the endless hallway to take a bath that afternoon. I protested feebly because of my stitches, but they insisted. The bathroom was occupied when I got there. "Please," I moaned, "will you be long? I've just given birth, I'm desperate!" One very grand clipped voice called back, "Sorry. I'm holding the next place for Mrs. Reginald Bosenquet, you'll have to ask her!" Hobble hobble down the corridor. Bosenquet was a very popular celebrity anchor and newscaster of the day. Knock knock, "Hello, you don't know me, Mrs. Bosenquet, but I've just had a baby and I've got to have a bath. I've got 7,042 stitches and I'm going to faint, please please can I go next."

A high-pitched even more upper-crust voice called back, "Poor old you. Of course!"

As I worked my way back to the bathroom I thought fondly of Bosenquet's newscasts and vowed to watch only him in future.

Once bathed, they wouldn't allow me to nurse our Benjy right away, and wouldn't even let him stay with me.

"No dear, he's had a rough time, he needs lots of peace and quiet," and off they sent him to the shrieking inhabitants of the overcrowded nursery.

Next morning they agreed to let me try to breast-feed him. His bruises were nearly gone and I held him to me. A little experimentation, and to my immense pride I found that we both seemed to know just what to do. I immediately phoned John and he said he'd be there for the next feeding at lunchtime.

Matron bustled in holding the beautiful Benjy.

"Now then, Mr. Clark, husbands can't stay in the room while we breast-feed."

John and I looked at each other, horrified. This special moment was about to be ruined.

"I want him to stay, Matron," I begged.

"No dear, it's against the rules. We just can't have the disruption."

Benjy and I began crying together.

"Now look what you've done, Mr. Clark, you're upsetting Mummy."

John stood up. "Matron, this is a private room, my wife wants me to stay, I want to stay, and this baby did not get conceived with me pacing up and down in the corridor. Now I would like *you* to leave."

We checked out of the hospital the next morning and went home to start our family life. I vowed that if humanly possible I would never give birth in a hospital again. Of course, that was 1968.

I didn't want to go back to work until Benjy was five months old, and meanwhile we took him with us everywhere. We went to stay with Vanessa and her new flame, Franco Nero, who were making a film together in northern Italy. In their rented farmhouse near Brendola, we ate homemade pasta and drank the farmhouse wine, and I reveled plumply in motherhood.

Looking back, I can think of nothing to beat this scene.

A little champagne, a little pasta, a little fruit, a little cheese, a little wine. . . . A baby asleep in my arms, John at my side, candles on the table, Vanessa sitting across from me. . . .

Franco downs his last forkful of fettucini and leans back in his chair, the picture of fulfilled Italian manhood.

"Now about circumcision," he opens. "How can you English be so barbaric?"

John explains that while there are lots of cases of people having to have circumcisions later in life, a horrible thing to happen, he had never met anyone circumcized as a baby who grew up and wished he wasn't.

"But I tell you. The problem." Franco won't let it drop. "I tell you what happens if you are circumcized. At thirty you are impotent."

John deadpans, "Well, I'm thirty-five, Franco."

Pause. Pause.

"Okay, maybe forty. Just wait and see."

A little more wine, some more conversation, a little cold chicken, a Perugina chocolate truffle, a little more pasta as we clear the table. . . .

Then we boarded a steamer in Venice and sailed down the coast to the Greek island of Corfu to visit our friend Peter Bull, our new and best friend from the cast of *Black Comedy*, who had a little house on the nearby island of Paxos. Poor Bull, so anxious, no doctors on his tiny little island, and our new baby only six weeks old. Those were irresponsible days, I suppose.

There we ate olives and lamb and eggplant moussaka, and the ubiquitous taramasalata made with cod's roe, garlic, and olive oil, until Benjy complained loudly for a whole night about the garlic in his milk.

As the time for my return to work approached, I got back to my postponement diet and dropped the excess pounds. But again and again I would fall off the food wagon, and feel Fat Ogre dangerously close to enveloping me once more. So I began to combine my two methods of control.

Nothing for breakfast, an apple or salad for lunch, and for dinner a huge feast which I would then get rid of.

Fat Ogre had undergone a strange mutation. There was

never a morning that I would wake without thinking of food, but now I knew I could feast later. In fact, it was starve and feast, because my new solution could only work with a full stomach.

I became hooked. Weeks of near starvation were then followed by weeks of a method that became progressively more distasteful but more obsessive. I knew how self-destructive I was being, but so frightened was I of the power of food that I was prepared to live this way.

I continued to work. A trip to Singapore to shoot *The Virgin Soldiers*, a first film for John Dexter of the National Theatre, *The Last of the Mobile Hotshots* in Louisiana for Sidney Lumet, and a play at the Edinburgh Festival. But the battle with Fat Ogre continued.

We conceived our second baby, so once again I had a reprieve. Eating to make a baby was okay because when you're pregnant you're not fat—you're pregnant, right?

Once again we planned a home birth, and this time Kelly's delivery was as calm and glorious as Benjy's had been violent. I'd been told that first babies can be complicated, and subsequent births are usually better.

We were living now in a large old house in the middle of Barnes Common, which seemed a perfect setting for the event. Labor began just after midnight on February 26th, 1970. Mrs. Ridley, our midwife, and her assistant came immediately and stayed till early evening when Kelly was born. A long slow first stage was accompanied by soothing Beatles' music throughout the day, mostly our favorite "Strawberry Fields" and "Penny Lane." And at the moment of birth, after some hard pushes, John made sure that Vivaldi's *Four Seasons* boomed forth, and there in our own brass bed was a delicate little baby girl. She lay for the briefest of seconds in purpley gray skin.

"Make her breathe," I gasped, and suddenly she cried while a life-giving pink color flowed from her face through to her toes, contrasting with the dark wisps of her hair.

How sweet it was to lie with our new baby in our own bed. Benjy, only twenty-two months old, himself born fuzzily bald, saw her just moments after she was born. She was dressed in her own clothes, no hospital gowns this time, and Mrs. Ridley

gently brushed her hair, giving it a little parting. The front
doorbell rang. It was the little girl who lived in the house at the
bottom of our garden.

"Mummy and Daddy say congratulations," she said, hand-
ing John a bottle of champagne.

In the excitement of Kelly's arrival we had forgotten to
draw the drapes, and so the neighborhood had shared in the
miracle of our birth.

We raised our babies in London to begin with, but gradually
found ourselves feeling dissatisfied with life in England. Maybe
I was beginning to see it through John's eyes, who was beginning
to become disenchanted with Britain. It could have been the
high taxes, or perhaps the continual long trips to Family Court
in Toronto where John vowed that he would continue to fight
for access to his son, over his former wife's continuing resistance.

We moved fractionally west to the Republic of Ireland for
two years, and lived in a little stone house on the edge of a tall
cliff outside Dublin, overlooking tiny Ireland's Eye. We'd bought
the house as a vacation retreat, but as we began to renovate it,
we began to realize that Ireland was a wonderful place to raise
small children, and the people were so friendly. The main excitement seemed to come from exotic weather changes, from
sun to rain showers to rainbows sometimes in the space of an
hour. Across the bay to the north on a good day we could just
discern through our living room window the faint outline of
the mountains of Mourne sixty miles distant. Locals had it that
if you can see the mountains of Mourne, it's going to rain, and
if you can't, then it's already raining.

We brought my Nanny over to a cozy little nursing home
a few miles away from Howth. Well into her eighties and quite
adorably dotty now, Nanny needed proper round-the-clock
care. She loved the nuns who looked after her and we visited
her regularly. She always knew me and John. "What do you
take me for, a fool?" She'd laugh, her sweet round face so full
of love. Otherwise she lived a marvelously happy fantasy life.
All of her favorite people who had died now magically visited
her and took her out to lunch, usually, according to Nanny, in
a Rolls-Royce.

It was hard trying to work from Ireland. Though only an

hour away from London by plane, the British think of it as totally off the beaten track. Wishing to blend in with the local scene, we produced a play at Dublin's venerable Gate Theatre, *A Better Place.* For me it was notable as John's first directing job, and turned into a great adventure, but the offers from abroad got less and less as people seemed to assume that I'd dropped out exclusively to bake bread and have babies. We began to get restless again.

Of course, Fat Ogre took up residence with us. Ireland's food and drink and social life made it easy to not work, to not even feel the desire to work ever again. I loved my family, I loved Ireland, and I just loved the life.

Then out of the blue came an offer from New York, a play that a few years earlier I would have easily turned down. *My Fat Friend* is the story of a 200-pound young woman who owns a small bookshop in London. She lives safely with a gay middle-aged stockbroker and a rather tongue-tied Scots writer. And into her store one day walks an American who falls in love with her. He has to leave for six months, however, and plans to return to claim her as his bride. In that time her well-meaning room-mates successfully slim her down, and in the final scene she is reunited with her lover, who takes one look, and promptly leaves her. No thank you. Yes, he liked fat better, and yes, it was a comedy. Ha ha! Of course, the moral was that while she lost her lover, she found herself. Pick and choose that one, I say. The play would be presented on Broadway, and cast already were John Lithgow and George Rose. We accepted it immediately.

Of course, the plot will tell you that I could not be fat for the role. Indeed, logistics and realities being what they are, it was necessary for me to be gorgeously thin for the triumphant but mordant ending. Even I could not slim down during the unwinding of a two-hour play, but I could put on padding. It was now 1974, and I put Fat Ogre firmly in his Irish closet while we prepared to leave for New York in February, just before Kelly's fourth birthday. Nanny had suffered a severe stroke a few days before our departure and I went to say good-bye to her for what I feared would be the last time.

Working on *My Fat Friend* was strange for me. It contained a message, and I wanted to get it right.

Vicky begins on a wave of belligerence provoked by an eating binge the night before. How well I remembered and identified with that! She comes down to breakfast with her roommates Henry and James, and suddenly they notice she's wearing her Fat Dress, the only thing she can get into. I knew what it was to carry fat, but I had a tough time making the scene completely real, something about my attitude for Vicky was wrong. Too quiet? Too depressed? I felt I needed help. Even at my heaviest I'd never been as big as Vicky.

I looked up Weight Watchers in the yellow pages and placed a call. I was referred to my nearest location and the lecturer was surprised at my request to come and observe a meeting. She explained that it was really important the members feel completely uninhibited, allowing a stranger to watch them would be against everything Weight Watchers was trying to do. But as I told her the story of the play, she began to see how important it was for me to portray Vicky accurately and sympathetically. I didn't want her to be a caricature, a stereotypical funny fat woman. Maybe the play well done could help people.

We agreed that I would come in as if I was a member from another meeting, but that I'd sit at the back and keep a low profile. Early on in the weighing-in process I found what I was looking for. A young woman burst into the meeting. About twenty-five years old, she was of medium height, short carrot-colored hair, a huge shapeless pink dress, gray cardigan, and bare feet thrust into wooden Dr. Scholl's sandals which beat out a furious tattoo on the shiny linoleum floor. She was clearly angry, but kept up a line of jokey repartee in a bright voice, as if defying anyone to feel sorry for her. She approached the screened-off weigh-in area at full steam, shedding jacket, book, bag, purse, wristwatch, and earrings as she walked. I heard her jumping up and down on the scale and then she emerged the other side of the screen hurling comments left and right mindless of whether anyone was listening or not. She was the first person to get up and speak after the lecturer had given her opening talk to the group.

Apparently the night before, Mary, as I shall call her, had gone on an eating binge to end all binges. It had all started with a call from her boyfriend, who had been out of town for a week. They made a date for the weekend and happy and elated Mary, who had just lost three pounds, imagined how pleased he would be when he saw her again. She decided to celebrate with just one chocolate chip cookie, and then another and another. . . . As she spoke she started to cry, but brushing away her tears she began telling jokes and stories about her day at work, her bus ride to the meeting. She had us all in stitches.

That is Vicky, I realized. I had to start the play with all that anger, and then try to cover it with the humor that so many of us resort to in our effort to feel liked and loved in spite of our own self-hate feelings I could so easily relate to.

The lecturer addressed us again. She was fun and energetic and obviously loved what she was doing. I don't now remember the details of her comments, but two things stood out. Weight Watchers is "people helping people" to become self-motivated, and with the group support we could learn "self-love." I was to remember these words eight years later.

I went back to rehearsal the next day and hit exactly the right note for the first scene. Now that I had the feelings in the right place, I wanted it to look as realistic as possible. I wore a lightweight fiber-filled fat suit reaching to my knees and elbows, and a bra over silicone prostheses which would move as I moved. Costumes on top of that. A long full wig, no makeup, and to help myself walk heavily, Dr. Scholl's wooden sandals. The perfect touch, thanks to Mary. The audience so completely believed in Vicki's weight that when I took off my coat at the end and revealed a slim body, they would gasp in bafflement, and applaud. I got a lot of letters from audience members who said that even though they realized it was a theatrical trick, seeing me fat and thin in the space of two hours made them feel that they could surely lose weight too. So my message was getting through! During that run, Fat Ogre stayed firmly behind in Dublin, and I never wanted to meet him again. I ate miniscule amounts, still no breakfast, preferably no lunch, and yet I was able to function.

A few weeks into the run, while John was on a quick trip back to Ireland, he phoned me to say that Nanny had died. Another stroke, from which she had not regained consciousness. The call came just before a matinee and I fought to control my emotions at the loss of so dearly a loved one.

The Catholic sisters who had so beautifully cared for her,

thoughtfully respected her religious faith and gave her a Protestant burial. Sadly, I could not attend it as the play was still running.

Now all that remained in Ireland were a few memories, no ties. The New World began to feel like home. So when *My Fat Friend* ended after a run of almost a year, we decided to stay in America.

John had taken out his citizenship many years before, and so he was able to apply to immigration to have the status of Benjy, Kelly, and me changed to that of "resident alien," an identity that to this day sometimes makes me feel like a friendly visitor from another planet. The fact of being issued a "Green Card" does nothing to dispel that feeling—but anyway, I was one proud wife and mother when I, accompanied by John and the children, made my way down to the office of U.S. Immigration and Naturalization Service District Director Maurice Kiley for our final interview and the official card-receiving ceremony. It was no coincidence that this milestone in our lives took place on January 2, 1976, making us the first people to be officially admitted to the USA in the Bicentennial Year. I guess the irony of the date was not lost on Immigration, and the press was called (not by me) to immortalize this solemn event for posterity. Just as the photographer squeezed off his picture, Kelly chose to lean over and yank Benjy's hair. Benjy howled, and a tremendous fight ensued, and so it was that we were blazoned across the front page of the *New York Daily News*.

As the years went by I felt that I really had got myself under control. I accepted my obsession with food as something I had to put up with, and assumed that low metabolism was my cross to bear. It seemed okay to me that I had to use special measures to live with this condition, and so I resigned myself to a lifetime of self-trickery. I had several weapons in my armory, to choose as I saw fit. The trouble was, my choices were becoming less and less effective, rather like the alcoholic or drug user who needs a larger and larger fix. My pattern of starving all week during work, and pigging out the night before my day off, seemed to work most of the time. If my willpower deserted me and I wanted to give myself a "special treat," I could for short periods of time resort to my other method of control, although I began to notice tiny telltale signs on my face. Little broken blood vessels around the eyes, swollen eyelids. I knew I couldn't do it if I had to film early in the morning. But it was my well-kept secret, and I almost felt a special proprietary fondness for the trick. Certainly, I thought I was the only person in the world who could do it.

Until one day I was on a flight from Toronto where we'd made yet another family court appearance to enforce visitation with Jonathan, when I found myself sitting next to Gilda Radner, the comedienne who had recently made a big name for herself on *Saturday Night Live.* We were having a drink when she suddenly confided in me that she was bulimic. She said she was totally out of control with it, and just had to tell somebody. I told her that I had the same problem. She was as amazed about me as I was about her, and somehow sharing our confidences shook me a great deal. I think we'd been affected by it in different ways; I know I thought about it for days afterward, and came to the decision to just stop doing it anymore. I saw big problems further down that road. It proved a struggle, but gradually over the next few years I was able to escape from this particular form of self-destruction.

We spent several years in New York. Benjy and Kelly attended P.S. 59 on East 57th Street, and John and I worked in the theater, often together, doing whatever attracted us. We found that once I was no longer the Visiting British Actress, we needed to create our own opportunities, produce our own plays. So with John directing and me acting, we toured around the country in plays by George Bernard Shaw, Neil Simon, and Michael Frayn. Our favorite collaboration was Shaw's *Saint Joan,* which we played at the Goodman Theatre, Chicago, and then, with a nearly new cast, at the Circle in the Square off Broadway.

Joan is the big classical test for an actress, in much the same way that *Hamlet* challenges an actor. It's vocally tough, with long and complex speeches (she never stops arguing). Emotionally and physically draining too. Each night you have to convince the audience that Joan is ready to burn at the stake for her beliefs. That takes a special kind of discipline and concentration.

I loved Joan. A medieval liberated woman, if you like, who

has shown us all the way to hold firm to our beliefs. I learned from her.

Television had begun to lure me away from New York to the West Coast. It began with an interesting part in a Universal Studios miniseries called *Centennial*, and this time my character didn't go from fat to thin, but from eighteen to ninety. We shot it over twenty weeks in Colorado, and soon after an offer came in for the job that was to become my Trial of Fire, the TV sitcom *House Calls*.

Based on a Walter Matthau and Glenda Jackson movie, this was a hospital story. A kind of Tracy/Hepburn relationship between me as a hospital administrator and Wayne Rogers as a surgeon. Ann Anderson was witty, disdainful, vulnerable, and British to the core. Charley Michaels was attractive, chauvinistic, romantic, street-smart, and from Alabama.

The show, a half-hour comedy shot on film, again for Universal, was an instant hit.

6

Annabel

*ouse Calls* had been a mid-season replacement on CBS, debuting before Christmas 1979. But the night before we were due to commence filming our second season of shows in July 1980 the Screen Actors Guild called a strike, over conditions controlling the burgeoning videotape and cable market.

Earlier in the year John and I had begun talking about having another child. Maybe it began with Kelly and Benjy, then ten and twelve years old, desperate for a little brother or sister. Knowing a little about the birds and the bees, they assumed that *their* parents wouldn't be doing that kind of thing anymore.

"Oh please have a baby," they begged week after week. Finally, in desperation, they took me aside.

"Oh come on, Mom, let him do it—just one more time."

So I did! Besides, with the strike on, there were lazy days at home instead of daily tensions at the studio. Actually, having another baby seemed about the nicest thing we could do for each other and for the children, and this time, being true professionals, we were timing things. We figured to conceive during the strike, gestate over the shooting season, and give birth during the following summer's hiatus. So much for family planning!

Rail-thin and food-obsessed and sticking to "postponement" with the recent addition of appetite suppressants, I knew that I had to make some major changes in my eating habits if I were going to "cook" a nice healthy baby. I wasn't pregnant yet, but I knew that good health and good habits would be needed, starting at the very moment of conception.

First I decided that I should cut out drinking, diet pills, and overeating. Drink and pills for obvious reasons, and less food so that I could put off the inevitable "pregnant look" as long as possible, because it was my guess that CBS would refuse to allow Ann Anderson to be pregnant on the show. Not that I was asking them for permission, but the character was single, Middle American morals had to be respected, and not least, Wayne Rogers would probably not like it.

On the morning of November 2, 1980, a home pregnancy test gave proof positive that our efforts had produced results. Due date, Independence Day, 1981. We all went out to celebrate, keeping our dark secret for the time being, although the strike was now over and work had started up again.

This new state of affairs caused me to rethink my whole approach to the subject of weight control as it affected me, for now I knew I could not take a selfish approach any longer, with another human being to consider.

This time I didn't look on my pregnancy as an excuse to "eat for two" as I had all those years before. People were better informed, and this time I began asking questions. I found out that at four months the fetus still only measures about six inches and needs no extra body fat of its own. The words of my English midwife, Mrs. Ridley, came back to me. "You are what you eat, and so is your baby!" So this time, I took care, knowing that what I ate would play a critical part in our baby's development and growth.

My doctor told me all I needed to know, I read all the books I could lay my hands on, and resolved that no matter what, I would stick to the rules. After all, I was older and much wiser, at least while I had this little body inside my own.

On January 22, 1981, Ronald Reagan became the fortieth

President of the United States. And I was leaving the lobby of the UCLA Neuro-Psychiatric Unit, having just received an amniocentesis test. Quite an astonishing experience for me, for I lay there in bed, and saw "it" on the screen, saw its heart beating, face toward my spine. Raised its hand to its face, and kicked out, it did. Then I felt the sharp prick of a needle entering my abdomen, and I remembered my breathing exercises, which helped. Tears ran down my face, part fear, part excitement. So now I had with me a Polaroid of—what would it be? Three weeks later, I was able to stop referring to "it." Because now "it" was a "she."

At the five-month point I was starting to show. My pregnancy was not a secret any longer, and if the producers and network boys had any negative feelings they certainly didn't show it. No, Ann Anderson would not become pregnant (what an opportunity they missed to be innovative), and it actually became a fun game trying to come up with different ways of hiding the baby from the camera. Mostly, it involved clever wardrobe. Chuck Waldo, our costume designer, came up with busy prints above the waist, dark skirts, and long jackets. One clever dress had navy blue and white stripes making an inverted V pattern from where my waist should have been, totally confusing the eye and making the baby invisible.

So I was always safe standing directly facing the camera, but of course sometimes I had to turn sideways. It became second nature to raise my hand holding a progressively larger and larger clipboard or briefcase just as I turned in profile.

I stood behind filing cabinets, potted palms, life-support systems, and short actors. I sat behind a desk that was raised higher and higher till in the final week it was almost under my chin. I incorporated bits of business which involved my entering a room carrying four bags of groceries and my coat, then as I set them down the camera could move in for a close-up.

My tummy grew steadily with the baby that we had all named differently—Sashimi Hannah Lucy Leila Rose Murgatroid. Our cat, Emmy, gave birth to three adorable black kittens in the middle of the night on April Fool's Day. Then the orange canary laid three eggs. It seemed as though everything in the house was breeding.

Time flew by. I finished shooting the season's twenty-two

shows and six more for the fall season as insurance against a possible directors' strike, which took me within six weeks of B day.

I secretly wished that it would have been possible to have our little girl at home, but not only is there not the medical backup system available for home deliveries in this country that we enjoy in Britain, but I was sensible enough to know that at my age I should not put the baby at risk for any reason at all. Besides, John and I had carefully chosen the Family Birthing Center facility at the Valley Presbyterian Hospital in Van Nuys, the heart of the Valley, and they were as close to a "home" feeling as one was likely to get.

On July 2nd, during the second act of *Chekhov in Yalta* at the Mark Taper, contractions began. I wanted to go backstage to see a friend, but they were coming every four minutes. John went back after the curtain and left a note of explanation. I leaned against the wall by the stage door.

Then we went home, called the doctor, and at 4 a.m. went to the hospital! At 6 a.m. we left the hospital! It all died down and left me feeling totally exhausted and not a little foolish.

Well, I thought, she shouldn't come till her due date anyway. What a patriotic gesture it would be to give birth to my first American baby, born in "the Valley" on the Fourth of July!

I slept well and was feeling great. Since there was no sign of the baby yet, I started a huge late Spring Clean of the house. I took a break to write a letter to my dad, telling him the baby was expected any day, licked the envelope and stuck on the stamp, when Boom!

It was about 11 a.m. and I decided to keep right on cleaning up, changing beds, vacuuming rugs, and ironing shirts, but by noon I had to stop and sit down to concentrate hard so that I could breathe through the contractions.

The doctor said she wanted me in without delay, so I rushed out and sat naked on the lawn and John took the last pictures of me and my tummy!

When we got to the hospital, about an hour's drive away, they said a lady was delivering in the birthing center and maybe we couldn't use it.

Contractions were now very strong and close. At about 4:30 p.m. I wanted to push so badly but they said not to, not yet.

The two nurses, Marion and Sue, were not being very helpful, Sue chewing gum all the while. Dr. Kelley said I wanted to push because the bag of waters was bulging and if she broke it things might go too fast to get me into the family birthing room, which was now being made ready. But by five o'clock I was into the queen-size bed, rocking chair and television set at the ready, and it was all starting to happen.

They tell me to blow, I want to push, but oh God it's hard. Awful pains in my legs. They give me a small shot of Demerol because I'm finding it impossible to relax when I'm not having the contraction. They want to put the internal monitor on the baby, it goes into the scalp. I'm scared (flashback to Benjy), "Don't hurt my baby!"

They say I can push, but lying on my side or on my back is totally painful. The big double bed won't let me get a grip with my feet. "Squat on the floor," suggests Nurse Van after I've even tried being on all fours on the bed.

So I squat and grab the bed—or Van—it's much better, at least the pushes are feeling like they are doing something. I get in about three to each contraction. She's still high, her head presented wrongly, face pressed up hard against my bones, and she's finding it difficult to turn. The actual pushes feel almost pleasurable in an odd way.

One hour later and it's getting desperate. "Help me, help me," I keep calling out. Dr. Kelley stands up and she says to my greatly bemused hubby, "We may have to do a forceps or a C section," which John explains to me because I'm almost ready to throw it all in. Anything just to get this baby out. But Van—bless her—says, "I know you can do it—come on, come on—get angry, get that kid out—get mad!"

Incredible effort—"Get out of here," I yell at the baby. She starts her move and then her turn. Each heave they say there's progress, and finally they say they can see the hair— "It's coming—come on, more contractions!" But now I can sense concern that the baby may eject head first on the floor, so it's back on the bed now, legs up on portable leg rests, hold the metal below, and really push. "One more . . . now stop!"

A suspended moment.

"Now pant . . . don't push." . . . Oh God, Oh God, it's

*my baby! Covered in thick vernix, her head bulging like mad.
Let me touch her, let me touch her! John is taking pictures,
they cut the cord and suction her mucus and lay her on my
tummy. Is she all right, does she look okay? Yes, yes.*

*I look at John and we kiss. We are filled with pride and
he says I did great and I say sorry I made a fuss and everyone
is talking and laughing and thrilled that we didn't give in—
and our love child gift to each other feels warm and strong
and gorgeous and I talk to her and love her at sight just as
I knew I would when she was in me. It is twelve minutes past
eight in the evening.*

*They get her on the scales, 9 pounds, 2½ ounces. She's
also 21½ inches long—no wonder it was hard work.*

*They bring in a little bath and John bathes her in warm
water. A little suck at my breast, it feels good and she knows
what to do. . . .*

*We look at our beautiful creation and talk to her and
gently kiss her.*

*Finally the work is done, I'm cleaned up, and the bed is
changed. John is hungry and goes out to get something to eat.
He had to leave the room briefly during labor, and I panicked
totally, couldn't focus. His being there was the one thing that
made it possible to get through it.*

*John returns and we lie down together in the big bed
and I feel exhilarated and content.*

It was only then that we realized that this baby had shown the
true spirit of her independence by deciding not to arrive until
July 5th.

The next morning we made our choice of names. Annabel
Lucy. Annabel because she looked so sweetly old-fashioned and
it seemed to suit her perfectly, and Lucy in memory of my idyllic
childhood days at Whitegate, Bromyard, Herefordshire.

After an early farewell lunch brought to our room complete
with tiny birthday cake, we loaded into the car and headed for
home.

Benjy and Kelly were waiting at the door as we pulled into
the driveway. Jumping, laughing, pushing and shoving each
other, they tried to get the best look at their baby sister. "Let's
take her upstairs," we told them. So we carried the precious

new family member up to our bedroom and laid her in the middle of our big brass bed, birthbed of Kelly eleven years before.

Brother and sister carefully snuggled up on either side of Annabel, kissed her sweet pale cheeks, tears of happiness wetting her fine red-gold hair. Then they held her hands and played "This Little Piggy" with her toes. She was welcomed into the family fold with so much elation I thought she might start crying too. Instead, she fell asleep.

7

Salvation

nnabel was breast-fed by me for thirteen months, despite a great deal of unpleasantness caused when I was fired from my *House Calls* job by Universal Television/MCA. Why? I don't know to this day, although I have pretty strong suspicions. I became known as "the actress who wanted to breast-feed her baby on the set." Also, "the actress who used her baby to try to renegotiate her contract." Well, that was awful misrepresentation. All I wanted was my baby nearby in my dressing room, so that I could be with her and feed her during my breaks, and as for the other accusation, I think I was the only actress who demanded to be let in to work (with the baby in tow) under the existing terms of her contract. As everyone knows, it is not unknown for actors to walk off a show in order to be tempted back at a higher fee. Well anyway, this case of mine lingers on . . . and that's the subject of another book! But what is worth saying here is that I think the situation helped to bring about a change in Hollywood, for there are other more enlightened studios today who have gone out of their way to create day care facilities for their staff, not only because it is the humane thing to do, but because parents who have young children can be better workers, and that should make sense to industry and the workplace, or so I should have thought!

I moved on to a new sitcom at NBC, *Teachers Only*, playing a rather warm and happy high-school teacher opposite the bachelor principal of Norman Fell. And oh yes, an early episode produced a sharp performance of a minor character played by a soon-to-be-famous Michael J. Fox. I couldn't have been happier with the care and understanding from everyone. With the thoughtfulness of my producer and now excellent friend, Aaron Rubin, I found a crib in my dressing room, and a little wicker basket should I want my baby next to me in the studio commissary during my lunch break.

During this period I was about twelve pounds over what I call my "fighting weight." Perfect, I thought. The La Leche League recommends a certain amount of body fat for nursing mothers, extra energy for a good milk supply. When she'd finished nursing, I told myself, I'd drop it just like that. For me, twelve pounds meant three or four days fasting and then back to the old postponement routine.

I was on hiatus from *Teachers Only* and imagined my return to work, how pleased everyone would be to see me back to my old thin self.

I had thought I could starve but was so used to eating three meals a day I didn't want to anymore. I'd had nine months of pregnancy, thirteen months of nursing, all the time eating to make a healthy baby. Now I had to return to my old way of life. Experience that horrible empty feeling. Brace myself for the return of Fat Ogre. I was so vulnerable.

When your baby doesn't nurse anymore, you move on with a mixture of pride and regret to the new phase of her development. She doesn't need you anymore in quite the same way. My body was no longer the provider. I was no longer Mother Earth. Anyone can give her a bottle. I felt empty, lonely. Comfort that sadness. Fill that void. Eat.

An actor friend of mine who goes to OA and AA in an effort to control his food addiction once said to me, "You know,

I actually envy alcoholics, all they have to do is stop drinking, but the food addict can't stop eating because he'll die."

That's what I was, a food addict and a scale addict. I began to weigh myself every few hours. But I was gaining, not losing. Come on, Lynn, you don't need to eat.

Panic—during the two weeks that followed the end of nursing, I gained another 17 pounds.

My Fat Friend, Vicky, the Fat Dress. Weight Watchers.

What had the lecturer in Manhattan said to us all those years ago? "People helping people." "Self-love."

I knew the Weight Watchers program was nutritionally sound, and that you could eat three good meals a day, and I knew I didn't want to get into any strange diet gimmicks, I'd had enough of those. But above all, I realized that for the first time in my life I was ready to be good to me, to my own self. Self-love. Not meant narcissistically or selfishly or arrogantly. But I'd always been sensible only toward that which existed outside of me. I could be thin for a role, I could eat properly to make a healthy baby. Now it was time to do that for *me.* Time to reassess, start over, to begin a new life.

It goes without saying that I wanted to lose weight, but I also wanted to gain control. After all those years of waking to a rising sense of panic, I wanted to live normally. A program that would allow me to eat with my family, go to restaurants, go on vacation. I recognized how important eating had been to me and I knew I had to stop being held hostage in the never-ending war between my twin mutually exclusive needs to overeat and to lose weight.

I had to admit that, when I truly thought about it, none of my previous diets had really worked. It seemed to me that my kind of dieting had been an awfully lonely and private experience. The ingredient that I found missing was the emotional support of others. Could I find it in a group program?

I looked at myself in the mirror, and I didn't like what I saw. Where was I? Hiding under hair and a shapeless dress, I was still Georgy Girl.

I thought back to my one visit to Weight Watchers in New York, seeking information. What did I now want from them? Why would they be the key to success?

I called directory inquiries for the Weight Watchers number, and rather nervously asked for the nearest location and meeting times.

Our daughter Kelly, then twelve years old, wanted to come too. Only the day before, I'd found her crying because she didn't want to go to a school swimming party looking overweight in a bikini. There's definitely something in heredity, I thought. It was hard for me to walk in that first day. I hated being fat again, after years of professional slimness. Would people recognize me? After all, there had been a lot of public controversy, and understandable curiosity. Would it be embarrassing? I looked pretty ghastly; no makeup, dark glasses, elastic-waist pregnancy-jeans (the ones with the ugly inset made of stretchy material) covered by an old faded Indian gauze top, and I weighed 161½ pounds, down a bit from my absolute worst, which had only recently been 170!

I nervously fantasized how the conversation might go.

"Isn't that Lynn Redgrave?"

"No, couldn't be, she's too fat!"

"Excuse me, but didn't you used to be Lynn Redgrave?"

"What happened?"

"Hello, are you Lynn Redgrave's mother?"

The meeting was in a small bare room in a sprawling shopping-mall area, and the three of us lined up in front of a desk and paid our membership fee.

Annabel content in her stroller, me feeling sick with pounding heart, and grateful for Kelly clutching my other hand. I knew that if anybody paid us special attention we'd just want to fall through a hole in the floor.

Over at the weigh-in scale, two women were dealing with a long line of people of more shapes and sizes than I'd have thought possible. I noticed that a piece of card was flipped over the front of the scale so that the lecturer could read the result from her side but the rest of us couldn't. Nice touch, I thought. My turn at last.

She smiled at me, no flash of recognition, so I relaxed.

I had signed up as Lynn Clark, my married name, and if anyone suspected, they weren't letting on.

I expected to be simply handed a diet sheet, but instead our lecturer explained to Kelly and me that the Weight Watchers Program had four elements, all interrelated.

The Food Plan, based on various categories of food.

The Self-Management Plan, designed to reshape our eating habits and give us understanding of our weight problem.

A Group Support System and The Exercise Plan.

The meeting began with a greeting to us (the new members) and to some returning members, and a follow-up on the previous week's theme, how to manage eating out.

Our lecturer stressed the importance of keeping a food diary, and about recipes, and encouraged everyone present to participate in airing both their successes and challenges (no one talks about failure). Our lecturer was herself a Weight Watchers success story. That seemed a smart thing to do, I thought, much better that we get tips from someone who's been there too. She showed us her "before" picture. What looked like a huge down comforter with a face poking out got a big laugh. Now she had turned into and remained a trim and attractive woman. I felt encouraged. I liked the atmosphere, I liked the stories. It helped to talk to another Weight Watchers member who had lost fifty pounds and still had another thirty to go, to hear the enthusiasm in everyone's voices.

Our group was a mixed bag of ages, sexes, races, and body shapes.

There was a priest who was well on his way to goal weight. He had joined because he felt hypocritical preaching self-control while he himself was eating his way out of the pulpit. A tall woman, about 300 pounds I guessed, had her newborn baby along, determined to get herself back to the size she was ten years and five babies ago.

On the cover of my Weight Watchers attendance book were the words "Some Talking, Some Listening, and a Program That Works," and that certainly did seem to sum it up. But it took time to fully absorb this new truth. I was so accustomed to doing battle with food or the denial of it, that the idea that I could reach a point where I would no longer consider myself on a diet, seemed unthinkable. I knew as well as anybody that after my years of yo-yo behavior there was no such thing as a miracle cure. That all those quick-fix diets I'd tried had not helped me change the rotten habits that Fat Ogre and I had concocted.

The first couple of weeks on the program were wonderful.

I lost over six pounds the first week, and another four the second, before I settled down into my steady one to two pounds per week. It seemed to me that I was actually eating more food than I was used to. The choice was wide, and I was surprised to find that no food was really forbidden. The quantity was limited, yes, but nothing was looked on as being "bad." Different ingredients could be substituted to satisfy individual tastes, to make dishes that looked and felt like their fat-laden equivalent, but weren't.

As the weeks went by, I began to realize just how important the lecturer's role was in helping us change. This was not a quick-fix program. I'm sure most of us joined to drop unwanted pounds quickly, but I began to realize that fast was not necessarily good. Weight Watchers was telling us that while we had a number of choices in dealing with our need to change, the changes had to be made gradually.

To allow us to get personal solutions to our common problems, the lecturer had to promote interaction within the group. She had to learn what was going on with all of us, talk about it in meaningful ways. And keep our interest and attention.

"What do I do when the kids are screaming, my husband's home late from work, the table is loaded with food, and all I want to do is eat it all?" asked one woman. And of course most people in the room identified immediately.

Some people felt a little strange at first, talking in front of a group. I was one of them—odd, I thought, considering my profession. But soon it was easy, and I found myself able to open up and actually contribute to the meeting. In myself I felt calmer, no longer waking each morning with a sense of rising fear and apprehension about the day's food. Above all, I no longer felt solitary, isolated, and alone; I was easily able to accept the Weight Watchers lifestyle.

We learned very specific techniques to see us through what I called "fridge panic," those awful moments when a well-stocked refrigerator is beckoning one to the final downfall. "Lock yourself in the bathroom for ten minutes," suggested an experienced middle-age blond computer programmer who had successfully lost forty-nine pounds and had no intention of backtracking.

"Drink lots of water!"

"Play the radio so loud that it blots out everything." This from a mother of four who had joined the same week as me and Kelly.

"Stand on your head and recite your mantra." Only in Southern California, I thought.

"Go to the zoo."

"Go to the beach."

"Call a friend."

"Call the fire department."

It's very odd, but now that I am looking back at those first weeks in the meeting room, I discover that the one thing I never talked about was my Fat Ogre. I guess I didn't want to sound weird. Well, over the years I've gotten over that. Now I'm prepared to talk about anything and everything, and I'd advise others to do the same. But stop at the point of boring oneself and others, I'd say. I think that Weight Watchers lecturers must have an advanced degree in "tact."

For me, at least, I think that my first and best decision was not to tell any of my friends that I was trying to lose weight. Through all of my years of dieting I found that the words "I'm on a diet" could be fatal. I would immediately feel that I had divested myself of all power over myself. And that I had somehow bestowed this power on that other person. By what rule of life is it that others seem to feel they have the right to challenge one with "I can't believe you're on a diet—you're *so* skinny! Now you *must* try this chocolate mousse/mocha/almond/frosted/layered/banana shortcake torte which I made myself!" If I was still heavy the response was almost identical but more depressing. "I can't believe you're on a diet—you've got such great skin and big bones—have this double chocolate, etc., etc."

"We'll tell *no one*, especially not Granny Rachel," I told Kelly as she and I and Annabel prepared for a visit to Wilks Water, England, four weeks after we'd joined our Weight Watchers group.

John and Benjy saw us off at the airport armed with our Food Plan booklet, food scale, and diaries.

My first problem hit me on board. The drinks trolley! I tried to remember if I'd ever taken an airplane trip without automatically having a glass of wine after takeoff. Even though

I was now allowing myself three glasses of wine a week, I knew that a glass on board at this early stage of my eating retraining could be a disaster. At high altitude, alcohol hits faster and harder, and I could see myself losing all inhibitions toward even cardboard airline meals.

"Hi Miss Redgrave, my name is Kimberley. How are you today?" The smiling flight attendant was clutching her twin green bottles of California Chardonnay, looming over me. "Nice to have you on board. And are these your lovely daughters? How cute. So this is the famous baby—I read about your problem over breast-feeding. A little Chardonnay today?" Her voice rapidly descended a couple of octaves, while her head seemed to spin madly 'round and 'round, *Exorcist* fashion.

"Fat Ogre," I scream silently, "I'd know you anywhere."

"Excuse me," I smiled tightly. "I have to go to the bathroom." How long had my Weight Watchers classmate said? Ten minutes?

Alone in the tiny cubicle, I touched up my makeup, re-combed my hair, and recited Rudyard Kipling's "If."

By the time I emerged fifteen minutes later, a line had formed outside the toilet but the drinks trolley had gone and at least for now my Chardonnay crisis was over.

The gravel and dirt driveway was almost hidden from view by the overhanging branches of the familiar old oak tree. Ferns, bracken, and cow parsley, still soaking wet from the morning downpour, brushed the sides of our rented Ford Fiesta as we bumped and slid our way over unremembered potholes. The woods had grown so densely during the spring that the August sun didn't have a chance until we rounded the last corner into the clearing, and there it was, Wilks Water.

Mum came running out to greet us with Barney, the golden labrador. She'd been listening for our arrival for the last two hours. As always when we meet, we both were awash with love and family sentiment.

It had been over two years since I'd been back, four years for Kelly, but for Annabel this was to be her first visit.

Into Wilks to see Dad. Living full-time now in this tiny cottage, he slowly fought his way to his feet, looking like an elderly bear who'd just come out of hibernation. His condition was getting worse. Lots of hugs and kisses, and as always I found myself prattling on as amusingly as I could about the saga of our journey, still uncomfortable if silence should fall between us. My problem, I couldn't help thinking. He was genuinely delighted to see us, especially Annabel. This was his first meeting with his youngest grandchild. She smiled at him, dribbled, and pulled his shaggy beard. Kelly took her bag up to the little room at the back with the oeil-de-boeuf window before arriving in the kitchen at the same moment as Annabel and I. We were starving!

Kelly and I exchanged glances. Mum was loading shortbread biscuits and a Mr. Kipling's Treacle Tart (Dad's favorite) onto a tea tray. Thrusting Annabel into Kelly's arms, I opened the larder door and hunted through the vegetable basket for carrots. What a mistake! "Carrots for tea!" declaimed Mum, sounding like Edith Evans. "You're not on a diet, are you?"

"Er, yes, Granny," said Kelly, always brutally truthful. "Mommy and me have joined Weight Watchers." Here we go, I thought. Rule one—never tell anyone you are on a diet—out the window, sunk in the weed-choked depths of Wilks Water Lake!

Annabel let out a loud burp.

So it began. Our two-week stay, and our toughest test yet. Although I had promised myself that we'd look up the nearest Weight Watchers meeting room in England and go to at least one meeting, my good intentions slipped away from me. Dad was getting so frail it seemed cruel to disappear when he saw us so seldom. Mum already showed signs of strain, living with an invalid. Unable to escape the devastation that Parkinson's disease brings to both the victim and the family, they needed us for cheering-up purposes.

We were still in our early days with Weight Watchers, but I rationalized that resisting Mum's food pushing could only make us stronger and our new habits more firmly entrenched. The heck with the support group. We'd invent our own.

"Now about the shopping for today," she began, "I'll come with you. I like to get out and go to the village. Now I've ordered a nice chicken from Mr. Monks and two pounds of his sausages. Ah, but of course you and Kelly can't have anything, can you?"

"Yes Mum, we'll have some chicken."

"Really? I thought you couldn't eat anything but carrots on this diet?"

"No Mum, really, don't worry about us, you carry on and make whatever you'd like, we don't have to have special food."

Fade out. . . .

Fade in. . . .

"What's the time, Lynny? Ah yes, six o'clock—Mikey! Do you want your Scotch? Lynny darling, pour me a glass of wine please. You're not having one? I thought you said you could have a little white wine on this diet. I can't see what harm a little white wine could do, it's a very *dry* white, gin yes, I could understand that would be quite fattening, but wine? Oh well, you know best. Now are you eating *anything* tonight? . . . Well I'm sorry, I thought you and Kelly were on such a terribly strict diet that you couldn't have a thing except a few old carrots. Now it's not fair—tomorrow you mustn't do the shopping or the cooking, because you are being so terribly good I can't bear it. Here's me eating in front of you—it's too cruel. Now I've got Mr. Kipling's Treacle Tart for pudding and some of that lovely Loseley's Jersey cream to go with it because it's Mikey's favorite—can you have just a taste of that? Oh no, of course you mustn't and of course I shouldn't either, but I don't know. I don't seem to put on too much weight, I really eat quite lightly, just a grapefruit for breakfast, well sometimes a boiled egg and maybe some toast and butter. . . ."

I did sometimes make special things for me and Kelly. Steamed fish with lemon and a little ginger and a salad with local dressing on a night when Mum and Dad were tucking into beef bourguignon with potatoes mashed in almost a pound of Normandy butter.

I'd practice my "imaging" technique. Mentally creating the image of myself eating the butter-laden mashed potatoes. Feeling them inside myself. Seeing myself half an hour later wishing I hadn't eaten them. Projecting myself forward to the next morning when I would wake angry and depressed. Then back to reality to savor and enjoy what was on my plate. I was glad of my actors' training. Mum gradually got used to our ways and stopped making it the chief topic of conversation.

It wasn't all plain sailing, of course. We had visits to John's parents, all that beautiful Scandinavian food prepared by my

Danish mother-in-law, Greta. Liverpastaj and roast beef and Frickerdeller and suet pudding.

We had the nightly TV watching at Wilks, a huge box of Cadbury's Milk Tray Chocolates illuminated by the flickering screen. And, during the first week, nightly fun and games in the kitchen with Annabel, who had no idea about the eight-hour time difference, wide awake, laughing and crawling at two o'clock in the morning.

I'd sit with her, nursing a cup of tea, and close my ears to the plaintive cries of Mr. Kipling's Treacle Tart emanating from the large cake tin in the larder.

Back in California we returned to our weekly Weight Watchers meetings in the Fallbrook Shopping Mall. Surprisingly, we hadn't done at all badly in England, even lost a few more pounds. But then I got news that my new television series, *Teachers Only*, was being postponed for another three months. A mixture of frustration at the lack of work and relief that I didn't have to report back to NBC at my fighting weight pressed all the old buttons.

The first thrill of healthy eating and diminishing poundage was wearing off, and I'd been wishing that I didn't have to make that trek. On the morning of my next Weight Watchers meeting, the bathroom scale told me the horrible truth. I'd gained back five and one half pounds. It took every scrap of reason and willpower to get myself to that meeting. In fact, if it hadn't been for Kelly's single-mindedness, I probably wouldn't have gone. "Come on, Mum, you keep telling me not to feel guilty, to think positive. You must keep at it!"

At the meeting, everyone told their horror stories about how they fell off the wagon—I felt an enormous sense of relief. A trouble shared is a trouble halved, I found. I got back on the program filled with new resolve and Kelly's example.

As the weeks went by the rituals of the meeting and the techniques offered there became more comfortable.

It became automatic to write down everything I ate. The Food Plan had a nice simplicity to it. How much easier I found following this plan than counting calories. To begin with I tended to follow the menu planner rather than branch out on my own, but as I gained confidence and my weight continued to drop, I became more creative in terms of handling my food.

Our lecturer really was prepared for all eventualities.

A game plan was instantly available for the member who had reached a weight plateau and became stuck. There was even a vegetarian plan. "Weight control" was referred to as a "skill," which of course it is but I'd never thought of it in such a way. Controlling my weight in the past had always been a miserable and lonely affair, utterly devoid of skill. Now I began to think of my Weight Watchers meetings and this period of learning in the same way that I approached other new things I'd learned. Whether taking lessons in wallpapering or visiting my vocal coach for breathing and voice-strengthening workouts. Computer or Chinese cooking classes—same thing.

At last I could take a clear look at my lifelong habit of feeding my feelings. For years I had turned to food whenever I was sad, depressed, or joyful and elated. I knew when I was doing it and why I was doing it. A part of me was amazingly clear-headed about my problem, yet I had been unable to find a way to change. Now, in our meetings I could confront the problem and deal with it.

We were given steps designed to help us identify and manage the feelings that led to our urge to eat. Steps to "deal with our feelings," rather than feed them.

I made a list of the feelings which were comfortable for me and not linked to food, then listed those dangerous feelings that pressed the automatic "eat" button.

I listed for myself all the soothing, self-nurturing activities I could turn to when provoked. Writing a letter to a friend or loved one. Playing my record of Vivaldi's *Four Seasons*, going out into my garden and picking flowers and then arranging them.

Looking at my collection of art books. Allowing my senses to enter the paintings. Taking some deep breaths and then singing a favorite song.

I began to recognize success in this area. I took pride in my new ability to manage my feelings. I became increasingly more confident that I could manage my feelings tomorrow and the next day and the next.

Now I realized something that I hadn't truly believed till

now. I need never again suffer as I had for the last twenty years.

I was acquiring a skill that once perfected could be mine for the rest of my life. Like all learned skills it might need a refresher course from time to time. It might need a little updating every now and then, but the knowledge I possessed was indestructible.

I'm walking through the woods near Wilks Water. The leaves crackle underfoot. It's fall. It's windy. I'm climbing out onto the ridge now above Dogmersfield Lake. Across the lake the big manor house is lit up—it used to be the scene of festive banquets, with footmen and chandeliers and string quartets. Now it's a monastery, a silent order of Franciscan brothers.

A choir boy's thin voice floats to me on the wind—soaring high above my head. "Kyrie."

I'm by the water now—the wind drops, no sound, all still. I look at my reflection. I like the face I see.

The Fat Ogre is dead. Gone without a sound, without a struggle. I needn't look for his grave, it has no interest for me.

I'm Free.

Goal weight at last, and I celebrated by going back to work on *Teachers Only*. At the first read-through, everyone from the NBC network brass to the craft servicemen complimented me on my new figure. Annabel continued to accompany me to work and was now old enough to join me in the actors' commissary for lunch. She'd sit in her little baby chair, proudly conducting the flow of conversation with her spoon, and sometimes if the shop talk got boring she'd just fall asleep! Kelly was back at school now. She had stopped accompanying me to meetings but had successfully absorbed much of the Weight Watchers philosophy and was carrying it forward into her teen years.

I was on maintenance at my Weight Watchers meetings and found myself reveling in the delightful treat of learning how to add back foods so I could monitor my weight. This was a potentially scary time for us all, and our lecturer encouraged us to voice any goal weight fears that we were experiencing.

Christa, who had joined Weight Watchers shortly before me, admitted feeling alienated from her friends who in the past had supported her desire to lose weight. They were still battling their own problems and she felt they were envious of her new figure. She found herself looking in the mirror and wondering who the person in the reflection was. Jane, one of the senior members of our group, who had reached goal after a 120-pound loss, wondered what on earth she would do with all her free time now she didn't have to focus on losing weight. She said she felt sort of "exposed" now that she was no longer protected by her extra pounds.

This was nothing new to our lecturer, who talked about it, and offered us all some simple reenforcement techniques.

For myself, I faced and accepted the fact that the nourishment that was sustaining me was no longer food, but the positive feelings that had blossomed inside. Boldly, I gave away all my maternity clothes and went shopping and bought some outfits. My perception of my size and figure were still a little off. I'd pick out a pair of pants that looked just right, only to discover they were two sizes too big. Well that was ego-boosting. But best of all was the ease with which I now handled a situation that in the past would have led to a ghastly night of bingeing.

I was facing a major personal challenge because *Teachers Only* was not going as well as we had all hoped. This second season we had a mostly new cast and an entirely new producing and writing team. Norman Fell and I were the only holdovers. With the kind of logic that only exists in TV land, it had been decreed that the location of the school, laid-back West Coast Beverly Hills, should now be inner-city, explosive, East Coast Brooklyn. No one would provide an answer to the obvious. "So how come Lynn and Norman are suddenly working in a different school on a different coast?" Whenever the networks decide on this kind of total revamp, they always resurrect the story of *Bewitched*, the long-running comedy in which Elizabeth Montgomery played a witch. The actor playing Elizabeth's husband got very ill and was replaced by another actor. The audience didn't question it.

Norman and I had now been joined by Tim Reid, from the television series *WKRP*, and the new and delightfully acerbic Jean Smart, now with *Designing Women*, as Norman's secretary, but the problem school premise simply wasn't working. We'd been promised episodes of hilarious but gritty reality. Instead, we found ourselves bogged down in scripts focusing on who was to baby-sit the science teacher's pet rat. The ratings were poor and I felt all the pressure and frustration that goes with being forced to wrestle to the ground unfunny, unbelievable material. All of this gave me more than enough reasons to hit the food wagon with a vengeance if I wanted to. But I didn't.

For the first time in my life, I dealt with the stress by dropping a few more pounds rather than allowing it to push me out of control.

When *Teachers* was not picked up for a third season, I suspect few mourned its demise. As usual, I tried to be practical about the situation and plunged into work in the theater—Christopher Durang's blackest of black comedies, *Sister Mary Ignatius Explains It All for You*. Sister Mary is one of the great roles in contemporary drama, and at the same time another new and different role had come my way.

8

Spokesperson

The call asking me to become spokesperson for Weight Watchers frozen foods came a few weeks into the season's new shows at NBC. The people at Foodways, in Boise, Idaho, and Doyle Dane Bernbach, the Madison Avenue ad agency in New York, learned I was a person with a famous fat past, thanks to my movie *Georgy Girl* and the play *My Fat Friend* all those years ago. I was certainly in favor of such a partnership. I was so thrilled with my new eating habits and grateful to the program for its help and support, and since I'd been using the frozen foods even before I'd joined Weight Watchers, it seemed a natural.

I'd assumed that all concerned must have somehow learned that I'd been a Weight Watchers member too, but one morning the phone rang, one of the DDB executives. "I feel really embarrassed to even call you about this," the voice said nervously to John, "we know how thin your wife is, but . . . for truth in advertising the client does insist that Lynn attend Weight Watchers meetings for a while."

"What do you mean?" said John. "Lynn's been a member since July."

Stunned silence, throat clearing.

"We had no idea, and—um—uh—you mean she lost weight on the program?"

"Yes, thirty-five pounds."

Noise of champagne corks popping, ad agency people falling off chairs, and hysteria. Ticker tape parade down Madison Avenue. . . .

It was decided that the first commercial would be called "Red Dress."

I'd talked quite a lot to the creative people at DDB and had reminded them that in *My Fat Friend*, Vicky's "Fat Dress" was an ideal symbol of that final frontier of fatness that so many people arrive at. "The morning after" as it were, the last bit of clothing you can fit into. We talked about the effect it made on the audience when I threw off my coat in the final scene, revealing myself as thin and gorgeous.

So the "Red Dress" came to be the Fat Dress. I'd step out of it and toss it aside, discarding the heavy me. (Of course I'd be wearing another "thin dress" underneath.)

For some time the commercials kept the red garment as large as possible to show the contrast with the new me. But over the years the symbol has been transformed into a red boa, a matador's cape, a hair ribbon, a blouse, a little sheepskin vest, and many more. It must be a successful campaign. If ever I wear red in public someone invariably comes up and asks me to "take it off!" "Shan't for asking" is my standard reply.

Weight Watchers even gave me an unexpected chance to be a "stage mother," a role I would never wish to seek. I'd never realized how much hard work it could be.

Annabel was playing me as a two-year-old in a Weight Watchers Dessert commercial, showing how in childhood I developed a "fat" habit. She was looking especially fetching, in a little pale pink smocked dress with a Peter Pan collar, sitting at a table with an actress dressed as a 1945 nanny.

NANNY: "Now eat your veggies, or you can't have dessert."

On cue, she had to eat a green vegetable, putting it into her mouth immediately the line was spoken. The whole piece of action was to run two seconds.

We arrived at the studio in the morning. I shot some of my segments including the red dress toss and Annabel played upstairs in the dressing room with a baby-sitter and the other little girl who'd been hired "just in case." Although I generally feel very ambivalent about children working in TV and film, this seemed like a fun idea for Annabel, and after all, she did look exactly like me in my two-year-old baby pictures.

The "Rival Mother" was not so thrilled. Although it was obvious that there could be no doubt as to whose child looked most like me, this didn't prevent her feeling that Annabel was an upstart amateur with no credentials.

"Of course Brianna has a lot of experience," she began, her knitting needles click click clicking. "Timing! Timing is *every-thing* in commercials, you know. The kids must be able to bring in a take exactly on time. Brianna did her first spot at two months and now she's up for a feature."

I almost felt guilty, Brianna was adorable—not a lot like me to look at, but adorable. How awful after a career like hers to be merely a standby to the star's precocious child.

As Annabel's two-second scene ran into its twenty-seventh take I really appreciated the importance of "Rival Mother's" words. Timing *was* everything.

The only way I could stop Annabel from eating on each take and therefore becoming full and bored too soon was to stand behind "Nanny" and mime eating the broccoli in the hope that she'd mimic me. I couldn't talk to her because that would ruin "Nanny's" line. If the take looked like running long, the director would say cut and I'd say to Annabel, "Don't eat it yet, it's too hot." Good as gold, she'd obediently put down her fork, looking longingly at what she thought was her boiling hot veggie. I began to feel like a child actor abuser. My darling baby was hungry and I was saying don't eat! On the twenty-ninth take, "Rival Mother" came in to see what was going on. I began to sweat. At take thirty, Annabel, with impeccable timing, gobbled up her broccoli to everyone's satisfaction.

I was a wreck. Tough work, this stage mother stuff.

Farewell to My Father

My newfound freedom coincided with the closing stages of my father's last illness. Parkinson's disease led to his death in early 1985. I had an overwhelming desire to make peace with him before he died. Having bidden farewell to my Fat Ogre, I wanted now to make whole my relationship with him.

I felt that there had been moments when I had almost broken through. Five years earlier, I called him to recount that on a working visit to Sydney, Australia, with my family, after much hard work, we had found his father's grave. He was stunned.

It was in the Sydney Opera House library where we had gone to research Roy's history that John made the discovery. He was leafing through a book on the Australian silent film industry of the early part of the century when he suddenly let out a whoop. There it was, Roy Redgrave, star of such classics as *Robbery Under Arms*, had died on May 25, 1922, and was buried in South Head Cemetery, Vaucluse, just outside the city. We scooped up the kids, who were playing in the Opera House lobby, hailed a taxi, and raced out to South Head.

The cemetery sits high on a cliff overlooking the bay on one side, and the open sea on the other, a stone's throw from a great old lighthouse.

The custodian greeted us as we tumbled out of the taxi, for the Opera House had called ahead to warn him of our arrival. He took us into his tiny office where he searched yellowing files and index cards for the name Roy Redgrave. Nothing. But then another book revealed the names of people who had been buried without a marker, and that was where he was. Under the footpath. The receipt of his burial showed that fifteen shillings had been paid by a mysterious Minnie Redgrave, the identity of whom still eludes us. The cost of a headstone was obviously out of the question. But of course!

A photo-taking session followed, and nine-year-old Kelly helpfully suggested that we should "dig him up and take him home to Grandpa"!

Before we left Australia, we spoke to an elderly lady in an old people's home in Adelaide. Her mother and father were producers for the J.C. Williamson Theatre Company with Roy, and she remembered him in many different roles.

Upon our return to London, I took Dad to dinner at the Savoy Grill, his favorite restaurant, to recount our adventures. I also told him how on the way to Australia we had stopped in Hong Kong and visited my half cousin, the newly knighted head of the British Armed Forces, Sir Roy Redgrave. Roy is the son of Robin Redgrave, Dad's elder half brother, who had married a Romanian actress. That made us both grandchildren of the first Roy Redgrave.

I had told cousin Roy how we hoped to find out information about grandfather Roy when we got to Sydney. "Good luck to you," he said, and then rather wistfully looking out across Hong Kong harbor he confessed, "I've never really understood why I became a soldier. I've always wanted to be a poet."

Dad listened intently to the story.

"John and I have been in contact with a stone mason in Sydney, Dad. We'd like to mark your father's grave for you."

He looked at me, that strange, still, uncommitted look that used to frighten me so as a child.

"What would you like inscribed on the headstone, Dad?" I persisted.

His hand was shaking, Parkinson tremor or emotion, I couldn't tell. Then he smiled a small, secret smile.

"Just this. Roy Redgrave. Actor."

That said it all, I thought.

I later came to treasure the memory of that dinner. Talking to my father had always been so difficult. The strange intimidating lack of reaction with which, even before the onset of his illness, he greeted every encounter. But even though he had not been very forthcoming during dinner, had not illuminated in any way his feelings toward his father, I like to feel that I perhaps helped him tie up some loose ends of his relationship with his own father, the stranger down under.

I know we cannot completely extricate ourselves from the power of the parent/child relationship, perhaps should not, but certainly we need to contain it and give it meaning. For me, my father had wielded a strong influence, although I am fairly sure he was not aware of it. But in my mind, at least, he was the source and the cause of the things that had gone wrong.

I had to change these feelings toward him if I was to finally grow up. I needed to banish the negativity I had toward my father just as I had banished the other destructive elements in my life.

I think I never truly came to understand the fear and hatred that I felt toward my father when I was little. I know that he was never there when I wanted him to be; it seemed to me that he did not take into account my presence in the world. I knew that he didn't want a third child. He had a six-year-old daughter and a four-year-old son, and had become more thoroughly entrenched in his "other life." Perhaps he was unwilling to take on the responsibility that comes with fatherhood. I don't want to imply that my father's homosexuality necessarily had anything to do with this. Interestingly, I did not know of his sexual orientation until I was a married adult, information carefully imparted to me by my husband. Although how it had escaped me till then I'll never fathom. Maybe I didn't want to know.

At any rate, knowing somehow finally made sense of much of his behavior. It became possible to stop hating him for his emotional neglect of my mother. That was something I always

knew about, because I was always aware that my parents maintained separate rooms and that my friends' parents shared a
bed. Tension was ever-present in our house, cushioned for me
by my beloved Nanny. I longed all my life to know and to feel
that he loved me, and only in his decline and illness did he begin
to show it. For my part, sadly, it was only as I became more the
parent to his ever-weakening child that I could reach out fear-
lessly to him.

Now I needed to forgive.

It was during rehearsals for *Aren't We All* with Rex Harrison
and Claudette Colbert for Broadway. He died the day after his
seventy-seventh birthday—March 21, 1985. Joan Hirst called
early to break the news. I was so glad it was she who told me.
Her voice, gentle and calm, generously trying to conceal her
own grief from me. He'd died in his sleep at midday in London,
she explained, Corin with him. Just stopped breathing.

I first called Corin. He'd told Mother when she got back
from work. At first distraught, he told me, she became "omi-
nously cheerful," her voice high, loud, and commanding.

Then I called my Godmother Edith, now ninety-one years
old. She cried and cried uncontrollably. As Dad's greatest ad-
mirer, she'd lived her life, I believe, in terms of his existence,
never dreaming that she would live to see his death. For myself,
I was glad to have a play to do, in which to lose myself.

Now it was Sunday, and after two long days of almost manic
rehearsal energy, I had awakened early as usual, limbs like lead.
I turned on the radio. Ralph Vaughn Williams's "Fantasia on a
Theme" by Thomas Tallis. Suddenly, I was six years old. As in
my childhood, he'd just come home. Fear. Pain.

*In the front garden, Rudi, Daddy's horrifying brown and
white bull terrier, is taking a flying leap at me as usual,
knocking me backward onto the flagstone path. I am screaming
an ear-piercing "Help!" Daddy runs down the front steps,
picks me up, takes me into the dining room, and spanks me.*

*"You're always screaming. No wonder the dog gets ex-
cited, stop screaming!"*

*The next day, Rudi attacks Nanny on her way to feed
the chickens, bites into her arm till you can see the bone. I*

scream again, but this time Daddy doesn't hear. He's doing a matinee.

I'm in bed with the flu, writing in my journal. I'm eight. "Hooray Hooray Hooray, Daddy's going away today!"

"Now cross that out at once!" Nanny sounds angry. "You mustn't write things like that about your father."

But I know from the look on her face that she understands. She moves to our bedroom door, as if to check that Daddy isn't coming up the stairs. She needn't have worried. In all my childhood, through all the many colds and fevers, Daddy never came upstairs to see me.

I'm four. Nanny dressed me in the pretty viyella dress she'd made for me. Pale blue with white smocking on the front. Hand-knitted blue socks. Nanny knitted all our socks. During the war, she said she knitted socks for soldiers. She takes me down the three flights of stairs to the drawing room. Time for tea with Mummy and Daddy, the only time of the day I can see them. Mummy looks a little tense, but kisses me and smiles her best smile just for me. Nanny leaves. The room is very quiet. I sit on the little needlepoint footstool made by my grandpa Eric, my back pressed hard against Mummy's knees. Daddy and Mummy speak occasionally. To each other. Daddy smokes his pipe. Soon it's time for Nanny to take me upstairs for my bath. "Good night, Mummy!" Hugs and kisses, I don't want to let go of her. "Good night, Daddy!" A hug and kiss for the stranger who didn't seem to notice that I was there.

My Godmother Edith is coming to school with Daddy to see me as Theseus in A Midsummer Night's Dream. *I'm thirteen, shaking with nerves. Daddy never comes to concerts or school recitals. I'm sure he'll think I'm good as Theseus, I've worked very hard at it. I fantasize about his post-performance comments. "Brilliant, Lynny!" "I never knew you were so talented!" "You spoke so well!" "You looked just like a duke."*

Miss Borchard, my teacher, whispers, "Your father's arrived. Middle of the fifth row."

The stained blue velvet curtains in front of our little

stage part, the audience murmur quiets, just a few squeaking chairs. I speak first, my arms around Harriet, who's playing my Amazon Queen.

"Now fair Hypolita, our nuptial hour draws on apace. . . ." My voice feels strong and manly, the scene playing so well.

During the first Titania scene, I peek through the curtains to see how Daddy is reacting. His seats are empty.

In my loft, I cried out loud, and found myself sobbing. And then it went as suddenly as it came, leaving me shaking and exhausted. That was odd, I thought, because until now my grief had been for him, for the loss of his talent, and for his effect upon Mother. But not for myself.

I wanted so much to see Corin, Vanessa, and Mum. Hold them tight.

With only a day off from rehearsal, it meant Concorde there and back, to be able to be at my father's funeral.

The coffin was covered with flowers. White lilies from Mum, yellow and white roses from Vanessa and Corin. By mistake, someone had left my blue bouquet of grape hyacinths, freesias, and lilac outside with the other flowers. So my note to Antony, "I dreamed there was an Emperor . . ." would not enter the furnace with him as I had hoped. My throat hurt.

The chapel was full of his friends and colleagues. Harold Pinter, Yehudi Menuhin, Ian McKellen, Dorothy Tutin.

In the front row we sat, his family. White and shaking, hands holding hands, a linked chain of his children and his grandchildren. Mum on my right, Corin on my left.

The program, arranged by Corin, was just what Michael would have wanted. Songs and Shakespeare. No prayers.

His favorite song, "My Time of Day" from *Guys and Dolls*, was sung a cappella by Ian Charleson. He stood facing us at the foot of the coffin. My body started to melt and mingle with the family's tears. Soon I'd be flowing down the aisle toward the wooden box. My nails dug into Corin's hand and he was making a strange deep strangling sound and I wanted to put my arms around him but they weighed so much I couldn't lift them.

And now he rests—and how shall I remember him?
I shall remember the best of him.
I shall remember the songs around the piano.

I shall remember the dressing room door opening and there stands—the King—the Madman—Hamlet—Antony—Shylock—all of these my father. . . .

I shall remember my wedding day in New York City, holding Dad's arm. Walking toward the mirrored fireplace in our friend's house. Gardenias smothering the mantel, trailing down the fireplace moldings. John waiting there, smiling, my eyes filling with happy tears. I look up at Dad, tears tumbling out of his eyes too.

I shall remember the hugs we learned to give each other when my childhood was left behind and his second one was with us.

I shall remember . . . his hand shaking in mine, his eyes closed. Lunch has been eaten, his medication taken. His beard looks unkempt, crumbs caught in it. The shaking stops. I stop singing "All I Want Is a Room Somewhere" (he still loved musicals). "Don't stop!"—the voice is thin and papery—"Don't stop, I like it."

I shall remember that on our last day together he reached his hand out to mine and held it, so gently. I shall remember that he said "I love you" and that I said "I love you" and meant it.

I shall remember his very last words to me. He's in his hospital bed, the curtains drawn, and he thinks he's in a theater and the noise of the other patients' visitors is the hum of an audience coming in.

"Have you arranged the billing yet?" he asks. "Gosh, Dad," I say, trying to enter his fantasy world, "I'm sure the management will give you the billing you want." But what does he want?

"Well, you must arrange it ahead of time." (At this point, I think he's going to tell me bad luck stories about unscrupulous producers, but not at all.) "You must arrange it ahead of time—because if the billing isn't arranged when the audience comes to the play they won't know who's in it."

"By the way," he says as the nurse comes in to rearrange the bedclothes, "I had to bow out of Antony and Cleopatra."

*"Oh no, Dad," I say, stalling, trying to join in this
hallucination, "I'm sorry."*

*"Well, actually," he whispers, "I didn't bow out—I swept
out!"*

*I dreamed there was an Emperor Antony—
O, such another sleep, that I might see
But such another man!
His face was as the heavens, and therein stuck
A sun and moon, which kept their course, and lighted
The little O, the earth.
His legs bestrid the ocean: his reared arm
Crested the world. His voice was propertied
As all the tuned spheres, and that to friends;
But when he meant to quail and shake the orb,
He was as rattling thunder. For his bounty,
There was no winter in't; an autumn 'twas
That grew the more by reaping: his delights
Were dolphin-like; they showed his back above
The element they lived in: in his livery
Walk'd crowns and crownets; realms and islands were
As plates dropp'd from his pocket.
Think you there was, or might be, such a man
As this I dream'd of?*

10

On Location

y life leapt forward. Wonderfully happy times with my fast-growing family, and of course always the work. New plays, new films, and my increasing involvement with Weight Watchers. Now, for the first time ever on a Weight Watchers commercial, we were going on location, St. Thomas in the Virgin Islands, to shoot on a mountaintop overlooking the bay.

For John and me it would be the first time back to St. Thomas since our honeymoon there in 1967. We decided to take Annabel with us and stay on for a few days after the shoot was over.

It was almost the end of October and the weather was absolutely fabulous. Occasional rainstorms would race through for twenty minutes followed by a rainbow, sometimes double rainbows.

The first day's shooting was for Seafood Linguini and that St. Thomas mountaintop was doubling for the Amalfi coast in Italy. It looked remarkably similar, in fact, except for the fact that overnight four huge cruise ships had sailed into the harbor packed with tourists anxious to load up with "duty free."

Our Swedish director, Steve Hylen, had to reset the shot to avoid revealing the ships, only to have the giant *Norway* sail into the background of my closeup just as I was flinging off my red shawl and declaiming in my best Italian, *"Questa'è la vita—* This is living!"

Annabel was happily swimming in the pool by the set with Steve's daughter, Olivia, and John was busy exploring the area in a rented open-top jeep, trying to remember that for no good reason you drive on the left in St. Thomas even though the steering wheel remains on the left as in America.

The next day was to be a very early start for a one-hour boat ride to a tiny desert island off Tortolla where I would be shipwrecked in a tattered red dress along with a huge commercial-size freezer filled with—of course—all my favorite Weight Watchers frozen foods: Lasagna, Stuffed Turkey Breast, French Bread Pizza, etc.

I woke at 5 a.m. to discover that some dreaded tropical flying insect had bitten my right eyelid in the night. I looked really strange. The lid was swollen and the eye half closed.

Leaving John and Annabel still asleep, I rushed over to the room that had been set aside for makeup to see François, my makeup artist and hairdresser. He put ice on my eye and told me not to worry, they'd probably shoot the long shots first. Anyway, by the time they were ready for a closeup he was confident my eye would be better.

The resort we were staying at was on the northeast side of the island. Beautiful view across to the nearby island of St. John. As I sat on the balcony getting made up, I almost felt guilty. It didn't feel like work at all.

We were all aboard our little cabin cruiser boat early next morning with my friend Bill Belew, who'd designed my attractively tattered red dress and the Dorothy Lamour-style sarong for underneath. François had been putting artificial tanning lotion on me for the last two days—my own very white skin would look far too pale in the extra-bright Caribbean sunlight and body makeup would sweat off in the heat in no time—that is, if it didn't get splashed off by the seawater.

Arriving at the location we dropped anchor offshore along with the other production boats.

"Okay," said our captain, "time for immigration." I thought he was joking. No such luck.

"Didn't the company tell you to bring your passports or other proof of citizenship?"

John felt in his pocket. He hadn't even brought his driver's license, and Annabel and I had on our bathing suits, and that was it!

"Why on earth do we need passports?" I asked.

"This little desert island is British territory and St. Thomas is American. You've already left the U.S. and are now sailing in British waters; the local immigration service need to know that you are legal to re-enter U.S. territory when we sail back to St. Thomas this evening."

I couldn't imagine how anyone in St. Thomas could know or care where we'd been for the day, but I began to feel pretty nervous. If I wasn't allowed off the boat, how would we shoot today? An enormous amount of time and money had been spent getting the crew and equipment out here!

"Stay hidden in the downstairs cabin," he ordered. "I'll take François and Bill's passports over and pretend they are the only people on my boat."

Three illegal immigrants crouched below deck. I had changed into my costume, a tattered red silk dress and I looked like the shipwrecked heroine of an old Stewart Granger movie. I imagined how Deborah Kerr would have handled this. Probably she'd have stood nobly on the ship's prow gazing out to sea, the wind failing to ruffle her perfect hair, lipstick in place, waiting for fate or in this case immigration to take her away.

We peeked out through the porthole to watch how things were going for our faithful captain. John had his binoculars out. The man from immigration at Tortolla sat in an open boat, his papers in front of him on a makeshift desk. Our various production people and agency personnel were boat-hopping back and forth with permits and passports. The bemused and bespectacled official had never seen so much activity in one day.

We could see that he was trying to get a head count going, but without much success. It was sheer chaos, situation out of hand.

He took his documents and, looking extraordinarily like Peter Sellers, took off in his launch.

Which made for a jovial day of work. A smaller motorboat ferried us to the island's shore, the propman brought a step ladder so that I could climb out into the shallow water and then wade up onto white-gold sand.

With the commercial completed we could now relax and stay on for a few days' vacation in the islands. Steve and his wife, Katie, decided to stay on too, so there followed five heavenly days, much of the time spent on the Hylens' small boat exploring the neighboring beaches or playing in the crystal-clear waters.

Olivia and Annabel, five and six years old, learned to snorkel, sometimes swimming hand in hand, dark and blond hair flowing out behind them. We'd hear their laughter bubbling up through the snorkel tubes as they chased the shoals of fish that darted back and forth in front of them.

We spent Halloween on the nearby island of St. John. Lunched at Caneel Bay and spent the evening mingling with a student crowd at the wharf, dressed in outlandish monster costumes, the children laughing and squealing. This was the life!

On our final day, John and I went looking for the Sea Horse cottages where we had spent a belated honeymoon twenty-one years before. Not remembering the exact road they were on, we rounded a corner in our jeep and suddenly there was the driveway. We parked the car and ran down the familiar footpath and long stone steps to what had been our cottage.

A pair of blue bathing trunks hung out to dry on the rail of the porch, no owner in sight.

On down the twisting cliffside path till we finally reached "our" beach, our tiny hidden cove where no one ever came but us, all those years ago.

I thought I saw a chubby young girl in a green and white bathing suit, wearing a purple chiffon scarf on her head, picking up shells. She was smiling a happy-sad clown smile. John looked at me. "Remember that purple scarf you used to wear to keep your hat on?" he said. I got out my camera and we photographed each other as the sun began to turn the sky streaky with gold and red.

It's Christmas Eve, midnight, 1988. Our family is together again, in the Santa Monica Mountains. Mum arrived from London with Kelly, who is living there now, and Ben drove in from college in Colorado. Annabel's barely asleep.

On the record player is my much-worn copy of the Christmas Carol Service from King's College, Cambridge. Kelly sits by the fire with her patchwork quilt. She is looking beautiful, her own battle with Fat Ogre seems to be over. Mum reads, stretched out on our battered comfortable red couch. The guys are out with friends, late from doing their last-minute gift shopping probably.

I've drawn up a menu for tomorrow's Christmas dinner. Roast goose with apple and grape stuffing, red cabbage, mushrooms with garlic, carrots with rosemary. As each holiday season comes around, it gets progressively more natural to enjoy a feast without the awful button-pressing of old bad habits. I look back to the many times I sat down at the Christmas table ready to start my meal, already stuffed full of nuts and Santa's candies. Bloated with nibbling all through the cooking process.

I'm better able to be the mother of this family now, I feel. Better able to bend and flow with their needs, to listen, to advise, and to be there. I had less time for them before, when so much energy went into keeping my ogre at bay.

I walk over to the couch and sit by my mum, put my arms around her. She's wearing the same familiar perfume that she used when I was a child. I close my eyes. Right now, this minute, all that matters to me is that I still have my mother to love and hold.

"Once in Royal David's city. . . ." Mum's still-clear soprano sings along with the King's College choirboy.

This is peace.

11

Full Circle

nd so life continues. Busy, hectic. The challenge.

I tried my hand at situation comedy once again in 1989, with Jackie Mason in *Chicken Soup*. Everybody knows that Jackie is a comic of great originality, and it was great for me to be part of such a lively group of people, but once again I fell into the same old trap that we had encountered on *Teachers Only*. The writers made every effort to keep Jackie as lovable as possible. But Jackie is at his best being a maniacal curmudgeon, and I think I'm at my best when I can be somewhat "spiky." But I was made to be warmer and more sympathetic with every episode. When will they all learn that nice people do not make for good comedy?

The series was canceled after seven episodes—the highest rated show ever to get the ax. Undeterred, I did what I've always done. Kept moving. John and I returned to the stage together in A. R. Gurney's *Love Letters*. We played Broadway over Christmas week, with all the kids and Mum, plus Vanessa and her kids, to cheer us on. It had been twenty-three years since John and I had acted together, twenty-three years since that television play in London when I had walked into the rehearsal hall and bumped into a handsome young actor who shook hands and said, "Hi. I'm John Clark."

In Australia, as spokesperson for the Down and Under Weight Watchers people, I made a series of commercials in Melbourne before linking up with John in Sydney for Weight Watchers of Australia's twenty-first anniversary ball. Just in time for a celebration of our own.

April 2, 1990, our twenty-third wedding anniversary. A grand outdoor fish lunch at Doyle's on the Beach, ice-cold champagne to celebrate. John and I leaned back in our chairs and looked out across the water to Sydney's skyline.

A drenching rainstorm suddenly raced overhead, sending us scurrying for cover. Five minutes later it was gone and the sun shone through again, sparkling the water with dancing light. Time for us to trudge up the cliffside on our odyssey.

Up and up we climbed, the bay below us to the right, the open sea to the left, storm clouds still chasing across the horizon.

Past the two lighthouses till we reached our goal, the gates of South Head Cemetery.

Nothing had changed since our last visit, or so it seemed. We hurried up and down the pathways till we found it. A small red-brown headstone, where the path used to be.

ROY REDGRAVE
ACTOR
DIED MAY 25 1922
AGE 50
MARKED BY HIS SON MICHAEL

"There you are, Dad," I whispered. "For you."

On sudden impulse, I lay down on his grave, my head just below the stone, where he was surely lying. I thought of Roy and Daisy and Fortunatus and Cornelius. Of Michael and Rachel, of Vanessa, Corin, and me. Of all those actors before and still to come who had bravely stood upon the stages of the world, filling the empty space with countless heroes and heroines, Kings and Queens and ordinary people whose stories have transported audiences beyond their daily lives for "the two hours' traffick of our stage."

I looked up at the shimmering sky, and John laughed and took my picture, and I began to declaim a bit of *Henry the Fifth*.

> *Oh for a Muse of fire, that would ascend*
> *The brightest heaven of invention,*
> *A kingdom for a stage, princes to act*
> *And monarchs to behold the swelling scene!*

I closed my eyes from the blinding sun, and all of a sudden time seemed to stand still. I was back at Wilks Water, alone in the living room.

> *The clock in the living room chimed quietly, ting . . . ting . . . ting.*
> *Three o'clock.*
> *One last snap as a spark flew from the grate.*
> *There it was, Dad's journal for 1943, the year of my birth. I turned to my day, March 8th, but now it was a short entry and one of my own making. A small liberty would be allowed, perhaps. No. My dad would approve, wholeheartedly. I know it now.*
> *"Today my daughter Lynn was born. I love her."*

PART
2

Challenges

**W**hen I began to overeat, gain weight, and battle the Fat Ogre, I never could have imagined that the self-destructive spiral that I was in could lead to the life I have now. Even when I made that first "Red Dress" commercial, I had no idea that it would prove to be the first step to a new career.

Yet here I am—an actress, always wanting to metamorphose into other characters and a woman who needed to metamorphose from an unhappy caterpillar into a liberated butterfly. My life as an actress and my life as myself have intertwined. I have two careers now, and each one feeds the other.

As an actress I am now able to expand and fly as I never quite could when so much negative stress was going on in my day-to-day existence, when Fat Ogre awoke with me every morning.

As the spokesperson for Weight Watchers, each year brings me in touch with more numbers of people who want to change their lives. People thinking they are alone, searching for a renewed sense of purpose. Wanting to be free.

Whenever I can, I talk to groups, large and small, on many issues: *"The Working Mother," "On-Site Day Care," "The Problems of the 90s," "Superwoman," "Seeking Justice in Hollywood."* But whatever the subject, whether my audience is in Dayton or San Francisco, Norfolk or Phoenix, when it comes to the question-and-answer period, they all ask about my weight-loss experience.

Scene: Milwaukee, to host a Weight Watchers in Wisconsin "Member of the Year" competition, to give a talk, and to answer questions.

Meet Lynn Redgrave, Saturday, 1–2 p.m. A packed 5,000-seat auditorium, built in 1909.

I've just made my entrance, through a movie screen made of white vertical overlapping strips, center stage. A scene from *Georgy Girl* was projecting on it. As Georgy runs down some stairs, I stepped through the screen, through Georgy, shattering her image.

> *I'm in slim white pants and silk shirt, the audience is screaming and applauding, and I know I'm among peers who can identify. Validation. Hope. Behind me the screen dims, the caterpillar fades, and the tall white butterfly swoops and dives and soars in the bright white light. That's me, folks.*

How long have you maintained your weight?

I've maintained a 35-pound weight loss since October 1982. When I look back, I realize that in the great scheme of things 35 pounds of extra weight is not really a staggering amount. However, to the person battling the Fat Ogre, 35 pounds can be as frightening as 50 or 70 pounds. I was never what is commonly called obese, but I do not think that one's poor self-perception has a graduated scale. I believe that the fear of being out of control has tremendous impact no matter what one's overpoundage might be.

What was the toughest challenge you faced while losing weight?

Well, I've already related the saga of my trip back to my parents' home with Kelly and Annabel. But that was only for a couple of weeks. Undoubtedly the biggest challenge for me was accepting that while I joined Weight Watchers at first simply to lose weight, I was going to have to make a major sea change in myself, my eating habits, and my attitude to food. The challenge lay in the fact that I didn't really believe that was feasible.

Of course this meant that every time I went off the program and gained weight back, I was giving that belief credibility. A self-fulfilling prophecy. It would have been easier to fall into my old patterns of behavior and allow those feelings of self-hate to take over. To follow those bad periods with days of punishing deprivation. But the guidance I received at Weight Watchers again and again encouraged me to return to the program. Don't skip meals, don't starve, don't go hungry. The empty feeling was not allowed to return. Gradually, my body began to respond. To recognize when it was satisfied. It took me some time.

Do you still attend meetings?

No. It's true that Weight Watchers encourages lifetime members to weigh in once a month, but speaking just for myself, I haven't for the reason that when I show up, I tend to divert peoples' concentration from the serious work at hand. Mind you, I do sometimes drop in, when asked, for the purpose of saying a few encouraging words to the members. Sometimes, I get to talk with members in different parts of the country. Meet leaders too (we used to call them lecturers), and discuss what's going on within the organization. Since the program prides itself on being "state of the art," new information and helpful tips are added regularly. So I keep up with and maintain my weight on the latest program so I feel in touch and included, and know that if the day comes when I need to return I'll be welcomed with open arms.

How do you follow the Food Plan and Exercise Plan with a schedule like yours?

I make a game of it, mapping out a comfortable timetable for each day. My schedule is sometimes stable for a week or so at a time, and so I make my eating plans along with plans for preparing and carrying out the work. For example, I was in Melbourne, Australia, last year to shoot six thirty-second Weight Watchers commercials. One a day for six days. Each day began early, as I had to be at the studio by 7 a.m. for makeup. Each night ended late because I had to study my lines and "business" for the next day's work. I was alone, so was able to plan my day without any social or family obligations. All my concentration could be focused on looking good and staying fit. I like to have a comforting "sameness" around the beginning and middle of each day. This helps free me for the challenges of a day's shooting.

I'd order my breakfast for 6 each morning, having awakened at 5 to wash my hair and phone home. Orange juice, decaf coffee, and oatmeal with skimmed milk. "Porridge," as the Brits and Aussies call it, gives me a nice contented full feeling right through the long morning's work. Lunch was usually at 12:30, and while I could have ordered something special I liked the challenge of staying on program regardless of the studio cook's hearty choices. Half an hour's nap, then back to work, and in the middle of the afternoon a cup of tea and an arrowroot biscuit (cookie). I was usually back at the hotel by 5 or 5:30, so that was when I got my exercise. An hour's walk through Melbourne's beautiful Fitzroy gardens, where neatly tended flowers border the pathways that zigzag back and forth under avenues of towering trees. Or up to the health club in the hotel for a ride on a stationary bike and a swim in the pool.

Then supper, either in my room or downstairs in the "food hall," which is an atrium with assorted ethnic food boutiques surrounding a large and lively seating area. Fun to watch Melburnians relaxing after their day's work. I'd alternate between steamed veggies with a cheesy baked potato and a Greek plate. Vine leaves stuffed with rice, humus, feta cheese, a few black olives, field greens topped with grapes, and pita bread. Then a relaxing bath, study my lines, and into bed.

A nice change from the assorted demands that I must deal with each day when I'm home in California.

Do you ever go to exercise classes?

Well, not now, although when we first came to California both John and I went to Richard Simmons's classes in Beverly Hills.

This was before Richard was Richard, if you know what I mean. His classes were always packed with what seemed like hundreds of shiny leotards, topped with gold jewelry and endless acrylic nails. He was very popular and kept telling us how famous he was about to become, and of course we didn't have the good sense to believe him. We should have seen it coming, for Richard's hard work, unswerving faith, chutzpah, and good business sense made his destiny inevitable, and his own success story is an object lesson.

But I always felt out of place in class (my nails were too short), and I longed for a form of exercise that would be in some way useful.

Once we moved to our canyon and had horses and dogs and goats and Annabel and land that needed clearing, it was different. Suddenly, exercise had a purpose. I carried my ever heavier baby in a front or backpack as I went up and down the hill to feed the animals.

Now I walk to the state park with the children for a picnic. I ride the horse, unload bales of hay and eighty-pound sacks of alfalfa cubes, mow the lawn (my little patch of England), and cut brush with a heavy motor-driven cutter.

As I rhythmically swing my bladed weed-whacker back and forth, I say to myself, "Some people are paying Jane Fonda hard-earned money in order to keep this fit, and yet they hire someone to cut their brush!"

When in New York working in a play I make a point of walking to the theater every day, all weathers, winter or summer.

On location in Charlottesville, Virginia, or San Antonio, stuck in a hotel on the edge of a busy highway, I head for the swimming pool every day after work. No, I know it's not useful, but at least it's fun.

Swimming laps with different strokes, making a game of it for myself. I've got some inflatable arm bands that little kids use when they are learning to swim and put them on my ankles. Standing in chest-high water I do leg lifts, forward, side, and back, the arm bands acting as counter weights as I bring my leg down through the water. Or with the bands on my wrists and standing with the water at neck level, I raise and lower my straightened arms twenty times.

Last birthday, John bought me a Life Cycle and installed

it in my office. With my favorite tapes on my Walkman I can now exercise even if the rain is pouring down and I can't mow the lawn or cut the brush. Even if the summer heat is too intense for yard work or horseback riding, I put on my air conditioner and a Tracy Chapman tape, and off I go on my ride to health.

Do you have any food rules that you live by?

Yes. These ought to be ideas that you develop for yourself in order to be truly meaningful, but I'll tell you mine.

Rule 1. Never tell anyone you are on a diet.

The moment you say "I'm on a diet" it implies that someone else is in control of what you eat. This gives the saboteur, usually your best friend or your mother, the challenge of taking control themselves. "You shall eat this because I have slaved over a burning hot oven for forty days and nights and my happiness is more important than your body."

I've noticed that nobody tries to stuff food into a person who's not on a diet.

Rule 2. Always eat sitting down.

Don't eat anything standing up, walking, traveling in buses, trains, or cars, while on the phone, watching TV, or at the movies. With just this rule alone I realize I cut out several hundred unwanted calories a day.

Because food is sensual, food is attractive, food is to be enjoyed, savored.

Sharing food with others is one of the most sociable of human endeavors, but everything that goes into my mouth without my noticing will bypass my brain's own good sense about when I've had enough. How can I know if I'm really hungry or just eating out of habit if I'm not taking notice!

Even if I'm eating alone, I lay a place at the table with a pretty place mat, napkin, flatware.

I always keep a proper set of dishes and place settings in my dressing room when I'm working in the theater.

I prepare the whole meal, and then eat only that. No picking before, during, or after.

Rule 3. Keep to a schedule.

Eat three meals a day, and eat them as close as possible to

the same time each day. Which means, don't eat late at night, a rule I myself have to break quite often, due to the kind of work I do. When I'm in a play I like to join friends for supper afterward to wind down and relax. So I eat something very light, a small plate of steamed vegetables or mixed salad. You see, my third proper meal I already ate before the show.

Of course there can be complications. What do I do if I have to fly somewhere and change time zones? I adapt my eating times carefully by writing down my meals and the time they should be eaten in the new time zone.

I once flew from east to west on the Concorde, halfway around the globe. Paris, London, New York, Seattle (yes, a charter flight). Every time we took off, they served lunch! By the time we got to bed that night, I'd had breakfast in Paris, four lunches, and dinner in Seattle!

By the way, before going to a party, I eat a piece of fruit or a few crackers, six small crackers being a program allotment for a serving of bread.

On arrival, I drink a mineral water, club soda, or diet soda first.

If there's a vegetable dip, I eat the veggies without dipping.

If it's a buffet, I take a plate, select small portions, avoid the mayonnaise, then sit down.

I am constantly dieting and I hate it. How do you face a lifetime of deprivation?

I don't. That's what I'm trying to get across to you. I spent more than twenty years either eating much more than I needed to satisfy hunger or depriving myself so badly that I sooner or later had to give in and fill that literal and emotional gap.

It is possible with the motivational support of the Weight Watchers meeting and the reinforcement of the leader, to change your life and your emotional responses to food. You don't have to live your life on a "diet." As a matter of fact, at Weight Watchers we really don't like that word.

I no longer wake in the morning with that word *diet* hovering in my consciousness. Yes, I will always be aware of what I am eating, but I have truly learned to run my life. It doesn't run me. I eat of my own free will, aided in my choice by the education that I received at Weight Watchers.

I love to eat. I need my food to taste good, and I never ever allow myself to go hungry. Part of the agony I went through in the past, and I know I share this with many people, was the feeling of isolation from my friends and family who didn't have a weight problem. Many times I'd make excuses not to eat at the same table. "I had an early lunch, just give me a cup of coffee," and I'd feel this awful empty feeling. Empty of food and empty because I was missing the fun and the camaraderie and the shared love that goes with shared food. I would avoid going to a party rather than face the stress of avoiding food.

What foods do you still crave?

Cheese and butter. I still eat a little more cheese than I should. I love the taste and texture and aroma of a good cheese, and unlike sweet things that can be duplicated in low-calorie form, cheese is cheese, there's no decent fake equivalent. My idea of food heaven is a wheel of Brie and a loaf of bread. I'm getting pretty good about butter. I usually pass it up quite easily at the dinner table. I've discovered that vegetables do taste great without it once you give your palate a chance to readjust.

A baked potato, with a spoonful of yogurt or a butter substitute sprinkled with a little sea salt and fresh cracked pepper, is delicious.

My mother loves butter. She keeps saying to me, "Now I must lose weight, Lynny, what should I do, you're the expert."

"Well, Mum darling, you could cut down on your butter. You're putting at least three ounces on your toast or bread at every meal. If you just limited it to a teaspoon per meal, you'd cut out hundreds of calories."

"Well, fine. Obviously, I'm never to eat butter again. I shall simply eat everything dry. Dry old toast and boring old bread. What about on a baked potato? You can't mean it! A little sliver on a baked potato won't taste like anything. Well, I won't have potatoes either. Life's going to be pretty awful, but never mind. Now I must just phone London and tell Jean, my housekeeper, to empty the fridge of all butter. Of course, she won't be able to get a refund on it. So she'll have to eat it or just throw it out."

Do people watch what you are eating?

You bet they do. In restaurants, hotels, on board ships, at a party. Everybody suddenly becomes an expert on what I should be eating. People who know little or nothing about Weight Watchers tend to butt in most forcefully.

"Is that Weight Watchers?" "Bread! Eh, caught you!" "Wait till I call my mother in Tallahassee and tell her you ate the pie crust!" "I suppose that's a Weight Watchers oyster?" "Go on, eat the butter, I won't tell."

Fellow Weight Watchers members, however, often watch my plate to compare theirs with mine.

At a Sunday brunch at Jimmy's club in New York waiting to hear the wonderful Maureen McGovern sing, a young woman turned around and clasped my arm. "Thank God you're here," she gasped. "I joined Weight Watchers yesterday. Then my boyfriend suggested brunch and I've been panicking all morning."

I told her what I was having. Orange juice without the champagne, mushroom omelet, sliced tomatoes with dressing on the side, bran muffin, and decaf. I suggested she halve her omelet and drink her tea or coffee without cream.

Later, Maureen McGovern came on and sang like an angel, and that put all thoughts of overeating right out of her head.

What do you eat when you want something sweet?

I've found sugar-free hot cocoa mix satisfies my sweet taste quite nicely.

Sometimes I make a cup, adding one teaspoon of Dutch chocolate mint coffee mix and a tablespoon of Half & Half. This brings the total calories up to about 90, but it tastes so rich and delicious that it's worth it.

I have a little espresso machine. Sometimes I make cappuccino with steamed, foamy lowfat milk and sprinkle a teaspoon of sugar-free hot cocoa mix on top.

What do you say to a host who keeps pushing food you don't want?

Well, of course you can always say you are full, thank you. But some hosts, particularly relatives, are hard to deal with, and with them I have been known to lie! I claim that whatever it is I have just turned down or not finished, won't go with the antibiotics I am taking. I pray that the host will be too polite to ask why I am taking them. But if they do, that old standby, "You remember my old sinus problem," comes in handy.

Have you raised your children with healthy eating habits?

I wish I could give an unqualified Yes, but the truth is, I didn't do such a good job with the first two. You see, when I first had babies I was in my twenties. Benjy was born in 1968 and then Kelly in 1970. I believed that tiny children had no taste buds and could only eat certain foods. When they were ready for solid food, I gave them jars of the available boringness—usually a squashy green-brown mess labeled "lamb and green beans" or "carrot custard and meat." Then as they began to handle spoons and forks, I continued with this ghastly legacy. Baked beans, peas, french fries, fish sticks, ketchup of course, and chocolate pudding. I often fed the children separately—my God, who'd want to eat what they were eating—and when we went out together as a family, I noticed with horror that they seemed only to want to eat the things they could recognize visually, especially if it was first anointed with reassuring ketchup.

John and I tried valiantly to broaden their horizons. "Please, just one mushroom." "Well, you won't know till you try it." Then "A dollar for the person who'll eat one broccoli spear." Hopeless.

Like thousands of mothers before me, I would give in to supermarket blackmail. "Stop making the selections and stop running up and down. I'll give you a candy when we get to the checkout counter."

Then Annabel was born in 1981. How much more we knew about nutrition, and about kids, and how to be sensible!

So with her it was different. No food pushed at her—and especially no jars of prepackaged goo. Let her come to it. Just natural hunger and a child's curiosity. At my baby shower I was given a wonderful little processor gadget. You put the food in and pushed it through a little mincer and Annabel could sample anything, and did.

All the childhood no-no's dispelled, broccoli, yummy mushrooms raw or cooked, delicious snow peas, green beans, fish (no, not fish sticks, but shark or bass, sole or mahi mahi), fruit, cooked or raw, yogurt, nuts, cereal of all kinds.

The little food processor was small enough to take to restaurants, and easy enough to wash, so it was no big deal.

Of late, Annabel has started reading labels. She enjoys checking how many mg's of sodium and fat, or what percentage of the RDA of iron, calcium, vitamins, and so on, is available. Doesn't yet know how to interpret the numbers but she's on the right track. She asks me questions all the time, often forcing me to admit to myself and her that I don't know all the answers. But this makes me reach for my nutrition book and together we discuss what it all means. With a child's natural curiosity, she's fascinated by all of this and takes pride in selecting good healthy food.

Of course, like any kid she sometimes wants to eat a candy, but it doesn't seem to be something she's obsessed with. She has lots of exercise at school and at home, and seems to have no self-consciousness about her ever-increasing height. She stands tall and proud and looks healthy and serene.

It really had never before occurred to me that I could easily guide a child to sensible eating, that it could be done quite naturally.

I'm able to see the fruits of my new lifestyle rubbing off on her. Being emulated, acting as her role model, makes me quite proud.

When Annabel wants to take the horse out, I not only welcome the opportunity to share my passion for riding with her, but look forward to the exercise I'm going to get by walking alongside. While we are out, we sing songs and tell stories and bird-watch, and stop for me to help her climb her favorite tree.

When eating out, she keeps an eye on her daddy, who's just lost 48 pounds, and offers him her vegetables when she sees his eyes looking longingly at the dessert trolley.

I look at both of them and smile from ear to ear.

Are you concerned that Annabel will become obsessed with dieting?

No. You see, I had practiced on my older children—badly, I'm sorry to say. They saw me alternately stuffing food and starving. They saw me load the table with rich food and then not eat it because "I was on a diet." I passed on to them all the bad food messages that my parents passed on to me and I spent years and years blaming my upbringing and thinking that I was powerless to stop the vicious circle.

I never knew that it was possible for a child to be raised with a "normal" attitude to food and health. My own perception of food and my body had always been so abnormal that I believed that very abnormality to be the norm. Just as the family of an alcoholic receives early messages that can help them perpetuate the legacy, so the overeater or the unhealthy eater hands down his or her legacy.

Which is to say that Annabel is receiving the benefits of the things I got to learn the hard way.

Do you drink alcohol?

Yes, from time to time. On special occasions I drink wine or champagne. Until recently, I drank wine every night. I still depended on it as my reward. A glass of wine or two. Or three. The habit of thinking about a drink and the relaxation it would bring would automatically kick in as I changed out of my costume after an evening's performance or a day's shooting. Driving to a dinner engagement, my mind and taste buds would relish in advance the sense memory of a cold glass of Pouilly-Fuissé or Chardonnay or anything.

Whenever I stopped in order to feel guilty about this, I would remind myself that I had successfully turned around thirty years of food addiction, but it was too soon to have a go at changing my desire to drink. But when I was honest with myself I had to admit that I was placing myself at the mercy of the grape in exactly the same way I had allowed myself to be ruled by food.

Since I was drinking much more than I'd been advised by Weight Watchers, I dealt with the calories in wine by eating less in direct proportion to the glasses I drank. When it came to work, I was easily able to discipline myself, as I could usually do with food. I never drank before a show or during a day's filming, never wanted to, but when work was over and as long as I didn't have to drive . . . I feared I wouldn't sleep well if I didn't have a glass of wine at night. I learned to live with the slightly muddy feeling I would experience first thing in the morning. And every six months or so I would just not drink for perhaps three days to prove to myself I could do without. In January 1988, a one-woman play was offered me to perform on British television. *A Woman Alone*, by the Italian playwrights Dario Fo and Franca Rame, is about a suburban wife who has been locked into her flat for three months by an abusive husband. During the course of this fifty-minute monologue, she progresses from a happy, house-proud, gadget-conscious ditz into a mental breakdown which leads to her breakthrough. Well, a kind of breakthrough, in the tradition of Fo's black humor. The final minutes show her aiming a loaded gun at the door waiting for her husband to walk through.

The dialogue was brilliant but complicated, and the director wanted to shoot the thing right through without stopping. It being a solo piece, there was no one to help with a cue. Now, it's a well-known fact that a certain amount of alcohol will impair a person's ability to drive a car. But I also know that even the smallest drop will impair an actor's ability to remember precisely his lines. And a glass of wine before a learning session can work on the brain rather as though it was a computer screen. Turn it off, go to sleep, and next morning nothing will be there. The nightcap would impair my learning ability. The next morning before breakfast, before the house wakes up, my very best learning time.

So I quit. When I felt tempted, I'd conjure up and re-create the sensation of wine's effects and remind myself how I'd be letting down my own high standards of work if I chose sleepy oblivion over creativity.

By the end of this play I knew for the first time that I wouldn't have to go back to my old drinking habits. Having straightened myself out with food, I welcomed the relief I experienced when I found that I felt better, and could even sleep better than ever before.

I still drink from time to time, but I can and do eat dinner in a restaurant, or go to a party, without feeling that my enjoyment depends on it.

Do I like myself more because I'm no longer obsessed with food and drink, or am I able to eat healthfully because I now like myself? Chicken and egg question.

How do you feel about coffee?

Well, delighted with my triumph over the grape, I decided to look at my other addiction, caffeine. And when we look at that, of course, we are also looking at other liquids that contain caffeine. I'm told that there really is nothing wrong with a moderate intake of the stuff, and that there is no reliable data on what actually constitutes too much. But for me, I decided to see if I couldn't cut it out completely. I had never successfully abstained except when I was pregnant with Annabel. I'd been a heavy-duty coffee drinker for at least twenty years so I couldn't remember whether it felt better without it or not.

All I did know was that wonderful feeling of rising half sleep and being kicked into full awareness as my giant mug of coffee was consumed.

It was John's example that turned me around. He joined a doctor's weight-loss program for lowering blood pressure and cholesterol and was advised to cut out caffeine completely.

Funny, for the second time in my life, doing something for someone else's well-being allowed me to step back from myself enough to figure I could do something for my own.

To start with, it made no sense to make two separate pots of coffee. I bought water-processed decaf beans and mixed and blended different roasts just as I always had with the regular beans. I fresh-ground them, then brewed them, and I had to ask myself as I sniffed the delightful results, "What on earth is different about this?" It looked, smelled, and sounded like coffee.

It didn't jolt me awake, it's true, but neither did I get that slightly nauseous feeling after my third mug. As the weeks went by, I realized I felt better, livelier, and more alert. And able to drop off to sleep better.

Now that this last barrier to my good health is down, I seem to have renewed creativity in me. I've never questioned my creative juices in theater, television, and film work (although others may have!), perhaps because of my training. But at home I've never seemed to have enough energy, or interest even, in being creative around the house. Now I find myself keeping a journal, making photo albums, creating collages of our family life, both for ourselves and as gifts for others; and writing letters and cards to friends and relatives comes to me with the greatest of ease.

I found stacks of old photos in drawers and boxes and spent a couple of days sorting them into years, marking packets of negatives, all the time wondering why I hadn't done this before. I had made albums up during the first two or three years in America, but then chaos had set in.

As I delved back through the years, I could document my self-destruction. The weight changes, the bulemic days, puffy face, shiny watering eyes. What a long time I had taken to grow up in the fullest sense of the word. A time for reassessment inside and out, and I felt sad that I had spent so many years fighting my ogre.

I remembered back to when I always so desperately needed the approval of others. To be popular, to be liked. To be loved. One dissenting voice in my direction and I would judge myself too harshly. Even in my "thin" photos, something is missing from my face. And it wears a subtly defiant smile. The apparent poise is ill at ease, covering as it does an anxious heart.

Have your healthy eating habits made a noticeable difference to your work?

Absolutely. There was a time when I would never dream of looking at myself at the "dailies," those being the processed rushed prints of the previous day's work. Now that has changed, and I nearly always insist on seeing them. Because I can make notes about what I know, and not get these observations mixed up with personal and usually negative vanity feelings about what I see.

I've also noticed a change in my work. Braver, no longer afraid of losing control. Improved discipline. Better concentration.

Particularly on a film, the required concentration is enormous. To block out the presence of twenty or thirty people surrounding the acting area in order to distill and focus truthful material in a few seconds of screen time is tough. To be alive to the many minute technical requirements of screen behavior while leaving your character free to just "be" is sometimes impossible.

My old obsession and lack of confidence in my body had always made this concentration doubly difficult, like working in a prison with a handicap.

My new freedom allowed me to have such confidence in my body that I was able to let it freely become the character's body. Able to move and react and feel and sense as that character, instead of always having that little bit of anxious Lynn looking over my shoulder, holding me back from total immersion in the new person's life.

In my everyday life I felt released from my prison. I'm more sure, more reasonable. Food and drink are no longer used as rewards or punishment, but loved for what they are. I'm more appreciative, more tranquil, more at peace. Savoring each day.

What do you do to help yourself eat slowly?

One of the aspects of eating that we used to talk about endlessly in the Weight Watchers meetings had to do with noticing what you eat. On reflection, I realized how often I had gobbled my food, but eating slowly gave me time to connect with the taste and aroma.

Eating slowly gave my stomach time to tell my brain when I'd had enough. Savoring my food gave me a chance to let my memory and imagination join in to make each meal, whether simple or lavish, a rich experience.

It was easier to do this alone at first (company means conversation), and I found I could go on fun memory trips eating almost anything.

Alone one lunchtime in New York, I was sitting at my kitchen table with an attractive earthenware bowl of rotelle, the curly corkscrew pasta. I had tossed the pasta with chopped fresh basil, two cloves of minced garlic, a quarter of a cup of part-skim ricotta, two chopped tomatoes, and a teaspoon of olive oil,

ABOVE: This photo of me and my soon-to-be husband John Clark was taken on the eve of our wedding in New York City in 1967. (PHOTO BY MICHAEL CRAWFORD) BELOW: Here we are slicing our already half-eaten wedding cake the next day. (PHOTO BY KIND PERMISSION OF MICHAEL CRAWFORD)

TOP: The proud parents at home with newborn son Benjy in 1968.
(USED BY KIND PERMISSION OF ARALDO DI CROLLALANZA) ABOVE:
One-day-old Kelly yawns for Mommy in London, 1970. (PHOTO BY
JOHN CLARK)

TOP: One-year-old Annabel meets her Grandpa
Michael at Wilks Water, 1982. (© ASSOCIATED PRESS)
ABOVE: Here I am with John and his mother,
Greta Clark, in New York, 1977. (PHOTO BY KIND
PERMISSION OF HENRY GROSSMAN)

John with Kelly, Benjy, and his eldest son Jonathan in New York, 1974. (PHOTO BY LYNN REDGRAVE)

Annabel and I board the *Queen Elizabeth II* at Southampton, 1988. (AUTHOR'S COLLECTION)

ABOVE: I conferred at length with Weight Watchers International executives Barbara Warmflash and Doug Fisher in preparation for their contribution to *This Is Living*. (© WEIGHT WATCHERS INTERNATIONAL. PHOTO BY DAVID G. HENNINGSEN.) BELOW: I also spent some time in the kitchens of Weight Watchers International working on new recipes. (© WEIGHT WATCHERS INTERNATIONAL. PHOTO BY DAVID G. HENNINGSEN.) RIGHT: John took this snapshot of me having fun down under on a Weight Watchers food commercial shoot in Australia. (PHOTO BY JOHN CLARK)

My friend, the costume designer Bill Belew, does umbrella duty in the Virgin Islands where I was filming a 1988 Weight Watchers food commercial. (PHOTO BY JOHN CLARK

I flew to Texas to clown around with Vanessa when she was filming on location in 1990. (PHOTO BY ANNABEL CLARK)

My son, Benjy, with his Granny Rachel in London, 1990. (PHOTO BY LYNN REDGRAVE)

My daughter Kelly at home in Topanga, California, 1990. (PHOTO BY LYNN REDGRAVE)

Annabel in borrowed costume for *The Cherry Orchard* at La Jolla Playhouse, 1990. (PHOTO BY LYNN REDGRAVE)

Both John and I attended Weight Watchers' 25th Anniversary Ball in New York City in 1989. (© WEIGHT WATCHERS INTERNATIONAL. PHOTO BY LOU MANNA)

and sprinkled freshly ground black pepper on top. Closing my eyes and leaning over the bowl and breathing deeply, I was suddenly fifteen years old, on my very first trip to Italy. My mother, brothers, and I had taken a train from Rome to Venice.

In the Piazza San Marco was a wonderful old restaurant called Florians. Through the years this had been the place to sit and be seen, but now was losing favor because this particular year a new young upstart restaurant had opened its doors exactly opposite on the far side of the piazza. The new place had a big noisy orchestra whose music drowned out Florians' elderly violinist.

One night we thought we'd try the new place for a little pasta and maybe a Sambuca. We sat in vain trying to flag down the overworked young waiters and after about fifteen noisy foodless minutes my brother leaped to his feet. With a cry like Olivier going to battle in *Henry the Fifth*, he yelled, "To Florians, you mutinous dogs!" Mum and I took up the cry, "To Florians!" and the three of us swept out of the restaurant and across the piazza.

Nobody actually took any notice of us, they luckily didn't know what "mutinous dogs" were, but we fell into Florians giggling and feeling we alone would be responsible for its reinstatement as the place to be and be seen in Venice.

We ordered pasta, of course. Was it like this bowl in front of me? I can't be sure. I do know that each delicious mouthful kept me in Venice that New York lunchtime, and I left the table refreshed and satisfied.

More often than not if I'm on my own for lunch, I make a sandwich. Funny, I never have a sandwich in a coffee shop, but I do like them at home for lunch. A favorite. Reduced-calorie bread, so that two slices can remain around 80 calories, Weight Watchers low-sodium mayonnaise and Dijon mustard, very thin almost shaved slices of cucumber, some alfalfa sprouts, and ham. Ham sandwiches take me back to the hunting field.

I loved to go fox hunting when I was a young girl. Four in the morning I'd groom my pony Rosalinda and then slowly make my way through the still dark woods near Wilks Water, and out onto the road. A short walk through the village of Odiham, Rosalinda's hoofs echoing in empty streets, past the bakery where the finest doughnuts in the world were made fresh every morning, and in two hours I'd arrive at the meet, where the Hampshire Hunt would gather. Pink coats, top hats, tweed jackets, and bowlers. The gentry gleaming impeccably on glorious thoroughbreds, and us children on our shaggy ponies trying to keep out of the way as hounds came through.

Nanny always made sandwiches, usually ham, as the hunt could take me a long way from home. She'd pack them in a little metal-lined leather sandwich pack that I could strap onto my saddle.

At some point in the day as hounds tried to find a new scent, we'd stand quietly at the edge of a ploughed field, steam rising from our heavily breathing mounts. Just time to munch a welcome sandwich before the huntsman's horn would blow and we'd be off again.

My memory trips are often to my childhood where the taste connection can conjure for me a day, a place, and a time when life seemed perfect. A can of shrimps, drained, mixed with finely chopped celery, parsley, low-fat plain yogurt, and a pinch of paprika instantly takes me back to an English seaside.

At low tide we children would race out across what seemed like miles of wet rippled sand, then build sandcastles with turrets and tunnels and a moat that would fill with water. Later with our shrimping nets we'd catch the tiny creatures trapped in the tide pools and take them back to Nanny, who would boil them and make shrimp sandwiches for our tea.

What's your worst eating habit?

Eating too fast!

"Don't gobble your food," Nanny used to say, and I'd try to slow down, but the habit of speedy eating became worse as my compulsive behavior developed. The faster I consumed the forbidden food, the easier it was to pretend I hadn't overeaten.

At drama school, meals and snacks were dashed down between classes and once I was an actress I soon acquired the young actor's habit—eating as much as possible today in the shortest possible time for fear of being out of work tomorrow.

Even now I have to make a conscious effort to eat slowly, and probably always will. I now know that I have to allow my brain twenty minutes to get the message that I've had enough.

So when I've eaten my meal, I get up and clear my plate away if I'm on my own. If I'm in company, I engage someone in conversation while sipping some water or coffee.

I put my knife and fork down between bites rather than reloading my fork in readiness for the next one.

Eating too fast is definitely my worst habit, and the one I'm having the hardest time curing.

What's your best eating-out tip?

Ask for the doggy bag before your meal! Don't wait till the end, or chances are you won't be able to resist eating the whole thing.

What's the most important piece of advice you'd give to someone who wants to lose weight?

Set yourself a reasonable goal weight without a time limit. "I want to lose fifteen pounds" not "I must lose fifteen pounds in three weeks."

Giving yourself a time limit sets you up for failure.

How often do you weigh yourself?

Too often! It all began back in the old Polytechnic cooking days. I read in a magazine that Sophia Loren weighed herself every day and if she found she'd gained some weight, she'd starve until she had got rid of it. Well, I thought, if it works for Sophia, it's good enough for me. So I bought the first of an endless array of scales.

Bathroom scales, doctors' scales, traveling scales. I had to weigh myself every day, sometimes two or three times. My travel bags seemed to weigh a ton because I had to take a scale with me wherever I went. If I didn't, I felt out of control and found it impossible not to go on a nonstop binge.

When I joined Weight Watchers, they exhorted us not to become wedded to the scale. To weigh at the meetings, not in between.

Daily weighing can be misleading, they explained. Some days, extra fluid retention may cause a high reading, while a low reading following a big night out may give the false impression that you can indulge yourself again the next night. But the following day, your weight bounces up and you lose confidence and want to throw in the towel.

In spite of these remonstrations, I found it impossible to wean myself from the weigh scale dependency. Until this year. It's been seven years since I joined Weight Watchers, but for the first time I took a series of business trips scaleless, and for the first time didn't panic. It didn't stop me from jumping on the moment I got home, but at least it was an improvement.

Do you still use a food scale?

Not often. But when I do, it's for a good reason. I really do have a good sense now about portion sizes, but there are two items that I am still able to fool myself with. Yes, cheese and peanut butter.

When I feel my eye lying to me, I get out the scale and the measuring spoon and get serious.

Do you really eat the Weight Watchers food products?

Oh yes. I must be one of the few people you see on your television screen that actually sells something that was part of one's life before being asked to be spokesperson.

I was using the mayonnaise and margarine and of course the frozen entrées for myself and my family even before I joined Weight Watchers.

Now that all of us have been made aware of the hazards of too much fat in our diet, I find the foods particularly useful. On the Weight Watchers Food Plan, foods that are high in fat are limited but not eliminated. The frozen entrées help me keep down my daily fat intake because the calories, fat, and exchange information are listed on the packet.

The American Heart Association says that less than thirty percent of our daily calories should come from fat and I know that this also applies most importantly to children. So Annabel, who loves Italian pastas and pizzas, for example, can enjoy those Weight Watchers foods as part of a healthy low-fat diet.

A lot of people ask me about the sodium content of the food products. The American Heart Association recommends limiting sodium to 3,000 mg per day, which means if you divided that amount equally into three meals, you could safely have 1,000 mgs of sodium at each meal. Since the entrées provide an average of 790 mgs of sodium with some as low as 350 mgs, I find I can safely incorporate the foods into my overall weekly plan.

Which are your favorites?

I particularly like the Italian dishes. Ravioli, Lasagna, Spaghetti with Meat Sauce, Pasta Primavera, and Seafood Linguini. The pizzas are another favorite and so are the Mexican dishes, burritos, enchilladas, and fajitas. Getting to frozen treats, Annabel and I are Vanilla Sandwich Bar fans and John gets very grumpy if he opens the freezer and doesn't see a packet of Chocolate Dips. Favorite breakfasts include the Pancakes and French Toast with Savory Links, and I have recently become particularly fond of the Muffin with Egg, and Cheese and Canadian-style Bacon.

What's the funniest food diversion technique you've ever heard of?

A man phoned in to a television show I was on recently and said he keeps photocopied chapters of Stephen King's novels in separate plastic bags in his fridge and freezer. When he feels an overwhelming food attack coming on, he takes out a chapter and reads it instead of eating.

Feeding your senses instead of your stomach really does work as an intervention technique. Hobbies, handicrafts, letter writing, music, exercise, perfume, makeup. All can be put into service to help re-educate your pleasure and comfort centers.

When your hand wants to reach for food, stop for a minute to consider what else would give you pleasure at that moment. Then do it! (Within the bounds of propriety, of course!)

Do you ever cheat?

One of the best things about the behavior modification learned at Weight Watchers is the reworking of the concept of cheating.

They helped me put the power that I had previously given to food back into myself.

To say "I'm afraid I cheated and ate the chocolate cake" makes the cake bad, powerful. It tempted you to cheat on yourself, and having cheated, you feel the need to punish yourself for doing so. But when you give yourself the power, you can say "I choose to eat the chocolate cake or I choose not to eat the chocolate cake. If I eat it, I do so of my own free will as a conscious decision. Having eaten it, I need feel no shame nor need for retaliation. I shall just allow for it within my daily food plan."

It's such a deceptively simple concept, really, that when my Weight Watchers leader first talked about it, I didn't believe that it could work. But by using each confrontation with what I used to call "forbidden food" as an opportunity to practice this technique, I soon found it to be completely effective.

So, in answer to your question, no, I never cheat. But I sometimes choose to eat foods that I once would have considered untouchable.

Do you order a special meal when you go on an airplane?

No, never. Once again, I look on it as a challenge to eat well and stay on program regardless of the standard of meals served anywhere. It is getting better and most airlines are much more health-conscious than they used to be, but the fact is, because the Weight Watchers plan includes all the food groups and offers such an enormously wide range of food choices, you can eat comfortably anywhere on a train or a boat or a plane. You can eat out in a restaurant or at home with your family and still lose, or, as in my case, maintain your weight.

Do you prepare separate meals for your family?

When I first joined in 1982 and in the bad old days before that, I seldom ate the same food as my family. In fact, I only ate what they ate when I was overeating.

It's taken me a few years to adapt my cooking style, but now we all eat together and enjoy the same foods. Guests who come to my house don't get the feeling they are going to be put on a diet—in fact, mostly they find it hard to believe that this is the home of "Ms. Weight Watchers."

How has Weight Watchers changed over the years since you joined?

Well, as consumer needs have changed, so Weight Watchers has changed. The woman of the nineties has more nutritional information available to her through the media than ever before. Like most modern women, I want to be healthy. I know that the key to a longer, more productive life is in my own hands. It's not just good luck or ill fortune that will shape my future. So Weight Watchers constantly updates itself. It's always coming up with new ways to keep its members' interest, to reinforce motivation without deserting the ethic. When I joined I believed that I was going on a diet that would last for a few weeks and that I would have to follow it despite the fact that my family and friends would be marching to a different drummer. The biggest difference between then and now is that Weight Watchers had been able to devise a plan whereby you need no longer put your life on hold.

Do you ever want to "crash diet" to lose pounds before shooting a commercial?

No, thank God. The gradual weight-loss approach, 1 to 2 pounds a week, enabled me to take the time necessary to learn new ways and the skills of weight management. When a new role in the theater or films pops up out of the blue, or last-minute plans are made to shoot a commercial, I don't need to crash diet because I've learned how to keep the weight off. I'm ready.

Would you ever gain weight again for a role?

No. I have used padding and makeup to achieve a heavier look, and I truly don't have any vanity about my appearance if a role calls for it. But I don't believe I could survive the effect on my spirit of a real weight gain. Maybe this just proves that I'm not 100 percent cured of my addiction. What am I afraid of? That once I start eating to gain I won't be able to stop? Perhaps. All I know is I never liked the fat me and wouldn't want to live with her again.

In 1970, I was appearing in Michael Frayn's comedy *The Two of Us*. One night I got word that the legendary film director Billy Wilder was out front and would be coming to see me after the performance. I was over the moon with excitement. *Some Like It Hot* and *The Apartment* were two of my favorite movies, and I couldn't wait to meet the master responsible for them.

Mr. Wilder was all beams when he entered my dressing room. "My dear, you were very funny," he said, Austrian accent still intact, trademark spectacles rounding out his chipmunk face. "I'm making a film vit Jack Lemmon. It's based on a play called *Avanti*—"

"Oh, I know that play," I interrupted. I had read it only recently, a lovely May-September romantic comedy. Me and Jack Lemmon, my mind leaped ahead.

"I think you vood be perfect for it . . . but . . ."

"Yes, yes . . ."

"I saw *Georgy Girl*, you vere vonderful but . . . a little heavier . . . I vant ze girl in *Avanti* to be fat. I tink it's funnier."

"But Mr. Wilder, in the play she's not fat!"

"I know, but fat is funnier, and you are quite thin so I vood vant you to gain maybe twenty-five pounds."

"Couldn't I wear padding?" My lip was starting to quiver. "I don't mind padding, I don't mind pretending to be fat."

"Vell no. You see, dere is a nude svimming scene."

Long pause.

"Oh Mr. Wilder, I would so love to work with you, but . . . you don't realize how hard I've tried to get away from Georgy. Oh please please, couldn't the girl be thin? Or couldn't you cut the nude swimming?"

Mr. Wilder looked at me sadly. "No," he said. "Good-bye," and he was gone.

Back in Hollywood he cast the very thin Juliet Mills, who dutifully gained lots of weight, swam in the nude, and gave a charming performance.

I have no regrets about that one. The film was sweet, but not special, and could only have cemented the image I was determined to lose. But I wish I could have worked with Billy

Wilder, and wish he could have seen that fat doesn't always equal funny.

How do you cope with food management when on vacation?

I used to be constantly surprised by my new sensation of freedom, no longer waking in the morning with that feeling of doing battle with my fear of food. I guess enough time has passed for me to be comfortable with it. I look forward to my meals still, truly enjoy them, and that is as it should be.

It means I can now let myself go on structureless vacations in a way I never could before. Where, and what do we like to do, I'm often asked. The answer in our case is simple. A boat! I mean ship! (Never call a boat a ship, unless it is one of course, says John the sailor.)

We've cruised the Caribbean, traveled the Pacific, and leaped the Atlantic. Five days, New York to Southampton, is not too long and not too short. There are lots of activities if you feel like them, guilt-free rest if you don't, and perfect for family travel. Come with us for a moment, on our last crossing.

It was summer of '88 when John and Annabel and I sailed to England on the *Queen Elizabeth 2*. I'd only been on board an hour before at least ten people had asked me what was I going to do about the food. "Did you bring your Weight Watchers?" "You're so thin—wait till Southampton, ha ha."

An ocean liner is paradise for both kids and grown-ups. There are many temptations, of course. What will they do to us? we ask ourselves. Will we be charged less if we don't submit to them? (No!) Who will be the fools and who will be the smart ones? Of all the temptations, food is undoubtedly the greatest. It's easy to deceive yourself in this relaxed atmosphere. If your clothes feel a little tight, well, it could be the sea air or salt water shrinking the fabric.

You can't check your weight so easily either. As the boat gently rocks its way through the water the scale goes up and down—"Ooh look, I've lost twenty pounds—I mean ten I mean five, oh God I've gained. Well, only three, I mean ten, oh help, seventeen."

We sailed with the tide at three in the afternoon and immediately put our clocks ahead two hours. The captain later told me that this was necessary because we'd all missed lunch, so dinner had to be brought forward. Everybody wanted to stay on deck for the incredible Hudson River views. Annabel was already in the pool and making friends while John took videos and remembered a fun summer when he was a guide on the round-Manhattan sightseeing boat. "See the Chrysler Building, the Parachutist's Nightmare," he announced loudly, as in the old days. The sun glinted off the golden roof of the New York Life building. The newly restored "Statue of Liverty," as Annabel calls it, brought the usual lump to my throat as it receded from view, and soon we were under the Verrazano Narrows Bridge and on our way out to sea, the humidity of an August New York quickly forgotten. Time to clean up and give Annabel a bath, for she was salty from the pool. Then down to dinner.

I decided to have the very simple spa menu. Hearts of palm salad, followed by baked potato, steamed vegetables, fresh fruit and cheese. White wine, coffee, and a taste of one of the little petit fours rounded it off.

Next morning I took a good long walk (five rounds of the boat deck is one mile) and a swim and then it was breakfast. Coffee, orange juice, half toasted bagel and cream cheese and off to check out the childrens' nursery. Two lovely nannies. Patty and Jayne, immediately made Annabel feel very welcome.

Eighteen years ago I brought Benjy up there. The room looked the same, only the nannies were different—strange *Twilight Zone* feeling.

Lunchtime, so far so good.

John and I then tried the computer seminar, but it was rather hot so I jettisoned my resolution to learn to operate an IBM PC by the time we reached Southampton, and took to a deckchair and a good book from the library instead.

At 5:30 it was Childrens' Tea in the Columbia dining room. Annabel loved being with the other kids, and her new friend, the chief steward's daughter, Emma, was there. But the food, which she loved, had an English bias: hot dogs, shepherd's pie, baked beans, french fries, sausages, ice cream, and cake. Everyone tucked in, ravenous from the sea air, and I decided to turn a blind eye on this less than terrific meal. But should I?

Dinner was in the Princess Grill following the captain's

cocktail party, and I tried the *QE2* vegetarian selection. Eggplant Parisian with Buckwheat Noodles. Delicious, though rather more oil than I feel really comfortable with. John had thrown caution to the winds, rejecting the menued items. Roast Beef and Yorkshire Pudding was his choice, and in they wheeled an entire standing rib for him to play with.

Early to bed for me. Tired but happy. John took a ration of small change, and went down for a gamble in the gaming room.

The next day was very foggy. From the bridge, the officer of the watch in true deadpan English fashion announced, "As you may have noticed we are sailing through fog."

The trip was totally uneventful, the way I like it. We have more than enough excitement in our working lives, so I was feeling very good, and much rested. I'd eaten well and felt no temptation to fall back into any old bad habits. But for our last dinner we did go slightly berserk. "Challenge the chef and keep him happy," was the game. Champagne to prepare. Then the teasing starter, as much caviar as you could possibly put away, before Pheasant Under Glass for me, Lobster Thermidor for John, and hamburger for the little one (*when* will they learn?). Chocolate soufflés all around to end. An ancient Medoc to wash it down—"Very smooth, madam," assured our waiter. I could be wrong, but was that a teeny Fat Ogre riding shotgun on the waiter's trolley?

I thought back to past crossings and remembered those last-night blues, good-byes to friends you'll probably never see again, getting ready to face a chubby reality as you got off the boat. Thank God that's changed.

For this voyage, though, I knew the memory I would take with me.

I had been asked to bring my old movie *Georgy Girl* to show in the ship's theater one afternoon, after a chat with the passengers about how we made it, and the problems and fun we had. I answered lots of questions and could have left, but something made me stay behind to watch the film once more.

God how strange. Me but not me—shadows from another life. Looking at my young self, I see our daughter Kelly, and in one scene when Georgy pretends to cry, I see Annabel. . . .

I reflected that John and I met and married when it first came out, and sailed *Queen Mary*'s final trans-Atlantic crossing soon after. A feeling of extraordinary contentment came over me as I sat there, John on one side, Annabel on the other. So far so good.

Here Comes Food

14 One-Day Menu Plans from Weight Watchers

t last. After all our talk about weight-loss battles, here comes food. Arc we to be afraid of it? Not at all! For this is good food, genuine food, and healthy food.

I live in the real world, like most of us, and because of the demands of this world, I know that I have to make some adjustments if I want to be a part of it. Each day could present a problem if I allowed myself to think the way I used to. But now I see each day, foodwise, as a challenge and an opportunity, with its many meal colorations. For example, if I am on a normal workday, I plan my meals mainly for myself. But for evenings and weekends with my family, or with entertaining to think about, I have other people to consider. What will be good for me but also appealing to them? Shall we eat in or out? And beyond "what" to eat, there is also "how much?" And so, with the wisdom and insight of Weight Watchers, I give you the following menus.

Here are fourteen days of complete menu plans, each one

being uniquely devised for three levels. Menus are based on the Program for Women. Men and youths must add additional Selections. Level 1 is designed for a fairly fast, but healthy rate of weight loss (1 to 2 pounds per week). Level 2 offers a more moderate rate, and Level 3 is for those who believe in slow and steady (between 1,400 and 1,500 calories). And by the way, nowadays, unless I feel the need to dip into Level 1 or 2, I will probably be thinking of Level 3 for purposes of my own weight maintenance, with perhaps certain amounts added. (What and how much to add is something that is specific to each individual, and *that* I learned at my Weight Watchers classes.) So whether you are losing or maintaining weight, you will find a menu plan to make your real life easier.

Workday #1
Workday #2
Workday #3
Brunch Menu
Lunch in a Restaurant
Family Dinner
Dinner Party
English Family Dinner
French Dinner in a Restaurant
Italian Dinner in a Restaurant
Total Tote Day Menu
No-Cook Day Menu
Easter Dinner
Christmas Dinner

Bon Appetit!

WORKDAY #1: LEVEL 1

BREAKFAST

- ½ cup Orange Sections
- ¾ ounce Cold Cereal
- ½ cup Skim Milk
- Coffee or Tea

LUNCH

- Roast Beef on Rye (2 ounces sliced roast beef with 2 tomato slices, 2 lettuce leaves, and 2 teaspoons mustard on 2 slices reduced-calorie rye bread)
- ½ cup Broccoli Florets and 6 Carrot Sticks
- 1 small Pear
- Coffee, Tea, or Mineral Water

DINNER

- 2 ounces Broiled Flounder Fillet sprinkled with Paprika
- 1 serving **Dill Potato Salad** (page 263)
- 1 cup Cooked Sliced Zucchini
- 1½ cups Tossed Salad with 1½ teaspoons Buttermilk Dressing mixed with 2 tablespoons Plain Low-Fat Yogurt and ¼ teaspoon Mustard
- ½ cup Reduced-Calorie Cherry-Flavored Gelatin topped with 1 tablespoon Whipped Topping
- Coffee or Tea

SNACK

- Pineapple Yogurt (½ cup plain low-fat yogurt mixed with ½ cup pineapple chunks, topped with 1 teaspoon shredded coconut)

WORKDAY #1: LEVEL 2

BREAKFAST

- ½ cup Orange Sections
- ¾ ounce Cold Cereal
- ½ cup Skim Milk
- Coffee or Tea

LUNCH

- Roast Beef on Rye (2 ounces sliced roast beef with 2 tomato slices, 2 lettuce leaves, and 2 teaspoons mustard on 2 slices reduced-calorie rye bread)
- ½ cup Broccoli Florets and 6 Carrot Sticks
- 1 small Pear
- Coffee, Tea, or Mineral Water

DINNER

- ¾ cup Chicken Bouillon
- 3 ounces Broiled Flounder Fillet sprinkled with Paprika
- 1 serving **Dill Potato Salad** (page 263)
- 1 cup Cooked Sliced Zucchini
- 1½ cups Tossed Salad with 1½ teaspoons Buttermilk Dressing mixed with 2 tablespoons Plain Low-Fat Yogurt and ¼ teaspoon Mustard, sprinkled with 2 teaspoons Imitation Bacon Bits
- ½ cup Reduced-Calorie Cherry-Flavored Gelatin topped with 1 tablespoon Whipped Topping
- Coffee or Tea

SNACK

- Pineapple Yogurt (½ cup plain low-fat yogurt mixed with ½ cup pineapple chunks, topped with 1 teaspoon shredded coconut)

WORKDAY #1: LEVEL 3

BREAKFAST

- ½ cup Orange Sections
- 1½ ounces Cold Cereal
- ½ cup Skim Milk
- Coffee or Tea

LUNCH

- Roast Beef on Rye (3 ounces sliced roast beef with 2 tomato slices, 2 lettuce leaves, and 2 teaspoons mustard on 2 slices reduced-calorie rye bread)
- ½ cup Broccoli Florets and 6 Carrot Sticks
- 1 small Pear
- Coffee, Tea, or Mineral Water

DINNER

- ¾ cup Chicken Bouillon
- 3 ounces Broiled Flounder Fillet sprinkled with Paprika
- 1 serving **Dill Potato Salad** (page 263)
- 1 cup Cooked Sliced Zucchini
- 1½ cups Tossed Salad with 1½ teaspoons Buttermilk Dressing mixed with 2 tablespoons Plain Low-Fat Yogurt and ¼ teaspoon Mustard, sprinkled with 2 teaspoons Imitation Bacon Bits
- 1-ounce Roll
- 2 teaspoons Reduced-Calorie Margarine
- ½ cup Reduced-Calorie Cherry-Flavored Gelatin topped with ½ medium Banana, sliced, and 2 tablespoons Whipped Topping
- Coffee or Tea

SNACK

- Pineapple Yogurt (½ cup plain low-fat yogurt mixed with ½ cup pineapple chunks, topped with 1 teaspoon shredded coconut)

WORKDAY #2: LEVEL 1

BREAKFAST

- ½ cup Orange Juice
- ½ Whole Wheat English Muffin, toasted
- 1 tablespoon Whipped Cream Cheese
- ½ cup Skim Milk
- Coffee or Tea

LUNCH

- Egg Salad Sandwich (1 hard-cooked egg, chopped, with 1 tablespoon *each* chopped celery and red bell pepper, 2 teaspoons reduced-calorie mayonnaise, ¼ teaspoon mustard, and 2 lettuce leaves on 2 slices reduced-calorie wheat bread)
- ½ cup Mushrooms and 6 Cucumber Spears
- 1 cup Skim Milk
- Coffee, Tea, or Mineral Water

DINNER

- 1 serving **Shakespeare Sherry Scallops** (page 232)
- 3-ounce Baked Potato with 2 tablespoons Plain Low-Fat Yogurt, sprinkled with Chopped Chives
- 9 Cooked Asparagus Spears
- 1½ cups Mixed Green Salad with 2 tablespoons Plain Low-Fat Yogurt mixed with 1 teaspoon Mustard
- 1 cup Applesauce
- Coffee or Tea

SNACK

- 1 serving **Berries with Sweet Yogurt Sauce** (page 214)

WORKDAY #2: LEVEL 2

BREAKFAST

- ½ cup Orange Juice
- ½ Whole Wheat English Muffin, toasted
- 1 tablespoon Whipped Cream Cheese
- ½ cup Skim Milk
- Coffee or Tea

LUNCH

- Egg Salad Sandwich (1 hard-cooked egg, chopped, with 1 tablespoon *each* chopped celery and red bell pepper, 2 teaspoons reduced-calorie mayonnaise, ¼ teaspoon mustard, and 2 lettuce leaves on 2 slices reduced-calorie wheat bread)
- ½ cup Mushrooms and 6 Cucumber Spears
- 1 small Nectarine
- 1 cup Skim Milk
- Coffee, Tea, or Mineral Water

DINNER

- 1 serving **Shakespeare Sherry Scallops** (page 232)
- 3-ounce Baked Potato with 2 tablespoons Plain Low-Fat Yogurt, mixed with 1 teaspoon Imitation Bacon Bits
- 9 Cooked Asparagus Spears
- 1½ cups Mixed Green Salad with 2 tablespoons Plain Low-Fat Yogurt mixed with 1 teaspoon Mustard
- 1 cup Applesauce
- Coffee or Tea

SNACK

- 1 serving **Berries with Sweet Yogurt Sauce** (page 214)

WORKDAY #2: LEVEL 3

BREAKFAST

- 1 cup Orange Juice
- 1 Whole Wheat English Muffin, toasted
- 2 tablespoons Whipped Cream Cheese
- ½ cup Skim Milk
- Coffee or Tea

LUNCH

- Egg Salad Sandwich (2 hard-cooked eggs, chopped, with 2 tablespoons *each* chopped celery and red bell pepper, 4 teaspoons reduced-calorie mayonnaise, ¼ teaspoon mustard, and 2 lettuce leaves on 2 slices reduced-calorie wheat bread)
- ½ cup Mushrooms and 6 Cucumber Spears
- 1 small Nectarine
- 1 cup Skim Milk
- Coffee, Tea, or Mineral Water

DINNER

- 1 serving **Shakespeare Sherry Scallops** (page 232)
- 3-ounce Baked Potato with 2 tablespoons Plain Low-Fat Yogurt, mixed with 1 teaspoon Imitation Bacon Bits
- 9 Cooked Asparagus Spears
- 1½ cups Mixed Green Salad with 2 tablespoons Plain Low-Fat Yogurt mixed with 1 teaspoon Mustard
- 1 cup Applesauce
- Coffee or Tea

SNACK

- 1 serving **Berries with Sweet Yogurt Sauce** (page 214)

WORKDAY #3: LEVEL 1

BREAKFAST

- 1 cup Cantaloupe Chunks
- Caraway Toast (⅓ cup low-fat cottage cheese sprinkled with ½ teaspoon caraway seed on 1 slice reduced-calorie rye bread, toasted)
- 1 cup Skim Milk
- Coffee or Tea

LUNCH

- Spinach-Cheddar Salad (¾ ounce Cheddar cheese diced, with 1 cup spinach leaves, 6 tomato wedges, ½ cup sliced cucumber, 6 red bell pepper strips, and 1½ teaspoons French dressing mixed with 2 teaspoons lemon juice and ¼ teaspoon mustard)
- 3 Melba Rounds
- Coffee, Tea, or Mineral Water

DINNER

- ¾ cup Onion Bouillon
- 3 ounces Cooked Chicken
- 1 cup Cooked Rice with 1 teaspoon Chopped Parsley
- ½ cup Cooked Snow Peas
- 1 serving **Beet and Endive Toss** (page 265)
- ½ cup Fruit Salad with 2 teaspoons Shredded Coconut
- Coffee or Tea

SNACK

- 1 small Nectarine; 1 serving Reduced-Calorie Chocolate Dairy Drink

WORKDAY #3: LEVEL 2

BREAKFAST

- 1 cup Cantaloupe Chunks
- Caraway Toast (⅓ cup low-fat cottage cheese sprinkled with ½ teaspoon caraway seed on 1 slice reduced-calorie rye bread, toasted)
- 1 cup Skim Milk
- Coffee or Tea

LUNCH

- Spinach-Cheddar Salad (¾ ounce Cheddar cheese, diced, with 2 ounces rinsed drained canned chick-peas, 1 cup spinach leaves, 6 tomato wedges, ½ cup sliced cucumber, 6 red bell pepper strips, and 1½ teaspoons French dressing mixed with 2 teaspoons lemon juice and ¼ teaspoon mustard)
- 3 Melba Rounds
- Coffee, Tea, or Mineral Water

DINNER

- ¾ cup Onion Bouillon
- 3 ounces Cooked Chicken
- 1 cup Cooked Rice with 1 teaspoon Chopped Parsley
- ½ cup Cooked Snow Peas
- 1 serving **Beet and Endive Toss** (page 265)
- ½ cup Fruit Salad with 2 teaspoons Shredded Coconut and 2 tablespoons Whipped Topping
- Coffee or Tea

SNACK

- 1 small Nectarine; 1 serving Reduced-Calorie Chocolate Dairy Drink

WORKDAY #3: LEVEL 3

BREAKFAST

- 1 cup Cantaloupe Chunks
- Caraway Toast (⅓ cup low-fat cottage cheese sprinkled with ½ teaspoon caraway seed on 1 slice reduced-calorie rye bread, toasted)
- 1 cup Skim Milk
- Coffee or Tea

LUNCH

- Spinach-Cheddar Salad (1½ ounces Cheddar cheese, diced, with 2 ounces rinsed drained canned chick-peas, 1 cup spinach leaves, 6 tomato wedges, ½ cup sliced cucumber, 6 red bell pepper strips, and 1½ teaspoons French dressing mixed with 2 teaspoons lemon juice and ¼ teaspoon mustard)
- 3 Melba Rounds
- 1 teaspoon Reduced-Calorie Margarine
- 1 large Plum
- Coffee, Tea, or Mineral Water

DINNER

- ¾ cup Onion Bouillon
- 3 ounces Cooked Chicken
- 1 serving **Spicy Barbecue Sauce** (page 221)
- 1 cup Cooked Rice with 1 teaspoon Chopped Parsley
- ½ cup Cooked Snow Peas
- 1 serving **Beet and Endive Toss** (page 265)
- 1-ounce Roll
- ½ cup Fruit Salad with 2 teaspoons Shredded Coconut and 2 tablespoons Whipped Topping
- Coffee or Tea

SNACK

- 1 small Nectarine; 1 serving Reduced-Calorie Chocolate Dairy Drink

BRUNCH MENU: LEVEL 1

BRUNCH

- 1 cup Tomato Juice
- 1 serving **Creamy Mexican Dip** (page 217) with 4 *each* Carrot, Celery, and Cucumber Sticks
- 1 serving **Pepper-Mushroom Omelet** (page 274)
- ½ cup *each* Sliced Endive, Arugula, and Watercress with 1 tablespoon Weight Watchers French Style Salad Dressing
- 1 serving **English Cider Cake** (page 211) topped with 2 tablespoons *each* Raspberries and Plain Low-Fat Yogurt
- Coffee or Tea

DINNER

- ½ medium Grapefruit
- 3 ounces Broiled Swordfish
- 3-ounce Baked Potato topped with ¼ cup Plain Low-Fat Yogurt
- ½ cup Cooked Sliced Beets
- ½ cup Cooked Coarsely Grated Yellow Squash
- 1½ cups Tossed Green Salad with Balsamic Vinegar and Herbs
- 1 Weight Watchers Vanilla Sandwich Bar
- Coffee or Tea

SNACK

- 1 serving Weight Watchers Hot Cocoa

BRUNCH MENU: LEVEL 2

BRUNCH

- 1 cup Tomato Juice
- 1 serving **Creamy Mexican Dip** (page 217) with 4 *each* Carrot, Celery, and Cucumber Sticks
- 1 serving **Pepper-Mushroom Omelet** (page 274)
- ½ cup *each* Sliced Endive, Arugula, and Watercress with 1 tablespoon Weight Watchers French Style Salad Dressing
- 1 serving **English Cider Cake** (page 211) topped with 2 tablespoons *each* Raspberries and Plain Low-Fat Yogurt
- Coffee or Tea

DINNER

- ½ medium Grapefruit topped with 1 teaspoon Sugar and 1 Maraschino Cherry
- 3 ounces Broiled Swordfish
- 3-ounce Baked Potato with ¼ cup Plain Low-Fat Yogurt, sprinkled with 1 teaspoon Imitation Bacon Bits
- ½ cup Cooked Sliced Beets
- ½ cup Cooked Coarsely Grated Yellow Squash
- 1½ cups Tossed Green Salad with Balsamic Vinegar and Herbs
- 1 Weight Watchers Vanilla Sandwich Bar
- Coffee or Tea

SNACK

- 1 serving Weight Watchers Hot Cocoa

BRUNCH MENU: LEVEL 3

BRUNCH

- 1 cup Tomato Juice
- 1 serving **Creamy Mexican Dip** (page 217) with 4 *each* Carrot, Celery, and Cucumber Sticks
- 1 serving **Pepper-Mushroom Omelet** (page 274)
- ½ cup *each* Sliced Endive, Arugula, and Watercress with 1 tablespoon Weight Watchers French Style Salad Dressing
- 1-ounce Roll
- White Wine Spritzer (½ cup *each* white wine and club soda)
- 1 serving **English Cider Cake** (page 211) topped with 2 tablespoons each Raspberries and Plain Low-Fat Yogurt
- Coffee or Tea

DINNER

- ½ medium Grapefruit topped with 1 teaspoon Sugar and 1 Maraschino Cherry
- 3 ounces Broiled Swordfish
- 6-ounce Baked Potato with ¼ cup Plain Low-Fat Yogurt, sprinkled with 1 teaspoon Imitation Bacon Bits
- ½ cup Cooked Sliced Beets
- ½ cup Cooked Coarsely Grated Yellow Squash
- 1½ cups Tossed Green Salad with 1½ teaspoons Italian Dressing mixed with 2 teaspoons Balsamic Vinegar
- 1 Weight Watchers Vanilla Sandwich Bar
- Coffee or Tea

SNACK

- 12 large Cherries; 1 serving Weight Watchers Hot Cocoa

LUNCH IN A RESTAURANT: LEVEL 1

BREAKFAST

- ½ medium Grapefruit
- ¾ ounce Cold Cereal
- 1 cup Skim Milk
- Coffee or Tea

LUNCH IN A RESTAURANT

- 1 bowl Egg Drop Soup
- 1 cup Shrimp Chow Mein
- ½ cup Cooked Rice
- 1 cup Steamed Snow Peas
- ½ cup Steamed Sliced Mushrooms
- Tea

DINNER

- 1 serving **Vegetable-Cheese Spread** (page 219) on Cucumber Slices
- 3 ounces Sliced Roast Beef
- 1 cup Cooked Broccoli Florets
- 1 cup Cooked Spaghetti Squash
- 1½ cups Green Salad with 1 tablespoon Weight Watchers Italian Style Salad Dressing
- 1-ounce Roll
- Coffee or Tea

SNACK

- 1 medium Peach, sliced, mixed with ½ cup Plain Low-Fat Yogurt

LUNCH IN A RESTAURANT: LEVEL 2

BREAKFAST

- ½ medium Grapefruit
- ¾ ounce Cold Cereal
- 1 cup Skim Milk
- Coffee or Tea

LUNCH IN A RESTAURANT

- 1 bowl Egg Drop Soup
- 1 cup Shrimp Chow Mein
- ½ cup Cooked Rice
- 1 cup Steamed Snow Peas
- ½ cup Steamed Sliced Mushrooms
- ½ cup Pineapple Chunks
- Tea

DINNER

- 1 serving **Vegetable-Cheese Spread** (page 219) on Cucumber Slices
- 3 ounces Sliced Roast Beef
- 1 cup Cooked Broccoli Florets
- 1 cup Cooked Spaghetti Squash
- 1½ cups Green Salad with 1 tablespoon Weight Watchers Italian Style Salad Dressing
- 1-ounce Roll
- Coffee or Tea

SNACK

- 1 medium Peach, sliced, mixed with ½ cup Plain Low-Fat Yogurt, sprinkled with 1 teaspoon Shredded Coconut

LUNCH IN A RESTAURANT: LEVEL 3

BREAKFAST

- ½ medium Grapefruit
- 1½ ounces Cold Cereal
- 1 cup Skim Milk
- Coffee or Tea

LUNCH IN A RESTAURANT

- 1 bowl Egg Drop Soup
- 1 cup Shrimp Chow Mein
- ½ cup Cooked Rice
- 1 cup Steamed Snow Peas
- ½ cup Steamed Sliced Mushrooms
- 1 Fortune Cookie
- ½ cup Pineapple Chunks
- Tea

DINNER

- 1 serving **Vegetable-Cheese Spread** (page 219) on Cucumber Slices
- 4 ounces Sliced Roast Beef
- 1 cup Cooked Broccoli Florets
- 1 cup Cooked Spaghetti Squash
- 1½ cups Green Salad with 1 tablespoon Weight Watchers Italian Style Salad Dressing
- 1-ounce Roll
- 2 teaspoons Reduced-Calorie Margarine
- 1 cup Strawberries
- Coffee or Tea

SNACK

- 1 medium Peach, sliced, mixed with ½ cup Plain Low-Fat Yogurt, sprinkled with 1 teaspoon Shredded Coconut

FAMILY DINNER: LEVEL 1

BREAKFAST

- ½ medium Banana, sliced
- ½ cup Cooked Cereal
- ½ cup Skim Milk
- Coffee or Tea

LUNCH

- 1 cup Mixed Vegetable Juice
- Roast Beef on a Bagel (2 ounces sliced roast beef with 2 lettuce leaves, ¼ cup sliced cucumber, and 1 teaspoon *each* reduced-calorie mayonnaise and mustard on 1 small bagel)
- 6 *each* Carrot and Celery Sticks
- Coffee, Tea, or Mineral Water

FAMILY DINNER

- 1 serving **Spiced Yogurt Chicken** (page 237)
- ½ cup Cooked Noodles
- ½ cup Cooked Green Beans
- 1 cup Cooked Cauliflower Florets
- Watercress and Endive Salad (¾ cup *each* watercress and sliced endive with 1 teaspoon olive oil mixed with balsamic vinegar and herbs)
- 1 cup Strawberries topped with 2 tablespoons Plain Low-Fat Yogurt
- Coffee or Tea

SNACK

- 1 large Tangerine; ½ cup Reduced-Calorie Vanilla Pudding with 1 teaspoon *each* Shredded Coconut and Chocolate Syrup

FAMILY DINNER: LEVEL 2

BREAKFAST

- ½ medium Banana, sliced
- ½ cup Cooked Cereal, sprinkled with 1 teaspoon sugar
- ½ cup Skim Milk
- Coffee or Tea

LUNCH

- 1 cup Mixed Vegetable Juice
- Roast Beef on a Bagel (2 ounces sliced roast beef with 2 lettuce leaves, ¼ cup sliced cucumber, and 1 teaspoon *each* reduced-calorie mayonnaise and mustard on 1 small bagel)
- 6 *each* Carrot and Celery Sticks
- Coffee, Tea, or Mineral Water

FAMILY DINNER

- 1 serving **Spiced Yogurt Chicken** (page 237)
- ½ cup Cooked Noodles
- ½ cup Cooked Green Beans
- 1 cup Cooked Cauliflower Florets
- Watercress and Endive Salad (¾ cup *each* watercress and sliced endive with 1 teaspoon olive oil mixed with balsamic vinegar and herbs)
- 1 cup Strawberries topped with 2 tablespoons Plain Low-Fat Yogurt
- Coffee or Tea

SNACK

- 1 large Tangerine; ½ cup Reduced-Calorie Vanilla Pudding with 1 teaspoon *each* Shredded Coconut and Chocolate Syrup and 2 tablespoons Whipped Topping

FAMILY DINNER: LEVEL 3

BREAKFAST

- ½ medium Banana, sliced
- ½ cup Cooked Cereal, sprinkled with 1 teaspoon sugar
- ½ cup Skim Milk
- Coffee or Tea

LUNCH

- 1 cup Mixed Vegetable Juice
- Roast Beef on a Bagel (3 ounces sliced roast beef with 2 lettuce leaves, ¼ cup sliced cucumber, and 2 teaspoons *each* reduced-calorie mayonnaise and mustard on 1 small bagel)
- 6 *each* Carrot and Celery Sticks
- 1 small Apple
- Coffee, Tea, or Mineral Water

FAMILY DINNER

- 1 serving **Spiced Yogurt Chicken** (page 237)
- ½ cup Cooked Noodles
- ½ cup Cooked Green Beans
- 1 cup Cooked Cauliflower Florets
- Watercress and Endive Salad (¾ cup each watercress and sliced endive with 1½ teaspoons olive oil mixed with balsamic vinegar and herbs)
- 1-ounce Roll
- 1 cup Strawberries topped with 2 tablespoons Plain Low-Fat Yogurt
- Coffee or Tea

SNACK

- 1 large Tangerine; ½ cup Reduced-Calorie Vanilla Pudding with 1 teaspoon *each* Shredded Coconut and Chocolate Syrup and 2 tablespoons Whipped Topping

DINNER PARTY: LEVEL 1

BREAKFAST

- ½ medium Banana, sliced
- ¾ ounce Cold Cereal
- ¾ cup Skim Milk
- Coffee or Tea

LUNCH

- 1 serving **First-of-Spring Pasta** (page 251)
- ½ cup Cauliflower Florets and 6 Red Bell Pepper Strips
- Coffee, Tea, or Mineral Water

DINNER PARTY

- 1 cup Tomato Juice
- 1 serving **Curried Lamb with Fruits** (page 246)
- 2 Cooked Broccoli Spears
- ½ cup Cooked Sliced Yellow Squash
- Green Salad (½ cup *each* watercress, spinach, and red leaf lettuce with 2 tablespoons diced red onion and 1 teaspoon reduced-calorie mayonnaise mixed with 2 tablespoons plain low-fat yogurt and ½ teaspoon mustard)
- 1 serving **Kiwi Meringues** (page 283)
- Coffee or Tea

SNACK

- ½ cup Skim Milk

DINNER PARTY: LEVEL 2

BREAKFAST

- ½ medium Banana, sliced
- ¾ ounce Cold Cereal
- ¾ cup Skim Milk
- Coffee or Tea

LUNCH

- 1 serving **First-of-Spring Pasta** (page 251)
- ½ cup Cauliflower Florets and 6 Red Bell Pepper Strips
- 1 small Orange
- Coffee, Tea, or Mineral Water

DINNER PARTY

- 1 cup Tomato Juice
- 1 serving **Curried Lamb with Fruits** (page 246)
- 2 Cooked Broccoli Spears
- ½ cup Cooked Sliced Yellow Squash
- Green Salad (½ cup *each* watercress, spinach, and red leaf lettuce with 2 tablespoons diced red onion and 1 teaspoon reduced-calorie mayonnaise mixed with 2 tablespoons plain low-fat yogurt and ½ teaspoon mustard)
- 1 serving **Kiwi Meringues** (page 283)
- Coffee or Tea

SNACK

- ½ cup Skim Milk mixed with 1 teaspoon Chocolate Syrup

DINNER PARTY: LEVEL 3

BREAKFAST

- ½ medium Banana, sliced
- ¾ ounce Cold Cereal
- 1 cup Skim Milk
- Coffee or Tea

LUNCH

- 1 serving **First-of-Spring Pasta** (page 251)
- ½ cup Cauliflower Florets and 6 Red Bell Pepper Strips
- 1 small Orange
- Coffee, Tea, or Mineral Water

DINNER PARTY

- 1 cup Tomato Juice
- 1 serving **Curried Lamb with Fruits** (page 246)
- 2 Cooked Broccoli Spears
- ½ cup Cooked Sliced Yellow Squash
- Green Salad (½ cup *each* watercress, spinach, and red leaf lettuce with 2 tablespoons diced red onion and 1½ teaspoons French dressing mixed with 2 teaspoons red wine vinegar)
- 1-ounce Roll
- 1 teaspoon Reduced-Calorie Margarine
- 4 fluid ounces Red Wine
- 1 serving **Kiwi Meringues** (page 283)
- Coffee or Tea

SNACK

- ½ cup Skim Milk mixed with 1 teaspoon Chocolate Syrup; 1 small Pear

ENGLISH FAMILY DINNER: LEVEL 1

BREAKFAST

- 1 cup Honeydew Balls topped with ¼ cup Plain Low-Fat Yogurt
- ½ English Muffin, toasted
- 1 teaspoon Reduced-Calorie Margarine
- 2 teaspoons Weight Watchers Raspberry Spread
- Coffee or Tea

LUNCH

- Cottage Cheese Fruit Salad (⅔ cup low-fat cottage cheese topped with ½ cup fruit salad)
- 6 *each* Green and Red Bell Pepper Strips
- Coffee, Tea, or Mineral Water

ENGLISH FAMILY DINNER

- 1 serving **Shepherd's Pie** (page 245)
- 1 cup Steamed Brussels Sprouts
- ½ cup Steamed Spinach
- 1½ cups Tossed Salad with 1 tablespoon Weight Watchers Caesar Salad Dressing
- 1 serving **O'Redgrave's Irish Soda Bread** (page 275)
- 1 teaspoon Reduced-Calorie Margarine
- 1 serving **English Trifle** (page 281)
- Coffee or Tea

SNACK

- 10 small Grapes; 1 serving Reduced-Calorie Vanilla Pudding

ENGLISH FAMILY DINNER: LEVEL 2

BREAKFAST

- 1 cup Honeydew Balls topped with ¼ cup Plain Low-Fat Yogurt
- ½ English Muffin, toasted
- 1 teaspoon Reduced-Calorie Margarine
- 1 tablespoon Weight Watchers Raspberry Spread
- Coffee or Tea

LUNCH

- Cottage Cheese Fruit Salad (⅔ cup low-fat cottage cheese topped with 1 cup fruit salad)
- 6 *each* Green and Red Bell Pepper Strips
- Coffee, Tea, or Mineral Water

ENGLISH FAMILY DINNER

- 1 serving **Shepherd's Pie** (page 245)
- 1 cup Steamed Brussels Sprouts
- ½ cup Steamed Spinach
- 1½ cups Tossed Salad with 1 tablespoon Weight Watchers Caesar Salad Dressing
- 1 serving **O'Redgrave's Irish Soda Bread** (page 275)
- 1 teaspoon Reduced-Calorie Margarine
- 1 serving **English Trifle** (page 281)
- Coffee or Tea

SNACK

- 10 small Grapes; 1 serving Reduced-Calorie Vanilla Pudding

ENGLISH FAMILY DINNER: LEVEL 3

BREAKFAST

- 1 cup Honeydew Balls topped with ¼ cup Plain Low-Fat Yogurt
- 1 Scrambled Egg
- 1 English Muffin, toasted
- 2 teaspoons Reduced-Calorie Margarine
- 1 tablespoon Weight Watchers Raspberry Spread
- Coffee or Tea

LUNCH

- Cottage Cheese Fruit Salad (⅔ cup low-fat cottage cheese topped with 1 cup fruit salad)
- 6 *each* Green and Red Bell Pepper Strips
- 1 small Apple
- Coffee, Tea, or Mineral Water

ENGLISH FAMILY DINNER

- ¾ cup Beef Bouillon
- 1 serving **Shepherd's Pie** (page 245)
- 1 cup Steamed Brussels Sprouts
- ½ cup Steamed Spinach
- 1½ cups Tossed Salad with 1 tablespoon Weight Watchers Caesar Salad Dressing
- 1 serving **O'Redgrave's Irish Soda Bread** (page 275)
- 2 teaspoons Reduced-Calorie Margarine
- 1 serving **English Trifle** (page 281)
- Coffee or Tea

SNACK

- 10 small Grapes; 1 serving Reduced-Calorie Vanilla Pudding

FRENCH DINNER IN A RESTAURANT: LEVEL 1

BREAKFAST

- ¼ small Cantaloupe
- 1 serving **Yorkshire Pudding (American Style)** (page 277)
- ½ cup Skim Milk
- Coffee or Tea

LUNCH

- 1 Weight Watchers Broccoli and Cheese Baked Potato
- Tomato-Sprout Salad (4 tomato wedges with ½ cup alfalfa sprouts and 1 teaspoon reduced-calorie mayonnaise mixed with ¼ teaspoon mustard and 2 tablespoons plain low-fat yogurt on 1 cup torn lettuce leaves)
- Coffee, Tea, or Mineral Water

FRENCH DINNER IN A RESTAURANT

- 5 ounces Fish Véronique
- 6 Steamed Asparagus Spears
- 1 cup Steamed Sliced Leeks
- 1½ cups Mixed Green Salad with 1½ teaspoons Vinaigrette Dressing
- 1 ounce French Bread
- ½ cup Fresh Fruit
- Coffee or Tea

SNACK

- 1 Weight Watchers Chocolate Mousse Bar; ¾ cup Skim Milk

FRENCH DINNER IN A RESTAURANT: LEVEL 2

BREAKFAST

- ¼ small Cantaloupe with 2 tablespoons Part-Skim Ricotta Cheese
- 1 serving **Yorkshire Pudding (American Style)** (page 277)
- ½ cup Skim Milk
- Coffee or Tea

LUNCH

- 1 Weight Watchers Broccoli and Cheese Baked Potato
- Tomato-Sprout Salad (4 tomato wedges with ½ cup alfalfa sprouts and 1 teaspoon reduced-calorie mayonnaise mixed with ¼ teaspoon mustard and 2 tablespoons plain low-fat yogurt on 1 cup torn lettuce leaves)
- Coffee, Tea, or Mineral Water

FRENCH DINNER IN A RESTAURANT

- 5 ounces Fish Véronique
- 6 Steamed Asparagus Spears, sprinkled with ½ teaspoon Sesame Seed
- 1 cup Steamed Sliced Leeks
- 1½ cups Mixed Green Salad with 1½ teaspoons Vinaigrette Dressing
- 1 ounce French Bread
- ½ cup Fresh Fruit
- Coffee or Tea

SNACK

- 1 Weight Watchers Chocolate Mousse Bar; ¾ cup Skim Milk

FRENCH DINNER IN A RESTAURANT: LEVEL 3

BREAKFAST

- ¼ small Cantaloupe with 2 tablespoons Part-Skim Ricotta Cheese
- 1 serving **Yorkshire Pudding (American Style)** (page 277)
- ½ cup Skim Milk
- Coffee or Tea

LUNCH

- 1 Weight Watchers Broccoli and Cheese Baked Potato
- Tomato, Sprout, and Bean Salad (2 ounces rinsed drained kidney beans with 4 tomato wedges on 1 cup torn lettuce leaves topped with ½ cup alfalfa sprouts and 1 tablespoon reduced-calorie mayonnaise mixed with 2 tablespoons plain low-fat yogurt and ¼ teaspoon mustard)
- 1 small Plum
- Coffee, Tea, or Mineral Water

FRENCH DINNER IN A RESTAURANT

- 5 ounces Fish Véronique
- 6 Steamed Asparagus Spears, sprinkled with ½ teaspoon Sesame Seed
- 1 cup Steamed Sliced Leeks
- 1½ cups Mixed Green Salad with 1½ teaspoons Vinaigrette Dressing
- 2 ounces French Bread
- ½ cup Fresh Fruit
- 4 fluid ounces White Wine
- Coffee or Tea

SNACK

- 1 Weight Watchers Chocolate Mousse Bar; ¾ cup Skim Milk

ITALIAN DINNER IN A RESTAURANT: LEVEL 1

BREAKFAST

- 1 Weight Watchers Strawberry Sweet Roll
- ¾ cup Skim Milk
- Coffee or Tea

LUNCH

- 1 cup Tomato Juice
- 1 serving **Spaghetti Squash Quiche** (page 273)
- 6 *each* Green and Red Bell Pepper Strips
- ½ cup Reduced-Calorie Vanilla Pudding
- Coffee, Tea, or Mineral Water

ITALIAN DINNER IN A RESTAURANT

- 1 bowl Lentil Soup
- 1 serving Shrimp Scampi (6 Shrimp)
- 1 cup Cooked Broccoli Florets
- ½ cup Cooked Zucchini Slices
- ¾ ounce Breadsticks
- 1½ cups Arugula and Endive Salad with 1½ teaspoons Italian Dressing
- Coffee or Tea

SNACK

- 1 small Orange

ITALIAN DINNER IN A RESTAURANT: LEVEL 2

BREAKFAST

- 1 Weight Watchers Strawberry Sweet Roll
- ¾ cup Skim Milk
- Coffee or Tea

LUNCH

- 1 cup Tomato Juice
- 1 serving **Spaghetti Squash Quiche** (page 273)
- 6 *each* Green and Red Bell Pepper Strips
- ½ cup Reduced-Calorie Vanilla Pudding
- Coffee, Tea, or Mineral Water

ITALIAN DINNER IN A RESTAURANT

- 1 bowl Lentil Soup
- 1 serving Shrimp Scampi (6 Shrimp)
- 1 cup Cooked Broccoli Florets
- ½ cup Cooked Zucchini Slices
- ¾ ounce Breadsticks
- 1½ cups Arugula and Endive Salad with 1½ teaspoons Italian Dressing
- Coffee or Tea

SNACK

- 1 serving **Lynn's Lemon Syllabub** (page 282); 1 small Orange

ITALIAN DINNER IN A RESTAURANT: LEVEL 3

BREAKFAST

- 1 Weight Watchers Strawberry Sweet Roll
- ¾ cup Skim Milk
- Coffee or Tea

LUNCH

- 1 cup Tomato Juice
- 1 serving **Spaghetti Squash Quiche** (page 273)
- ¾ ounce Cheddar Cheese
- 6 *each* Green and Red Bell Pepper Strips
- 1 small Orange
- Coffee, Tea, or Mineral Water

ITALIAN DINNER IN A RESTAURANT

- 1 bowl Lentil Soup
- 1 serving Shrimp Scampi (6 Shrimp)
- ½ cup Cooked Spaghetti
- 1 cup Cooked Broccoli Florets
- ½ cup Cooked Zucchini Slices
- ¾ ounce Breadsticks
- 1½ cups Arugula and Endive Salad with 1 tablespoon Italian Dressing
- 4 fluid ounces White Wine
- ½ cup Fresh Fruit
- Coffee or Tea

SNACK

- 1 serving **Lynn's Lemon Syllabub** (page 282); 1 serving Reduced-Calorie Vanilla Dairy Drink

TOTAL TOTE DAY MENU: LEVEL 1

BREAKFAST

- 1 small Orange
- Cottage Cheese 'n' Pita (2 tablespoons regular cottage cheese with 1 teaspoon imitation bacon bits on 1 small whole wheat pita)
- 1 cup Skim Milk
- Coffee or Tea

LUNCH

- ¾ cup Chicken Bouillon
- 1 Hard-Cooked Egg
- 1 serving **Mozzarella Via Veneto** (page 268)
- ¾ ounce Breadsticks
- 1 small Pear
- Coffee, Tea, or Mineral Water

DINNER

- 1 serving Weight Watchers Spaghetti with Meat Sauce
- 6 *each* Carrot Sticks and Green Bell Pepper Strips
- Spinach and Sprout Salad (¼ cup *each* bean sprouts and sliced mushrooms on 1 cup torn spinach leaves, topped with ¼ cup alfalfa sprouts and ½ teaspoon olive oil mixed with red wine vinegar and herbs)
- Berry Yogurt (½ cup plain low-fat yogurt mixed with 2 teaspoons reduced-calorie strawberry spread and 1 teaspoon shredded coconut)
- Coffee or Tea

SNACK

- 1 serving Reduced-Calorie Chocolate Dairy Drink

TOTAL TOTE DAY MENU: LEVEL 2

BREAKFAST

- 1 small Orange
- Cottage Cheese 'n' Pita (2 tablespoons regular cottage cheese with 1 teaspoon imitation bacon bits on 1 small whole wheat pita)
- 1 cup Skim Milk
- Coffee or Tea

LUNCH

- ¾ cup Chicken Bouillon
- 1 Hard-Cooked Egg
- 1 serving **Mozzarella Via Veneto** (page 268)
- ¾ ounce Breadsticks
- 1 small Pear
- Coffee, Tea, or Mineral Water

DINNER

- 1 serving Weight Watchers Spaghetti with Meat Sauce
- 6 *each* Carrot Sticks and Green Bell Pepper Strips
- Spinach and Sprout Salad (¼ cup *each* bean sprouts and sliced mushrooms on 1 cup torn spinach leaves topped with ¼ cup alfalfa sprouts and ½ teaspoon olive oil mixed with red wine vinegar and herbs)
- Berry Yogurt (½ cup plain low-fat yogurt mixed with 2 teaspoons reduced-calorie strawberry spread and 1 teaspoon shredded coconut, topped with 1 maraschino cherry)
- Coffee or Tea

SNACK

- 3 Graham Crackers; 1 serving Reduced-Calorie Chocolate Dairy Drink

TOTAL TOTE DAY MENU: LEVEL 3

BREAKFAST

- 1 small Orange
- Cottage Cheese 'n' Pita (2 tablespoons regular cottage cheese with 1 teaspoon imitation bacon bits on 1 small whole wheat pita)
- 1 cup Skim Milk
- Coffee or Tea

LUNCH

- ¾ cup Chicken Bouillon
- 2 Hard-Cooked Eggs, chopped and mixed with 2 teaspoons *each* Ketchup and Reduced-Calorie Mayonnaise
- 1 serving **Mozzarella Via Veneto** (page 268)
- ¾ ounce Breadsticks
- 1 small Pear
- Coffee, Tea, or Mineral Water

DINNER

- 1 serving Weight Watchers Pasta Rigati
- 6 *each* Carrot Sticks and Green Bell Pepper Strips
- Spinach and Sprout Salad (¼ cup *each* bean sprouts and sliced mushrooms on 1 cup torn spinach leaves, topped with ¼ cup alfalfa sprouts and 1 teaspoon olive oil mixed with red wine vinegar and herbs)
- Strawberries and Yogurt (½ cup plain low-fat yogurt mixed with 1 cup strawberries, sliced, topped with 1 teaspoon shredded coconut)
- Coffee or Tea

SNACK

- 3 Graham Crackers; 1 serving Reduced-Calorie Chocolate Dairy Drink

NO-COOK DAY MENU: LEVEL 1

BREAKFAST

- ½ medium Grapefruit
- ¾ ounce Cold Cereal
- 1 cup Skim Milk
- Coffee or Tea

LUNCH

- Cheese 'n' Tomato Sandwich (1 ounce Weight Watchers Natural Swiss Cheese with 2 *each* tomato slices and lettuce leaves and 2 teaspoons mustard on 2 slices reduced-calorie wheat bread)
- 6 *each* Yellow Squash Sticks and Green Bell Pepper Strips
- Coffee, Tea, or Mineral Water

DINNER

- Tuna Salad (3 ounces tuna mixed with 2 tablespoons *each* chopped celery and red bell pepper and 2 teaspoons reduced-calorie mayonnaise on 2 *each* lettuce leaves and red onion slices)
- 1 serving **Green Bean Salad with Yogurt Sauce** (page 266)
- 1-ounce Roll
- 1 teaspoon Margarine
- Blueberry Yogurt (½ cup blueberries topped with 2 tablespoons plain low-fat yogurt)
- Coffee or Tea

SNACK

- 1 serving **Melba Shake** (page 290)

NO-COOK DAY MENU: LEVEL 2

BREAKFAST

- ½ medium Grapefruit
- ¾ ounce Cold Cereal
- 1 cup Skim Milk
- Coffee or Tea

LUNCH

- Cheese 'n' Tomato Sandwich (2 ounces Weight Watchers Natural Swiss Cheese with 2 *each* tomato slices and lettuce leaves and 2 teaspoons mustard on 2 slices reduced-calorie wheat bread)
- 6 *each* Yellow Squash Sticks and Green Bell Pepper Strips
- Coffee, Tea, or Mineral Water

DINNER

- Tuna Salad (3 ounces tuna mixed with 2 tablespoons *each* chopped celery and red bell pepper and 2 teaspoons reduced-calorie mayonnaise on 2 *each* lettuce leaves and red onion slices, topped with 6 large olives)
- 1 serving **Green Bean Salad with Yogurt Sauce** (page 266)
- 1-ounce Roll
- 1 tablespoon Whipped Cream Cheese
- Blueberry Yogurt (½ cup blueberries topped with 2 tablespoons plain low-fat yogurt)
- Coffee or Tea

SNACK

- 1 serving **Melba Shake** (page 290)

NO-COOK DAY MENU: LEVEL 3

BREAKFAST

- ½ medium Grapefruit
- ¾ ounce Cold Cereal
- 1 cup Skim Milk
- Coffee or Tea

LUNCH

- Cheese 'n' Tomato Sandwich (2 ounces Weight Watchers Natural Swiss Cheese with 2 *each* tomato slices and lettuce leaves and 2 teaspoons *each* mustard and reduced-calorie mayonnaise on 2 slices reduced-calorie wheat bread)
- 6 *each* Yellow Squash Sticks and Green Bell Pepper Strips
- 12 large Cherries
- Coffee, Tea, or Mineral Water

DINNER

- Tuna Salad (4 ounces tuna mixed with 2 tablespoons *each* chopped celery and red bell pepper and 2 teaspoons reduced-calorie mayonnaise on 2 *each* lettuce leaves and red onion slices, topped with 6 large olives)
- 1 serving **Green Bean Salad with Yogurt Sauce** (page 266)
- 1-ounce Roll
- 1 tablespoon Whipped Cream Cheese
- Blueberry Yogurt (½ cup blueberries topped with 2 tablespoons plain low-fat yogurt)
- Coffee or Tea

SNACK

- 3 Graham Crackers; 20 small Grapes; 1 serving **Melba Shake** (page 290)

EASTER DINNER: LEVEL 1

BREAKFAST

- 1 cup Mixed Vegetable Juice
- 1 slice Reduced-Calorie Bread
- 2 tablespoons Part-Skim Ricotta Cheese
- 2 teaspoons Reduced-Calorie Strawberry Spread
- ½ cup Skim Milk
- Coffee or Tea

EASTER DINNER

- ¾ cup Onion Bouillon
- 1 serving **Greek-Style Lamb Chops** (page 201)
- ½ cup Cooked Noodles sprinkled with Chopped Parsley
- 9 Cooked Asparagus Spears
- Tomato and Cucumber Salad (½ cup cucumber slices with 3 cherry tomatoes and red wine vinegar and herbs on 4 lettuce leaves)
- 1 serving **Quick Apple Tart** (page 286)
- Coffee, Tea, or Mineral Water

SUPPER

- Bean Salad (2 ounces *each* rinsed drained canned red and white kidney beans with ½ cup cooked sliced green beans, ¼ cup diced red onion, and 1½ teaspoons Italian dressing mixed with 2 teaspoons red wine vinegar)
- 2 slices Melba Toast
- 6 *each* Red and Green Bell Pepper Strips
- 1 serving Reduced-Calorie Vanilla Pudding topped with ¼ cup Blueberries
- Coffee or Tea

SNACK

- 1 pouch Weight Watchers Apple Snacks; ½ cup Skim Milk

EASTER DINNER: LEVEL 2

BREAKFAST

- 1 cup Mixed Vegetable Juice
- 1 slice Reduced-Calorie Bread
- 2 tablespoons Part-Skim Ricotta Cheese
- 2 teaspoons Reduced-Calorie Strawberry Spread
- ½ cup Skim Milk
- Coffee or Tea

EASTER DINNER

- ¾ cup Onion Bouillon
- 1 serving **Greek-Style Lamb Chops** (page 201)
- ½ cup Cooked Noodles sprinkled with 1 teaspoon Grated Parmesan Cheese and Chopped Parsley
- 9 Cooked Asparagus Spears
- Tomato and Cucumber Salad (½ cup cucumber slices with 3 cherry tomatoes and red wine vinegar and herbs on 4 lettuce leaves)
- 1 serving **Quick Apple Tart** (page 286)
- Coffee, Tea, or Mineral Water

SUPPER

- Bean Salad (2 ounces *each* rinsed drained canned red and white kidney beans with ½ cup cooked sliced green beans, ¼ cup diced red onion, and 1½ teaspoons Italian dressing mixed with 2 teaspoons red wine vinegar)
- 2 slices Melba Toast
- 6 *each* Red and Green Bell Pepper Strips
- 1 serving Reduced-Calorie Vanilla Pudding topped with ¼ cup Blueberries and 2 tablespoons Whipped Topping
- Coffee or Tea

SNACK

- 1 pouch Weight Watchers Apple Snacks; ½ cup Skim Milk

EASTER DINNER: LEVEL 3

BREAKFAST

- 1 cup Mixed Vegetable Juice
- 1 slice Reduced-Calorie Bread
- 2 tablespoons Part-Skim Ricotta Cheese
- 2 teaspoons Reduced-Calorie Strawberry Spread
- ½ cup Skim Milk
- Coffee or Tea

EASTER DINNER

- ¾ cup Onion Bouillon
- 1 serving **Greek-Style Lamb Chops** (page 201)
- 1 cup Cooked Noodles sprinkled with 1 teaspoon Grated Parmesan Cheese and Chopped Parsley
- 9 Cooked Asparagus Spears
- Tomato and Cucumber Salad (½ cup cucumber slices with 3 cherry tomatoes and 1 teaspoon olive oil mixed with red wine vinegar and herbs on 4 lettuce leaves)
- 4 fluid ounces White Wine
- 1 serving **Quick Apple Tart** (page 286)
- Coffee, Tea, or Mineral Water

SUPPER

- Bean Salad (2 ounces *each* rinsed drained canned red and white kidney beans with ½ cup cooked sliced green beans, ¼ cup diced red onion, ¾ ounce shredded Cheddar cheese, and 1½ teaspoons Italian dressing mixed with 2 teaspoons red wine vinegar)
- 2 slices Melba Toast
- 6 *each* Red and Green Bell Pepper Strips
- 1 serving Reduced-Calorie Vanilla Pudding topped with ¼ cup Blueberries and 2 tablespoons Whipped Topping
- Coffee or Tea

SNACK

- 1 pouch Weight Watchers Apple Snacks; ½ cup Skim Milk

CHRISTMAS DINNER: LEVEL 1

BREAKFAST

- 1 cup Tomato Juice
- 1 slice Reduced-Calorie Wheat Bread
- 1 teaspoon Reduced-Calorie Raspberry Spread
- ½ cup Skim Milk
- Coffee or Tea

CHRISTMAS DINNER

- 4 ounces Sliced Baked Ham
- 3 ounces Baked Butternut Squash with 1 teaspoon Reduced-Calorie Margarine
- 1 cup Cooked Brussels Sprouts
- Spinach-Mushroom Salad (½ cup sliced mushrooms with 3 tomato slices, 2 tablespoons diced red onion, and 1½ teaspoons blue cheese dressing mixed with 2 tablespoons plain low-fat yogurt and ½ teaspoon mustard on 1 cup torn spinach leaves)
- 1 serving **Sweet Potato-Pecan Pie** (page 287)
- Coffee, Tea, or Mineral Water

SUPPER

- Cottage Cheese Fruit Salad (⅔ cup low-fat cottage cheese mixed with 2 tablespoons plain low-fat yogurt, topped with ½ cup *each* cantaloupe and pineapple chunks)
- 6 *each* Carrot and Celery Sticks
- Coffee or Tea

SNACK

- ½ medium Banana; ½ cup Reduced-Calorie Chocolate Pudding

CHRISTMAS DINNER: LEVEL 2

BREAKFAST

- 1 cup Tomato Juice
- 2 slices Reduced-Calorie Wheat Bread
- 2 teaspoons Reduced-Calorie Raspberry Spread
- ½ cup Skim Milk
- Coffee or Tea

CHRISTMAS DINNER

- 4 ounces Sliced Baked Ham
- 3 ounces Baked Butternut Squash with 1 teaspoon Reduced-Calorie Margarine and 1 teaspoon Honey
- 1 cup Cooked Brussels Sprouts
- Spinach-Mushroom Salad (½ cup sliced mushrooms with 3 tomato slices, 2 tablespoons diced red onion, and 1½ teaspoons blue cheese dressing mixed with 2 tablespoons plain low-fat yogurt and ½ teaspoon mustard on 1 cup torn spinach leaves)
- 1 serving **Sweet Potato-Pecan Pie** (page 287)
- Coffee, Tea, or Mineral Water

SUPPER

- Cottage Cheese Fruit Salad (⅔ cup low-fat cottage cheese mixed with 2 tablespoons plain low-fat yogurt, topped with ½ cup *each* cantaloupe and pineapple chunks)
- 6 *each* Carrot and Celery Sticks
- Coffee or Tea

SNACK

- ½ medium Banana; ½ cup Reduced-Calorie Chocolate Pudding

CHRISTMAS DINNER: LEVEL 3

BREAKFAST

- 1 cup Tomato Juice
- 2 slices Reduced-Calorie Wheat Bread
- 2 teaspoons Reduced-Calorie Raspberry Spread
- ½ cup Skim Milk
- Coffee or Tea

CHRISTMAS DINNER

- 5 ounces Sliced Baked Ham
- 6 ounces Baked Butternut Squash with 1 tablespoon Reduced-Calorie Margarine and 1 teaspoon Honey
- 1 cup Cooked Brussels Sprouts
- Spinach-Mushroom Salad (½ cup sliced mushrooms with 3 tomato slices, 2 tablespoons diced red onion, 1 teaspoon imitation bacon bits and 1½ teaspoons blue cheese dressing mixed with 2 tablespoons plain low-fat yogurt and ½ teaspoon mustard on 1 cup torn spinach leaves)
- 1 serving **Sweet Potato-Pecan Pie** (page 287)
- Coffee, Tea, or Mineral Water

SUPPER

- Cottage Cheese Fruit Salad (⅔ cup low-fat cottage cheese mixed with 2 tablespoons plain low-fat yogurt, topped with ½ cup *each* cantaloupe and pineapple chunks)
- 6 *each* Carrot and Celery Sticks
- Coffee or Tea

SNACK

- 1 medium Banana; ½ cup Reduced-Calorie Chocolate Pudding

100 Weight Watchers Recipes

I love to read cookbooks and have dozens of them. But I tend to use recipes that don't have too many ingredients, and don't need a lot of special shopping beforehand. The following dishes can be prepared quickly, and I guarantee will be as enjoyable to cook as they are to eat.

Working along with the professionals at Weight Watchers International, I started by choosing twenty-five of my favorites culled from hundreds in the Weight Watchers cookbooks. It was great fun assembling these recipes, with the advice and creative inspiration of Nina Procaccini and her staff of chefs and taster testers at the Weight Watchers kitchens.

Then I came up with seventy-five of my own recipes, newly created with the same expert help, and created exclusively for this book. Some of them are for dishes I never thought I'd be able to eat now, favorites from my childhood that have been specially adapted to fit the Weight Watchers program. Each recipe in this book is followed by a statement that tells you how one serving of the recipe fits into the Food Plan.

Also included is the per serving nutrition analysis for calories, protein, fat, carbohydrate, calcium, sodium, cholesterol, and dietary fiber.

You'll find here a wide variety of pastas and pies, meats and seafoods, breads and muffins, soups, salads, and dips. Sweet things, spicy things, even English things. Yes, I remember what I said about postwar British food, but nothing can curb my enthusiasm for shepherd's pie, scones, soda bread, English toffee, and lemon syllabub. They're all here, and more. Let's start with my Weight Watchers favorites.

My 25 Favorite Weight Watchers Recipes

▪ *Hummus* ▪

Makes 4 servings

I first met hummus when I was in drama school. At lunch in a little Greek restaurant nearby, we budding actors would spread it on pita bread, down several tiny cups of thick black coffee, and discuss Stanislavsky's influence on Chekhov. You don't have to do any of that, but you can try it as a raw-veggie dip.

4 ounces rinsed drained canned chick-peas (reserve 1 tablespoon liquid)
1 tablespoon lemon juice

2 teaspoons sesame seed, toasted
½ teaspoon Chinese sesame oil
1 small garlic clove

1. In food processor combine chick-peas and reserved liquid with remaining ingredients; process into a smooth paste.

Adapted from *Weight Watchers New International Cookbook*

Each serving provides: ½ Protein; 15 Optional Calories

Per serving: 49 calories; 2 g protein; 2 g fat; 6 g carbohydrate; 26 mg calcium; 98 mg sodium (estimated); 0 mg cholesterol; 1 g dietary fiber (this figure does not include sesame seed; nutrition analysis not available)

▪ *Eggplant and Tomato Appetizer* ▪

Makes 4 servings

Because I love eggplant (or aubergine as we call it in England), I was really glad to find this recipe. You can serve it with chicken or fish, but for my taste it really comes into its own alongside lamb.

*1 small eggplant (about
    ³/₄ pound), cut lengthwise
    into ¼-inch-thick slices
1 tablespoon plus 1 teaspoon
    olive oil, divided
3 tablespoons balsamic or red
    wine vinegar, divided*

*2 garlic cloves, minced,
    divided
¼ teaspoon salt, divided
⅛ teaspoon pepper, divided
2 tablespoons chopped fresh
    basil, divided
1 medium tomato, chopped*

1. On nonstick baking sheet arrange eggplant slices in a single layer; using a pastry brush, lightly brush half of the oil over eggplant and broil until lightly browned, 2 to 3 minutes. Turn eggplant over; brush with remaining oil and broil 2 to 3 minutes longer.
2. In 8-inch glass pie plate drizzle half of the vinegar. Arrange half of the eggplant slices over bottom of plate, overlapping edges slightly; sprinkle with half of the garlic, salt, pepper, and basil. Top with tomato and drizzle remaining vinegar over tomato. Top with remaining eggplant slices and sprinkle with remaining garlic, salt, pepper, and basil.
3. Set a 6- or 7-inch plate over pie plate and set a 2-pound weight on plate. Let marinate at room temperature for 30 minutes or refrigerate overnight.
4. To serve, remove weight and plate and cut into 4 equal wedges.

Adapted from *Weight Watchers Quick Success Program Cookbook*

Each serving provides: 1 Fat; 1½ Vegetables

Per serving: 73 calories; 1 g protein; 5 g fat; 8 g carbohydrate; 49 mg calcium; 141 mg sodium; 0 mg cholesterol; 2 g dietary fiber

▪ *Curried Cream of Carrot Soup* ▪

Makes 2 servings, about 1 cup each

I don't think anyone would argue that homemade soup is superior to its canned cousin; so if you're not in a hurry, then it's worth making time to prepare it. Remember to allow the hot ingredients to cool a bit before blending. Start at a low speed with no more than 2 cupfuls at a time.

2 teaspoons margarine
¼ cup chopped scallions
(green onions)
½ small garlic clove, minced
2 teaspoons all-purpose flour
1 cup water
1¼ cups sliced carrots

1 packet instant chicken broth
and seasoning mix
½ teaspoon curry powder
½ cup skim or nonfat milk
⅛ teaspoon salt
Dash white pepper

1. In 1½-quart saucepan melt margarine; add scallions and garlic and sauté over medium heat until soft, about 2 minutes.
2. Sprinkle with flour and stir quickly to combine; cook, stirring constantly, for 1 minute. Continuing to stir, gradually add water; add carrots, broth mix, and curry powder and bring mixture to a boil. Reduce heat to low, cover, and cook until carrots are very soft, about 20 minutes. Remove from heat and let cool slightly.
3. Pour soup into blender and process until smooth. Pour soup back into saucepan; stir in milk, salt, and pepper and heat (*do not boil*). Pour into 2 soup bowls; serve hot.

Adapted from *Weight Watchers Quick and Easy Menu Cookbook*

Each serving provides: ¼ Milk; 1 Fat; 1½ Vegetables; 15 Optional Calories

Per serving: 104 calories; 4 g protein; 4 g fat; 14 g carbohydrate; 108 mg calcium; 735 mg sodium; 1 mg cholesterol; 3 g dietary fiber

▪ *Autumn Soup* ▪

Makes 2 servings, about 1⅔ cups each

Soup. Say it smoothly, soothingly. *Sooo-o-o-o-oup.* This autumn soup makes me think of cozy evenings by a log fire, just home from a performance. Shoes off, feet up, my Autumn Soup gets served in a big blue willow-pattern cup, with toast points.

2 teaspoons margarine
½ cup each diced onion and
   sliced celery
2 cups water
1½ cups frozen cubed
   butternut squash (9 ounces)

1 packet instant chicken broth
   and seasoning mix
8 ounces rinsed drained
   canned small white beans
2 slices crisp bacon, crumbled

1. In 1-quart saucepan melt margarine; add onion and celery and sauté over high heat, stirring frequently, until tender-crisp, about 1 minute.
2. Add water, squash, and broth mix and stir to combine; cook until mixture comes to a full boil. Reduce heat to low, cover, and let simmer until squash is soft, about 15 minutes.
3. Using a wooden spoon, press some of the squash against inside of saucepan to mash; stir in beans and bacon and let simmer until flavors blend, about 5 minutes longer.

Adapted from *Weight Watchers Meals in Minutes Cookbook*

Each serving provides: 1 Fat; 2 Proteins; 1 Vegetable; 1½ Breads; 50 Optional Calories

Per serving: 292 calories; 14 g protein; 7 g fat; 46 g carbohydrate; 151 mg calcium; 1,056 mg sodium (estimated); 5 mg cholesterol; 1 g dietary fiber

▪ *Microwave Coquilles St. Jacques* ▪

Makes 2 servings

I like to serve this in individual white shell-shaped dishes, which we bought years ago in Valauris, France. Light the candles, dim the lights, put on a little flute music, and John and I have the loveliest supper.

½ pound bay scallops or sea scallops (cut into 1-inch pieces)
2 tablespoons dry white table wine
1 tablespoon minced shallot or onion
1 small bay leaf

¼ cup evaporated skimmed milk
1 tablespoon all-purpose flour
¼ cup sliced mushrooms
¾ ounce Gruyère or Swiss cheese, shredded
2 tablespoons plain dried bread crumbs

1. In 1-quart microwavable shallow casserole combine scallops, wine, shallot, and bay leaf; cover and microwave on High (100%) for 2 minutes, until scallops are opaque and cooked through.
2. Using a slotted spoon, transfer scallops to 1-quart flameproof casserole, reserving wine mixture. Remove and discard bay leaf.
3. Using a fork, in 1-cup liquid measure, combine milk and flour and stir well to dissolve flour. Stir flour mixture into wine mixture; add mushrooms and microwave, uncovered, on Medium (50%) for 3 minutes, until mixture thickens. Add to scallops in flameproof casserole and stir to combine.
4. Preheat broiler. In small bowl combine cheese and bread crumbs; sprinkle evenly over scallop mixture. Broil 5 to 6 inches from heat source until topping is lightly browned, 1 to 2 minutes.

Adapted from *Weight Watchers Meals in Minutes Cookbook*

Each serving provides: ¼ Milk; 3½ Proteins; ¼ Vegetable; ½ Bread; 15 Optional Calories

Per serving: 220 calories; 26 g protein; 4 g fat; 16 g carbohydrate; 237 mg calcium; 295 mg sodium; 49 mg cholesterol; 1 g dietary fiber

▪ *Scallops with Kiwi Fruit Sauce* ▪

Makes 2 servings

Kiwis first came to us from New Zealand, so this piquant sauce combining gingerroot, lemon peel, and lime juice makes me dream of the Antipodes, of blue skies and clouds that form into giants and dragons . . . If you don't have time to dream, just prepare and enjoy.

1 teaspoon each margarine and olive oil
10 ounces scallops
½ teaspoon minced pared gingerroot
¼ teaspoon minced shallot
¼ cup each canned ready-to-serve chicken broth and dry white table wine
1 tablespoon lime juice (no sugar added)

¼ teaspoon grated lemon peel
Dash white pepper
2 teaspoons all-purpose flour, dissolved in 2 teaspoons water
1 medium kiwi fruit (about ¼ pound), pared, cut in half lengthwise, then sliced

1. In 10-inch nonstick skillet combine margarine and oil and heat over medium-high heat; add scallops and sauté, turning occasionally, until scallops are lightly browned, 3 to 4 minutes. Using a slotted spoon, remove scallops to plate; set aside and keep warm.
2. In same skillet combine gingerroot and shallot and sauté until softened, about 1 minute; add broth, wine, lime juice, lemon peel, and pepper and stir to combine. Bring to a boil; add dissolved flour to skillet and stir quickly to combine.
3. Reduce heat to low, cover, and let simmer, stirring occasionally, until sauce is smooth and thickened, 5 to 10 minutes. Return scallops to skillet; add kiwi fruit and cook until heated through, 2 to 3 minutes longer.

Adapted from *Weight Watchers New International Cookbook*

Each serving provides: 1 Fat; 4 Proteins; ½ Fruit; 40 Optional Calories

Per serving: 227 calories; 25 g protein; 6 g fat; 14 g carbohydrate; 53 mg calcium; 379 mg sodium; 47 mg cholesterol; 2 g dietary fiber

▪ *Orange-Gingered Sea Bass* ▪

Makes 2 servings

So quick to prepare, this delicately flavored dish is perfect for a light supper when I get home after a long evening's work in the theater.

¼ cup each julienne-cut (matchstick pieces) red bell pepper, scallions (green onions), carrots, and diced red onion
2 tablespoons rice vinegar
1 tablespoon each thawed frozen concentrated orange juice (no sugar added) and orange zest*

1 teaspoon each grated pared gingerroot, vegetable oil, and Chinese sesame oil
2 sea bass fillets (¼ pound each)

1. In small mixing bowl combine all ingredients except fillets and stir to thoroughly combine; set aside.
2. On microwavable serving platter arrange fillets in a single layer; top each with half of the vegetable mixture.
3. Cover and microwave on Medium-High (70%) for 3 minutes, rotating platter ½ turn halfway through cooking. Let stand for 1 minute, until fish is cooked through and flakes easily when tested with a fork.

Adapted from *Weight Watchers Meals in Minutes Cookbook*

Each serving provides: 1 Fat; 3 Proteins; 1 Vegetable; ¼ Fruit

Per serving: 189 calories; 22 g protein; 7 g fat; 9 g carbohydrate; 36 mg calcium; 84 mg sodium; 47 mg cholesterol; 1 g dietary fiber

Variation: Orange-Gingered Halibut—Substitute 2 halibut fillets (¼ pound each) for the sea bass.

Per serving: 204 calories; 25 g protein; 7 g fat; 9 g carbohydrate; 78 mg calcium; 68 mg sodium; 36 mg cholesterol; 1 g dietary fiber

* The zest of the orange is the peel without any of the pith (white membrane). To remove zest from orange, use a zester or vegetable peeler; wrap orange in plastic wrap and refrigerate for use at another time.

▪ *Stir-Fried Oysters* ▪

Makes 2 servings

I love oysters, and make no bones about it; if ever I was to be shipwrecked, I'd be diving for them daily. Luckily, there's a great fish market within easy reach of my home, so I don't have to be in a wreck to enjoy this recipe.

1 teaspoon peanut oil
1 1/2 teaspoons each minced
    pared gingerroot and hoisin
    sauce
1 garlic clove, minced
18 medium oysters, shucked
1 1/2 teaspoons soy sauce

1 teaspoon dry sherry
1/2 teaspoon cornstarch,
    dissolved in 1 1/2 teaspoons
    water
1/4 cup diagonally sliced
    scallions (green onions)

1. In 10-inch nonstick skillet heat oil over medium heat; add gingerroot, hoisin sauce, and garlic and cook, stirring quickly and frequently, for 15 seconds (*be careful not to burn*).
2. Add oysters to skillet in a single layer, sprinkle with soy sauce and sherry, and let cook for 1 minute (*do not stir*); stir in dissolved cornstarch and cook, stirring constantly, until mixture thickens.
3. Transfer to serving plate and sprinkle with scallions.

Adapted from *Weight Watchers New International Cookbook*

Each serving provides: 1/2 Fat; 3 Proteins; 1/4 Vegetable; 10 Optional Calories

Per serving: 157 calories; 13 g protein; 6 g fat; 10 g carbohydrate; 88 mg calcium; 576 mg sodium; 93 mg cholesterol; 0.3 g dietary fiber

▪ *Vindaloo Beef Curry* ▪

Makes 2 servings

Though England's Empire came tumbling down, there has remained a strong tradition of Indian cuisine. Strangely, this dish is as ideal for a cooling effect at the height of a dry summer day as it is for a warming glow on a rainy winter's night. As it simmers, the kitchen fills with mouth-watering aromas.

10 ounces boneless beef round steak
2 teaspoons reduced-calorie margarine (tub)
1/2 cup chopped onion
1/2 garlic clove, minced
1 1/2 teaspoons white vinegar
1 teaspoon ground coriander
1/4 teaspoon ground turmeric

1/8 teaspoon each ground cumin, ground ginger, powdered mustard, black pepper, crushed red pepper, and salt
3/4 cup water
1 1/2 teaspoons lemon juice
1 cup cooked long-grain rice (hot)

1. On rack in broiling pan broil steak 4 inches from heat source, turning once, until rare; cut into 1-inch cubes.
2. In 1-quart saucepan melt margarine; add onion and garlic and sauté over medium heat until onion is translucent.
3. Add vinegar and seasonings and stir to combine; add steak and cook, stirring frequently, for 3 minutes.
4. Stir in water, cover, and simmer, stirring occasionally, until meat is tender, about 1 hour.
5. Stir in lemon juice and serve over rice.

Adapted from *Weight Watchers New International Cookbook*

Each serving provides: ½ Fat; 4 Proteins; ½ Vegetable; 1 Bread

Per serving: 388 calories; 36 g protein; 12 g fat; 33 g carbohydrate; 35 mg calcium; 256 mg sodium; 93 mg cholesterol; 1 g dietary fiber

▪ *Chicken à la Grecque* ▪

Makes 4 servings

4 chicken cutlets (¼ pound
each)
¼ cup lemon juice
2 tablespoons all-purpose flour
2 teaspoons oregano leaves
1 tablespoon plus 1 teaspoon
olive oil
1 tablespoon whipped butter
1 cup each sliced onions,
quartered mushroom caps,
and julienne-cut (matchstick
pieces) red or green bell
pepper

2 small garlic cloves, minced
¼ cup each dry white table
wine and water
1 packet instant chicken broth
and seasoning mix
2 tablespoons minced fresh
mint
1½ ounces feta cheese,
crumbled
Garnish: mint sprigs

1. In medium glass or stainless-steel bowl combine chicken and lemon juice and turn to coat with juice. Let marinate for 10 minutes.

2. On sheet of wax paper combine flour and oregano. Remove chicken from lemon juice, allowing juice to drip into bowl; reserve juice. Dredge chicken in flour mixture, coating both sides.

3. In 10-inch nonstick skillet that has a metal or removable handle heat oil; add chicken and cook, turning once, until browned on both sides, about 2 minutes on each side. Transfer chicken to plate; set aside.

4. In same skillet melt butter, stirring into pan drippings; add vegetables and garlic and cook over medium heat, stirring constantly, until tender-crisp, about 5 minutes. Add wine, water, broth mix, reserved lemon juice, and mint; stir and bring to a boil. Return chicken to skillet. Reduce heat to low, cover, and let simmer until chicken is cooked through, 5 to 10 minutes.

5. Preheat broiler. Sprinkle feta cheese over chicken and broil until cheese is softened, 2 to 3 minutes.

Adapted from *Weight Watchers Quick Success Program Cookbook*

Each serving provides: 1 Fat; 3½ Proteins; 1½ Vegetables; 45 Optional Calories

Per serving: 263 calories; 30 g protein; 10 g fat; 11 g carbohydrate; 96 mg calcium; 461 mg sodium; 79 mg cholesterol; 1 g dietary fiber

▪ *Greek-Style Lamb Chops* ▪

Makes 2 servings, 1 chop each

If I had to choose my favorite ethnic cuisine, it would be a close call between Italian and Greek. The aroma of rosemary and garlic being browned on sizzling lamb chops is enough to start me dancing on tabletops and breaking plates.

1 garlic clove, mashed
½ teaspoon salt
1 tablespoon lemon juice
2 teaspoons olive oil
1 teaspoon rosemary leaves, crushed
¼ teaspoon each *pepper and grated lemon peel*

2 lamb shoulder chops (5 ounces each)
1 small plum tomato (about 1 ounce), cut crosswise into 4 equal slices
¾ ounce feta cheese, crumbled

1. Using a mortar and pestle, mash together garlic and salt to form a paste; add lemon juice, oil, rosemary, pepper, and lemon peel and continue to mash until well combined; set aside.
2. On rack in broiling pan broil lamb chops until browned on top, about 5 minutes. Turn chops over and spread each chop with ¼ of the rosemary mixture; broil until browned, 4 to 5 minutes longer. Set 2 tomato slices on each chop, then top each with half of the feta cheese and half of the remaining rosemary mixture. Broil until cheese softens and is glazed, about 2 minutes.

Adapted from *Weight Watchers Quick and Easy Cookbook*

Each serving provides: 1 Fat; 3½ Proteins; ¼ Vegetable

Per serving: 276 calories; 29 g protein; 16 g fat; 3 g carbohydrate; 86 mg calcium; 750 mg sodium; 101 mg cholesterol; 0.2 g dietary fiber

Variation: Olive-Topped Chops—After topping chops with cheese, top each with 3 sliced pitted Greek olives, then remaining rosemary mixture; proceed as directed. In Serving Information increase Fats to 1½.

Per serving: 300 calories; 29 g protein; 18 g fat; 3 g carbohydrate; 92 mg calcium; 987 mg sodium; 101 mg cholesterol; 0.2 g dietary fiber

▪ *Pork Calvados* ▪

Makes 2 servings

This version of the classic French dish subtly combines apples
and pork. But the calvados gives it the stamp of the gourmet.
For accompaniment, I like to serve red cabbage.

10 ounces pork cutlets
2 teaspoons margarine
¼ cup each sliced onion and
    apple brandy (calvados)
2 tablespoons canned ready-to-
    serve chicken broth
2 teaspoons thawed frozen
    concentrated apple juice (no
    sugar added)

1 small apple (about ¼ pound)
1 tablespoon whipping cream
Dash each salt, pepper, and
    ground nutmeg

1. On rack in broiling pan broil cutlets 2 inches from heat source
about 6 minutes, turning once. Remove cutlets to work surface
and cut into 1-inch pieces.
2. In 1-quart saucepan melt margarine over medium heat; add
onion and sauté until translucent, about 2 minutes. Add pork
and cook, stirring frequently, for 1 minute; add brandy, chicken
broth, and concentrated apple juice and stir to combine.
3. Reduce heat to low, cover, and simmer until pork is fork-
tender, about 20 minutes.
4. Core and pare apple; cut into ½-inch-thick slices. Add apple
slices to pork mixture and cook until slices are soft, 8 to 10
minutes; stir in cream and seasonings.

Adapted from *Weight Watchers Favorite Recipes*

Each serving provides: 1 Fat; 4 Proteins; ¼ Vegetable; ½ Fruit; 115 Optional Calories

Per serving: 454 calories; 37 g protein; 19 g fat; 21 g carbohydrate; 23 mg calcium;
265 mg sodium; 121 mg cholesterol; 1 g dietary fiber

▪ *White Bean and Cheddar Casserole* ▪

Makes 2 servings

When my elder daughter Kelly is home from college, she makes this for me. Kelly loves it because she's crazy about beans: white beans, navy beans, lima beans, jumping beans. I open my china closet in the morning and there, bursting out of a tea cup, I'll see beans, left overnight to soak and now puffed up and tumbling over the sides. Kelly's home!

2 teaspoons olive or vegetable oil
½ cup chopped onion
1 garlic clove, minced
2 cups canned Italian tomatoes, seeded and chopped (reserve liquid)
2 teaspoons molasses
1 teaspoon red wine vinegar
¼ teaspoon ground nutmeg

⅛ teaspoon each salt and ground ginger
Dash each black and ground red pepper
6 ounces rinsed drained canned white beans
1 ounce day-old Italian bread, toasted and cut into cubes
¾ ounce Cheddar cheese, shredded

1. In 2½-quart saucepan heat oil; add onion and garlic and sauté over medium heat, stirring occasionally, until onion is translucent, about 3 minutes.

2. Add tomatoes with liquid, molasses, vinegar, and seasonings and stir to combine. Reduce heat to low and simmer for 5 minutes.

3. Add beans, stir to combine, and simmer until heated through, about 5 minutes.

4. In 1-quart flameproof casserole arrange bread cubes; spoon bean mixture over bread and sprinkle with cheese. Broil until cheese is melted and lightly browned, about 1 minute.

Adapted from *Weight Watchers Quick Success Cookbook*

Each serving provides: 1 Fat; 2 Proteins; 2½ Vegetables; ½ Bread; 20 Optional Calories

Per serving: 300 calories; 13 g protein; 9 g fat; 44 g carbohydrate; 235 mg calcium; 970 mg sodium (estimated); 11 mg cholesterol; 3 g dietary fiber

▪ *Linguine Verdi ai Quattro Formaggi* ▪

Makes 4 servings

Cheese has always been my favorite food, so how could I resist
four different kinds in one dish! I had my first taste of this dish
when I was fifteen, in a little restaurant on Rome's Via Veneto.
It was the first occasion when Father asked his family to join
him on location. He was shooting *The Quiet American,* and this
meal stands out in my memory as we stopped to eat on our way
from the airport, the first thing we did.

½ cup part-skim ricotta cheese
1½ ounces each mozzarella
 and Fontina cheeses,
 shredded
1½ ounces grated Parmesan
 cheese
3 tablespoons skim or nonfat
 milk

3 cups cooked spinach linguine
 (hot)
2 tablespoons plus 2 teaspoons
 reduced-calorie margarine
 (tub)

1. In small saucepan heat ricotta cheese until thinned, stirring
constantly with a wooden spoon; gradually add remaining
cheeses, stirring constantly after each addition until cheeses are
melted.
2. Continuing to stir, add milk, 1 tablespoon at a time, stirring
until thoroughly combined. Keep warm over lowest possible
heat.
3. In mixing bowl combine hot linguine and margarine, tossing
until margarine is completely melted. Transfer linguine to serving dish and top with cheese sauce; toss to combine and serve
immediately.

Adapted from *Weight Watchers New International Cookbook*

Each serving provides: 1 Fat; 2 Proteins; 1½ Breads; 4 Optional Calories

Per serving: 321 calories; 18 g protein; 17 g fat; 25 g carbohydrate; 375 mg calcium;
470 mg sodium; 69 mg cholesterol; 2 g dietary fiber

• *Thai-Style Noodles* •

Makes 4 servings

We love pork in our family, and this recipe is a great way to use leftovers from the Sunday roast. Besides, I'll take any excuse to exploit the wok. It's always fun, and only needs minutes.

4 small dried Chinese black mushrooms (stems removed)
1 cup hot water
1 tablespoon plus 1 teaspoon peanut oil
1/4 cup chopped scallions (green onions)
3 garlic cloves, minced
1/4 pound julienne-cut (matchstick pieces) cooked pork

1/4 cup julienne-cut (matchstick pieces) drained canned bamboo shoots
2 tablespoons Oriental fish sauce (nuoc nam nhi)*
1 tablespoon red wine vinegar
Dash pepper
2 cups cooked vermicelli (very thin spaghetti)

1. Place mushrooms in small bowl and add hot water; let soak for 10 minutes. Drain mushrooms, discarding water; slice mushrooms and set aside.
2. In wok heat oil over medium heat; add scallions and garlic and sauté until scallions are softened, about 1 minute.
3. Add pork, bamboo shoots, fish sauce, vinegar, pepper, and sliced mushrooms and sauté, stirring frequently, for 2 to 3 minutes; add vermicelli and sauté, stirring frequently, until spaghetti is lightly browned, about 3 minutes.

Adapted from *Weight Watchers New International Cookbook*

Each serving provides: 1 Fat; 1 Protein; 1/4 Vegetable; 1 Bread

Per serving: 233 calories; 14 g protein; 9 g fat; 24 g carbohydrate; 16 mg calcium; 24 mg sodium; 28 mg cholesterol; 1 g dietary fiber

* This sauce can usually be found in the section of the supermarket that stocks Oriental products; if fish sauce is not available, substitute soy sauce.

▪ *Most Delicious Cauliflower* ▪

Makes 2 servings

This is cauliflower with an Italian accent. Cauliflower, macaroni, Parmesan, and ricotta, an exotic version of my childhood favorite, Cauliflower Cheese.

½ cup part-skim ricotta cheese
1 cup cauliflower florets
½ teaspoon salt
1 teaspoon each *olive oil and margarine*
¼ cup diced onion
1 small garlic clove, minced
1 cup cooked elbow macaroni
1 tablespoon chopped fresh parsley, divided

1 tablespoon plus 1 teaspoon plain dried bread crumbs, lightly toasted
2 teaspoons grated Parmesan cheese
Dash freshly ground pepper
½ ounce toasted almonds, finely ground
Garnish: Italian (flat-leaf) parsley sprig

1. In order to eliminate chill, remove ricotta cheese from refrigerator and let stand 30 minutes before using.
2. In 1-quart saucepan add cauliflower and salt to *1½ cups boiling water*; return to a boil and cook until tender, about 10 minutes. Drain cauliflower, reserving ¾ cup cooking liquid.
3. In 9-inch skillet combine oil and margarine and heat over medium heat; add onion and garlic and sauté for 1 minute (*do not brown*). Add ¾ cup drained cauliflower and, using a fork or potato masher, mash cauliflower; add macaroni, reserved cooking liquid, and 2 teaspoons chopped parsley and stir to combine.
4. To serve, spoon macaroni mixture into serving bowl; top with ricotta cheese and sprinkle with remaining chopped parsley, the bread crumbs, Parmesan cheese, and pepper. Top with almonds. Arrange remaining cauliflower over ricotta mixture and garnish with parsley sprig.

Adapted from *Weight Watchers Favorite Recipes*

Each serving provides: 1½ Fats; 1½ Proteins; 1¼ Vegetables; 1 Bread; 30 Optional Calories

Per serving: 307 calories; 14 g protein; 14 g fat; 32 g carbohydrate; 249 mg calcium; 718 mg sodium; 21 mg cholesterol; 3 g dietary fiber

▪ *Baked Squash* ▪

Makes 4 servings, 1 stuffed squash quarter each

I had never met a squash, baked or otherwise, until I came to live in America. Now it ranks as one of my top favorite vegetables, in its many varieties. This version can be a great alternative for Thanksgiving yams.

1 tablespoon plus 1 teaspoon reduced-calorie margarine (tub)
1 small apple (about ¼ pound), cored and diced
¼ cup dry white table wine
2 tablespoons dark raisins (¾ ounce)

1 butternut squash (about 1½ pounds)*
1 tablespoon plus 1 teaspoon firmly packed dark brown sugar
Garnish: celery leaves

1. Preheat oven to 350°F. In 9-inch skillet melt margarine over medium heat; add apple and sauté until lightly browned, 1 to 2 minutes. Add wine and raisins and cook until liquid has evaporated, 2 to 3 minutes. Remove from heat and set aside.
2. Cut squash lengthwise into quarters, discarding seeds and membranes. In 10 × 10 × 2-inch baking dish arrange squash quarters, cut-side up. Spoon ¼ of apple mixture into seed cavity of each quarter; sprinkle each quarter with 1 teaspoon sugar.
3. Fill baking dish with water to a depth of about ½ inch; cover and bake until squash is fork-tender, 40 to 45 minutes. Arrange squash on serving platter and garnish with celery leaves.

Adapted from *Weight Watchers Favorite Recipes*

Each serving provides: ½ Fat; 1 Bread; ½ Fruit; 35 Optional Calories

Per serving: 139 calories; 2 g protein; 2 g fat; 29 g carbohydrate; 78 mg calcium; 48 mg sodium; 0 mg cholesterol; 1 g dietary fiber

* A 1½-pound butternut squash will yield about ¾ pound cooked squash.

▪ *"Down Under" Brussels Sprouts* ▪

Makes 2 servings

Hooray for Oz. Now that I get to visit Australia regularly, I just love to whip up this fast and easy side dish, all dressed up with chestnuts and sherry. Turns a good day into a G'day!

1 teaspoon margarine
6 small chestnuts (2 ounces),
*   peeled and cut into quarters*
1 ounce Canadian-style bacon,
*   chopped*
¼ cup sliced mushrooms
1½ teaspoons minced shallot
1 cup cooked brussels sprouts,
*   sliced*

2 tablespoons canned ready-to-
*   serve chicken broth*
1 tablespoon dry sherry
½ teaspoon grated lemon peel
¼ teaspoon salt
Dash pepper

1. In 9-inch nonstick skillet melt margarine over high heat; add chestnuts, bacon, mushrooms, and shallot and sauté, stirring occasionally, until mushrooms are lightly browned, 3 to 4 minutes.
2. Add remaining ingredients and mix well to combine. Reduce heat to low and cook until all liquid evaporates, about 5 minutes.

Adapted from *Weight Watchers New International Cookbook*

Each serving provides: ½ Fat; ½ Protein; 1¼ Vegetables; ½ Bread; 10 Optional Calories

Per serving: 171 calories; 6 g protein; 4 g fat; 27 g carbohydrate; 50 mg calcium; 580 mg sodium; 7 mg cholesterol; 3 g dietary fiber

▪ *Spinach Pie* ▪

Makes 6 servings

I got to try this recipe one day when John suddenly phoned to say he was bringing four Irish friends home for lunch, and they were all starving. My fridge was almost bare except for eggs and cheese, but when I opened the freezer the first thing I saw was frozen spinach. We all had a fabulous lunch.

2 tablespoons margarine	*8 eggs, beaten*
¾ cup chopped onions	*1½ cups well-drained cooked*
2 garlic cloves, minced	*spinach*
2 tablespoons all-purpose flour	*1½ ounces each Cheddar*
1 cup skim or nonfat milk	*cheese, shredded, and grated*
¼ teaspoon salt	*Parmesan cheese*
Dash each ground nutmeg	
and pepper	

1. In small saucepan melt margarine over medium heat; add onions and garlic and sauté until onions are softened, about 1 minute. Add flour and stir quickly to combine. Gradually stir in milk; cook, stirring constantly, until sauce is smooth. Add salt, nutmeg, and pepper, mixing well; cook, stirring occasionally, until mixture is thickened, 5 to 10 minutes. Remove from heat and let cool to lukewarm, about 5 minutes.

2. Preheat oven to 350°F. Transfer sauce to medium mixing bowl; add eggs and mix well. Add spinach and cheeses and mix until thoroughly combined.

3. Spray 9-inch pie plate with nonstick cooking spray and pour in spinach mixture; bake until top is puffed and lightly browned, 40 to 45 minutes (until a knife, inserted in center, comes out dry).

4. Remove from oven and let cool 5 minutes before serving.

Adapted from *Weight Watchers Favorite Recipes*

Each serving provides: 1 Fat; 2 Proteins; ¾ Vegetable; 25 Optional Calories

Per serving: 237 calories; 16 g protein; 15 g fat; 9 g carbohydrate; 302 mg calcium; 448 mg sodium; 297 mg cholesterol; 1 g dietary fiber

▪ *Whole Wheat-Banana Muffins* ▪

Makes 8 servings, 1 muffin each

¾ cup plus 2 tablespoons all-
   purpose flour
¼ cup whole wheat flour
1½ ounces ready-to-eat bran
   flakes cereal
1 teaspoon double-acting
   baking powder
¼ teaspoon baking soda
⅛ teaspoon ground allspice
1½ very ripe medium bananas
   (about 9 ounces), peeled

½ cup low-fat buttermilk
   (1% milk fat)
1 egg
2 tablespoons plus 2 teaspoons
   vegetable oil
2 tablespoons firmly packed
   brown sugar
1 teaspoon vanilla extract
4 pitted dried dates
   (1½ ounces), chopped

1. Preheat oven to 375°F. In medium mixing bowl combine flours, cereal, baking powder, baking soda, and allspice; set aside.

2. Spray eight 2½-inch muffin-pan cups with nonstick cooking spray; spoon ⅛ of batter (about ¼ cup) into each sprayed cup (each will be about ⅔ full) and partially fill any remaining cups with water (this will prevent pan from warping and/or burning).

3. Bake in middle of center oven rack for 20 minutes (until muffins are lightly browned and a toothpick, inserted in center, comes out dry). Remove muffins to wire rack and let cool.

Adapted from *Weight Watchers Quick and Easy Menu Cookbook*

Each serving provides: 1 Fat; 1 Bread; ½ Fruit; 40 Optional Calories

Per serving: 184 calories; 4 g protein; 6 g fat; 30 g carbohydrate; 59 mg calcium; 153 mg sodium; 27 mg cholesterol; 1 g dietary fiber

▪ *English Cider Cake* ▪

Makes 8 servings

I think of Somerset and cider and high teas; of cucumber sandwiches, strawberries and cream, and long summer evenings in
rose-scented gardens. But even if you can't go to England, you
can still enjoy a slice of English cider cake with a cup of Lapsang
Souchong. Very civilized.

1½ cups cake flour
1½ teaspoons double-acting
baking powder
1 teaspoon ground cinnamon
¼ teaspoon salt
⅛ teaspoon ground nutmeg
2 tablespoons plus 2 teaspoons
reduced-calorie margarine
(tub)
1 tablespoon plus 2 teaspoons
granulated sugar

2 eggs
⅔ cup unfermented apple cider
(no sugar added)
1 small apple (about
¼ pound), cored, pared,
and grated
2 tablespoons golden raisins
1 teaspoon confectioners' sugar

1. Into medium mixing bowl sift together flour, baking powder,
and seasonings; set aside.
2. Preheat oven to 375°F. In small mixing bowl, using mixer at
medium speed, cream margarine with granulated sugar; add
eggs, 1 at a time, beating well after each addition.
3. Add egg mixture alternately with cider to flour mixture, stirring until batter is smooth; fold in fruits.
4. Line bottom of 7⅜ × 3⅝ × 2¼-inch loaf pan with wax
paper; spray bottom and sides of pan with nonstick cooking
spray. Pour batter into pan and bake for 40 to 50 minutes (until
cake tester, inserted in center, comes out dry).
5. Let cake cool in pan for 5 minutes, then remove to wire rack
and let cool 10 minutes longer.
6. Using a sieve or tea strainer, sift confectioners' sugar over
loaf. To serve, cut into 8 equal slices.

Adapted from *Weight Watchers New International Cookbook*

Each serving provides: ½ Fat; ¼ Protein; 1 Bread; ¼ Fruit; 25 Optional Calories

Per serving: 147 calories; 3 g protein; 3 g fat; 26 g carbohydrate; 50 mg calcium; 205
mg sodium; 53 mg cholesterol; 0.4 g dietary fiber

▪ *Apple-Pecan Loaf* ▪

Makes 12 servings

Just as the cider cake takes me to England, this keeps me firmly in America. Baking it turned into a learning experience, as it incorporates nuts and cheese. Amazing!

1½ cups all-purpose flour
1 teaspoon each double-acting baking powder and baking soda
¼ teaspoon salt
2 ounces chopped pecans
½ cup reduced-calorie margarine (tub)
¼ cup granulated sugar

2 eggs
2 small apples (about ½ pound), cored, pared, and cut into ¼-inch cubes
1½ ounces sharp Cheddar cheese, shredded
1 ounce uncooked quick oats
½ cup skim or nonfat milk

1. Onto sheet of wax paper sift together flour, baking powder, baking soda, and salt.
2. In small bowl combine pecans and 1 tablespoon flour mixture, tossing to coat; set aside.
3. Preheat oven to 375°F. Using mixer at medium speed, in large mixing bowl beat together margarine and sugar until light and fluffy; add eggs, 1 at a time, beating well after each addition. Gradually beat in remaining flour mixture, apples, cheese, and oats; gradually add milk and continue beating until mixture is moistened. Fold in pecan mixture.
4. Spray 9 × 5 × 3-inch loaf pan with nonstick cooking spray and pour batter into pan; bake in middle of center oven rack for 40 to 45 minutes (until a cake tester, inserted in center, comes out clean).
5. Let loaf cool in pan for 10 minutes, then invert onto wire rack and let cool completely. To serve, cut into 12 equal slices.

Adapted from *Weight Watchers 1988 Engagement Calendar—25th Anniversary Edition*

Each serving provides: 1¼ Fats; ½ Protein; ¾ Bread; 50 Optional Calories

Per serving: 187 calories; 5 g protein; 10 g fat; 22 g carbohydrate; 66 mg calcium; 267 mg sodium; 39 mg cholesterol; 1 g dietary fiber

▪ *Grapes Brûlée* ▪

Makes 2 servings

I found this recipe when exploring my Weight Watchers cookbooks for crème brûlée. I couldn't find it, but settled for this delicious alternative. Now that I get to choose the recipes for my own book, you'll find crème brûlée on page 280 of the *This Is Living* recipe section.

40 small seedless grapes (about 6 ounces)
2 tablespoons sour cream

2 teaspoons granulated brown sugar

1. Rinse grapes with cold water and pat dry with paper towels.
2. Into each of 2 individual flameproof serving dishes arrange 20 grapes; spread half of the sour cream over each portion of grapes and then sift half of the sugar over sour cream in each dish.
3. Set dishes on sheet pan and broil 3 inches from heat source until sugar melts and is caramelized, about 1 minute.
4. Remove dishes from broiler and let cool slightly.

Adapted from *Weight Watchers Quick Success Program Cookbook*

Each serving provides: 1 Fruit; 55 Optional Calories

Per serving: 109 calories, 1 g protein, 4 g fat, 19 g carbohydrate; 20 mg calcium; 10 mg sodium; 6 mg cholesterol; 1 g dietary fiber

▪ *Berries with Sweet Yogurt Sauce* ▪

Makes 4 servings

The perfect end to luncheon, this sauce accompanies any variety of berries. Kelly and I tried it with raspberries for breakfast, because it's also a great way to start the day.

½ cup plain low-fat yogurt
2 tablespoons reduced-calorie raspberry spread (16 calories per 2 teaspoons), melted

1 teaspoon confectioners' sugar
⅛ teaspoon grated orange peel
2 cups strawberries, cut into quarters

1. In blender combine all ingredients except strawberries and process until smooth.
2. Into each of 4 dessert dishes spoon ¼ of the strawberries and top each portion with ¼ of the yogurt mixture (about 2 tablespoons); serve immediately.

Adapted from *Weight Watchers Quick and Easy Menu Cookbook*

Each serving provides: ¼ Milk; ½ Fruit; 15 Optional Calories

Per serving: 56 calories; 2 g protein; 1 g fat; 11 g carbohydrate; 63 mg calcium; 21 mg sodium; 2 mg cholesterol; 2 g dietary fiber

▪ *Honey-Sesame Popcorn* ▪

Makes 2 servings

Annabel loves this when she gets home from school. Sometimes we sit down in the kitchen and share a bowl while we swap stories about the day's adventures.

1 tablespoon whipped butter　　*4 cups prepared plain popcorn*
2 teaspoons each honey and
　sesame seed, toasted

1. In small microwavable cup or bowl combine butter and honey and microwave on High (100%) for 1 minute, until melted. Stir in sesame seed.
2. In medium mixing bowl arrange popcorn; pour honey mixture evenly over popcorn and toss to coat.

Adapted from *Weight Watchers Meals in Minutes Cookbook*

Each serving provides: 1 Bread; 65 Optional Calories

Per serving: 110 calories; 2 g protein; 5 g fat; 16 g carbohydrate; 32 mg calcium, 90 mg sodium; 8 mg cholesterol, 2 g dietary fiber (this figure does not include sesame seed; nutrition analysis not available)

75 New "This Is Living" Recipes

▪ *Herbed-Cheese Toasts with Olives* ▪

Makes 2 servings

A cocktail party, a light snack before a show, a glorious dinner party—all these events will be enhanced by a tray of these.

¼ cup part-skim ricotta cheese
3 tablespoons whipped cream cheese
1 tablespoon each chopped chives and fresh basil or ½ teaspoon basil leaves
6 large pitted black olives (1 ounce), minced

1 teaspoon each rinsed drained capers and red wine vinegar
2 ounces French bread, diagonally cut into 12 equal slices

1. In small mixing bowl combine cheeses, chives, and basil; stir well and set aside.
2. In separate small bowl combine olives, capers, and vinegar; stir and set aside.
3. On baking sheet arrange bread slices in a single layer and broil 5 to 6 inches from heat source until golden brown. Turn bread slices over and repeat procedure until both sides are golden brown.
4. Spread an equal amount of cheese mixture over each slice of bread. Broil until cheese is melted, 1 to 2 minutes. Top each slice of bread with an equal amount of the olive mixture.

Each serving provides: ½ Fat; ½ Protein; 1 Bread; 50 Optional Calories

Per serving: 200 calories; 7 g protein; 11 g fat; 19 g carbohydrate; 130 mg calcium; 399 mg sodium; 25 mg cholesterol; 1 g dietary fiber (this figure does not include capers; nutrition analysis not available)

▪ *Creamy Mexican Dip* ▪

Makes 4 servings, about ¼ cup each

Another great party dip, served best with crudités. My own favorite dipping veggie? Jicama.

¼ cup each *chopped scallions (green onions) and mild salsa*

2 tablespoons each *sour cream and lime juice (no sugar added)*

1 tablespoon plus 1 teaspoon reduced-calorie mayonnaise

½ teaspoon salt

4 drops hot sauce

Dash ground red pepper

1. In small bowl combine all ingredients and mix well. Cover and refrigerate until ready to serve. Just before serving, stir well.

Each serving provides: ½ Fat; ¼ Vegetable; 15 Optional Calories

Per serving: 37 calories; 0.4 g protein; 3 g fat; 2 g carbohydrate; 15 mg calcium; 453 mg sodium; 5 mg cholesterol; 0.2 g dietary fiber

▪ *Spicy Chick-Peas* ▪

Makes 2 servings, about ⅓ cup each

A friend drops by. We sit on the porch and gossip with a glass of minty iced tea and a small bowl of these crunchy delights.

*4 ounces rinsed well-drained
    canned chick-peas*

*¼ teaspoon each garlic
    powder and chili powder*

1. Preheat oven to 350°F. Pat chick-peas dry with paper towels. In small mixing bowl combine all ingredients, mixing to thoroughly coat with seasoning.
2. Spray nonstick baking sheet with nonstick cooking spray and arrange chick-peas on sheet. Bake for 15 minutes, stirring every 5 minutes, until dry. Set aside and let cool. Store in airtight container until ready to serve.

Each serving provides: 1 Bread

Per serving: 70 calories; 4 g protein; 1 g fat; 12 g carbohydrate; 21 mg calcium; 198 mg sodium (estimated); 0 mg cholesterol; 1 g dietary fiber

▪ *Vegetable-Cheese Spread* ▪

Yields ½ cup

This is my standby, around four o'clock in the afternoon on a heavy workday, when lunch is long past and dinner seems so far away. I like to spread a little on a rice cake or two.

½ cup whipped cream cheese
2 tablespoons each minced
  celery, scallion (green
  onion), red bell pepper, and
  carrot

1 tablespoon chopped fresh dill

1. In food processor* process cream cheese until fluffy.
2. Transfer to small bowl; add remaining ingredients and stir to combine.
3. Cover and refrigerate until flavors blend, at least 30 minutes.

Each 1-tablespoon serving provides: ⅛ Vegetable; 35 Optional Calories

Per serving: 34 calories; 1 g protein; 3 g fat; 1 g carbohydrate; 10 mg calcium; 38 mg sodium; 10 mg cholesterol; 0.1 g dietary fiber

* If food processor is not available, use electric mixer at medium speed and proceed as directed.

▪ *Sesame Spread* ▪

Makes 4 servings, about 3 tablespoons each

My daughter Kelly and I tried this together as a change from our old friend peanut butter. It seems to satisfy exactly the same taste buds, but is much lighter. Mini rice cakes underneath, I'd say.

½ cup plain low-fat yogurt
2 tablespoons tahini (sesame paste)
1 tablespoon each sour cream and toasted sesame seed

1 teaspoon lemon juice
½ teaspoon granulated sugar

1. In small mixing bowl combine all ingredients, mixing well until thoroughly combined.
2. Cover and refrigerate until flavors blend, about 30 minutes.

Each serving provides: ¼ Milk; ½ Fat; ½ Protein; 25 Optional Calories

Per serving: 85 calories; 3 g protein; 6 g fat; 5 g carbohydrate; 110 mg calcium; 31 mg sodium; 3 mg cholesterol; 1 g dietary fiber (this figure does not include sesame seed; nutrition analysis not available)

▪ *Spicy Barbecue Sauce* ▪

Makes 4 servings, about 2 tablespoons each

⅓ cup ketchup
1 tablespoon each teriyaki
  sauce and white wine
  vinegar
2 teaspoons each vegetable oil
  and firmly packed light
  brown sugar

¾ teaspoon powdered mustard
⅛ teaspoon salt
Dash each ground red pepper
  (optional) and black pepper

1. In small saucepan combine all ingredients and, over high heat, bring to a boil. Reduce heat to low and simmer, stirring frequently, until flavors are well blended, 5 to 10 minutes.

Each serving provides: ½ Fat; 30 Optional Calories

Per serving: 58 calories; 1 g protein; 2 g fat; 8 g carbohydrate; 14 mg calcium; 480 mg sodium; 0 mg cholesterol; dietary fiber data not available

▪ *Chunky Beef Soup* ▪

Makes 4 servings

A healthy, hearty favorite with Annabel and my whole family. Freeze extra portions of this soup in individual containers and you'll always have this meal-in-a-bowl available. Just reheat and relish!

15 ounces boneless beef for stew (cut into 1-inch cubes)
1½ quarts water
1 cup each tomato juice, diced turnips, and chopped green cabbage
6 ounces diced pared potatoes
½ cup each chopped celery, chopped onion, and quartered mushrooms

1½ ounces uncooked lentils, rinsed
¾ teaspoon salt
½ garlic clove, minced
⅛ teaspoon pepper

1. On rack in broiling pan broil beef, turning once, until rare and browned, about 5 minutes on each side.
2. Transfer beef to 4-quart saucepan; add remaining ingredients and bring liquid to a boil. Reduce heat to low, cover, and simmer, stirring occasionally, until meat and vegetables are tender, 40 to 50 minutes.

Each serving provides: 3½ Proteins; 2 Vegetables; ½ Bread

Per serving: 304 calories; 33 g protein; 9 g fat; 22 g carbohydrate; 54 mg calcium; 731 mg sodium; 86 mg cholesterol; 4 g dietary fiber

▪ *Spanish Gazpacho (Chilled Salad-Soup)* ▪

Makes 4 servings

Assorted raw vegetables are lightly processed in the blender to make this ice-cold soup. Perfect for that sultry summer day.

1 cup tomato juice
1 packet instant beef broth and seasoning mix
2 medium tomatoes, coarsely chopped
1 medium cucumber, pared and coarsely chopped
½ cup each coarsely chopped celery and red bell pepper

¼ cup coarsely chopped onion
1 tablespoon olive oil
2 teaspoons balsamic vinegar
1 teaspoon lemon juice
1 garlic clove
¼ teaspoon salt
2 drops hot sauce
Dash pepper
½ cup plain low-fat yogurt

1. In small saucepan combine tomato juice and broth mix and bring to a boil. Remove from heat and allow to cool.
2. In blender combine remaining ingredients except yogurt and process until vegetables are finely chopped. Turn motor off and add cooled tomato juice mixture; process just until combined (*do not puree*).
3. Refrigerate at least 2 hours. Before serving, top each portion with 2 tablespoons yogurt.

Each serving provides: ¼ Milk; ¾ Fat; 2¼ Vegetables; 3 Optional Calories

Per serving: 88 calories; 3 g protein; 4 g fat; 11 g carbohydrate; 80 mg calcium; 630 mg sodium; 2 mg cholesterol; 2 g dietary fiber

▪ *Boston Clam Chowder* ▪

Makes 2 servings

John and I courted in Boston, where I was performing in the pre-Broadway tryout of *Black Comedy*. He introduced me to all the fishy delights that Boston has to offer. Top of the list, of course, was Boston Clam Chowder. I make it often, in memory of those happy days.

1 tablespoon plus 1 teaspoon reduced-calorie margarine (tub)
½ cup chopped onion
6 ounces pared potato, cut into ½-inch cubes
4 ounces drained canned clams, chopped (reserve ¼ cup liquid)

¾ cup water
1 cup low-fat milk (1% milk fat)
⅛ teaspoon crushed thyme leaves
Dash each salt and white pepper

1. In 1-quart saucepan melt margarine; add onion and sauté until softened. Add potato, reserved clam liquid, and water and bring to a boil; cook until potato is tender, about 8 minutes.
2. Using a slotted spoon, transfer about half of the potato mixture to a small mixing bowl. Using a fork, mash potato; return to saucepan (this will thicken soup). Stir in clams, milk, thyme, salt, and pepper and heat (*do not boil*).

Each serving provides: ½ Milk; 1 Fat; 2 Proteins; ½ Vegetable; 1 Bread; 15 Optional Calories

Per serving: 250 calories; 21 g protein; 7 g fat; 27 g carbohydrate; 224 mg calcium; 341 mg sodium; 43 mg cholesterol; 2 g dietary fiber

▪ *Irish Fish Chowder* ▪

Makes 2 servings, about 1¼ cups each

One day when visiting us in Ireland, Vanessa went fishing off the rocks below our house. We heard her yelling for help and rushed outside to find her struggling with a five-foot conger eel. We plunged into the water to help her, and having taken her photograph with her giant catch, I then had to figure out a way to cook it. Here's what I did, but don't worry, you don't have to have conger eel. Try cod, halibut, or red snapper!

3 ounces diced pared all-purpose potato
¼ cup each diced green bell pepper, onion, and carrot and thinly sliced celery
1 teaspoon vegetable oil
1 cup canned ready-to-serve low-sodium chicken broth
½ cup canned Italian tomatoes, seeded and diced (reserve liquid)

2 teaspoons chopped fresh parsley
⅛ teaspoon each thyme leaves and salt
Dash pepper
3 ounces halibut, cod, or red snapper fillet (cut into ½-inch cubes)
1 slice crisp bacon, crumbled

1. In 1-quart microwavable casserole combine potato, bell pepper, onion, carrot, celery, and oil and stir to thoroughly coat; microwave on High (100%) for 3 minutes, stirring halfway through cooking.
2. Add broth, tomatoes with liquid, parsley, thyme, salt, and pepper; microwave on High, uncovered, for 2 minutes.
3. Add fish and stir to combine; microwave on High, uncovered, for 2 minutes, until fish is cooked through and flakes easily when tested with a fork. Let stand for 1 minute. Sprinkle chowder with bacon.

Each serving provides: ½ Fat; 1 Protein; 1½ Vegetables; ½ Bread; 40 Optional Calories

Per serving with halibut: 165 calories; 13 g protein; 6 g fat; 15 g carbohydrate; 58 mg calcium; 358 mg sodium; 16 mg cholesterol; 2 g dietary fiber

With cod: 153 calories; 12 g protein; 5 g fat; 15 g carbohydrate; 45 mg calcium; 358 mg sodium; 21 mg cholesterol; 2 g dietary fiber

With red snapper: 161 calories; 13 g protein; 5 g fat; 15 g carbohydrate; 52 mg calcium; 362 mg sodium; 18 mg cholesterol; 2 g dietary fiber

▪ *Lentil Stew* ▪

Makes 2 servings, about 1½ cups each

In Bromyard, Herefordshire, with Cousin Lucy, I'd get back from a hard day of minnow fishing to find this hearty, warming stew filling the house with its aroma. Lucy used regular parsley, but I prefer the Italian flat-leaf variety.

*2 teaspoons olive or vegetable
  oil*
2 cups thinly sliced onions
*½ cup each diced red and
  green bell pepper*
1 small garlic clove, minced
2 cups water
*3 ounces uncooked lentils,
  rinsed*

*2 ounces uncooked long-grain
  rice*
*½ cup canned ready-to-serve
  low-sodium chicken broth*
2 tablespoons sour cream
*Garnish: 2 teaspoons chopped
  fresh Italian (flat-leaf)
  parsley*

1. In 2-quart nonstick saucepan heat oil over high heat; add onions, peppers, and garlic and cook, stirring frequently, until tender, 8 to 10 minutes. Remove 1 cup of vegetable mixture to small bowl; set aside and keep warm.
2. Add water, lentils, rice, and broth to vegetable mixture remaining in saucepan and cook, stirring occasionally, until mixture comes to a boil. Reduce heat to low, cover, and let simmer until lentils and rice are tender, about 40 minutes.
3. Transfer to serving platter and top with reserved vegetable mixture; spoon sour cream onto vegetable mixture and serve sprinkled with parsley.

Each serving provides: 1 Fat; 2 Proteins; 3 Vegetables; 1 Bread; 45 Optional Calories

Per serving: 394 calories; 17 g protein; 9 g fat; 63 g carbohydrate; 93 mg calcium; 32 mg sodium; 6 mg cholesterol; 9 g dietary fiber

▪ *Hoisin Tuna* ▪

Makes 2 servings

1 boneless tuna steak
  (½ pound)
2 teaspoons peanut oil
1 teaspoon Chinese sesame oil
1 cup **each** snow peas
  (Chinese pea pods), stem
  ends and strings removed,
  and blanched carrot slices
1 teaspoon minced pared
  gingerroot

1 small garlic clove, minced
½ cup canned ready-to-serve
  low-sodium chicken broth
2 tablespoons reduced-sodium
  soy sauce
1 tablespoon hoisin sauce
1 teaspoon cornstarch

1. Preheat broiler. Brush each side of tuna with 1 teaspoon peanut oil; set fish on nonstick baking sheet. Broil 5 inches from heat source, turning once, until fish is cooked through and flakes easily when tested with a fork, 3 to 4 minutes on each side.

2. While fish is cooking, prepare vegetables. In 10-inch skillet heat sesame oil; add snow peas, carrot slices, gingerroot, and garlic and sauté over medium-high heat, stirring frequently, until snow peas are tender-crisp, about 1 minute.

3. In 1-cup liquid measure, combine broth, soy sauce, hoisin sauce, and cornstarch, stirring to dissolve cornstarch; add to skillet. Reduce heat to low and let simmer, stirring occasionally, until mixture thickens, 4 to 5 minutes.

4. To serve, transfer fish to serving platter and pour any juices from baking sheet over tuna; using a slotted spoon, arrange snow peas and carrot slices around tuna, then top fish with hoisin mixture.

Each serving provides: 1½ Fats; 3 Proteins; 2 Vegetables; 30 Optional Calories

Per serving: 313 calories; 31 g protein; 13 g fat; 17 g carbohydrate; 53 mg calcium; 935 mg sodium; 43 mg cholesterol; 3 g dietary fiber

▪ *Tuna España* ▪

Makes 2 servings

My ubiquitous eggplant joins forces with sherry, capers, and bell peppers to get the castanets clicking.

2 tablespoons each *dry sherry and minced fresh parsley*
2 teaspoons olive oil
1 teaspoon each *lemon juice and rinsed drained capers*
2 garlic cloves, minced
1 boneless tuna steak (10 ounces)

1 tiny eggplant (about ½ pound)
1 each *medium red and green bell peppers*
1 medium onion, peeled and ends removed

1. In glass or stainless-steel medium mixing bowl combine sherry, parsley, oil, lemon juice, capers, and garlic; add tuna and turn to coat with marinade. Cover and refrigerate for 1 hour.

2. On baking sheet broil eggplant, peppers, and onion 3 inches from heat source, turning frequently, until vegetables are charred on all sides. Remove from broiler and let stand until cool enough to handle, 15 to 20 minutes.

3. Fit strainer into medium mixing bowl and peel eggplant and peppers over bowl, allowing juice from vegetables to drip into bowl; remove and discard stem ends and seeds from peppers. Cut eggplant and peppers into 2 × ¼-inch strips; remove charred layer from onion and cut onion into wedges. Place vegetables in bowl with juice.

4. Drain tuna, reserving marinade. Place marinade in ½-quart saucepan and bring to boil over high heat. Cook 1 minute; pour into bowl containing vegetables.

5. Preheat broiler. On rack in broiling pan broil tuna 4 inches from heat source, turning once, until fish begins to brown, 4 to 5 minutes on each side. Transfer to serving plate, pour any juices from bottom of broiling pan over tuna, and serve with vegetables.

Each serving provides: 1 Fat; 4 Proteins; 4 Vegetables; 15 Optional Calories

Per serving: 335 calories; 36 g protein; 12 g fat; 17 g carbohydrate; 67 mg calcium; 103 mg sodium; 54 mg cholesterol; 4 g dietary fiber (this figure does not include capers; nutrition analysis not available)

▪ *Fillets with Almond-Orange Sauce* ▪

Makes 2 servings

When we lived on our Irish clifftop, I'd watch for the return of the fishing boats each evening. As the sun set, I'd buy my just-caught sole or flounder and run back up the cliff to prepare it with this almond-orange sauce.

2 *sole* or *flounder fillets*
 (*¼ pound each*)
1 *tablespoon plus 1 teaspoon*
 all-purpose flour
2 *teaspoons olive* or *vegetable*
 oil
1 *tablespoon whipped butter*
½ *ounce sliced almonds*
1 *small navel orange (about 6*
 ounces), peeled and
 sectioned; reserve juice

¼ *cup dry white table wine*
1 *tablespoon freshly squeezed*
 lime juice
⅛ *teaspoon* each *salt and*
 white pepper
1 *teaspoon chopped fresh*
 Italian (flat-leaf) parsley

1. On sheet of wax paper coat fillets with flour, lightly coating both sides and reserving remaining flour.
2. Spray 10-inch nonstick skillet with nonstick cooking spray; add oil and heat. Add fillets to skillet and cook over medium-high heat, turning once, until fish is lightly browned and flakes easily when tested with a fork, 2 to 3 minutes on each side. Transfer fillets to serving platter; set aside and keep warm.
3. In same skillet melt butter; add almonds and sauté over medium-low heat, stirring frequently, until almonds are lightly browned, 1 to 2 minutes. Add remaining reserved flour and stir quickly to combine; stir in orange sections and reserved juice, wine, lime juice, salt, and pepper. Cook, stirring occasionally, until mixture is reduced by ⅓ and slightly thickened, 1 to 2 minutes. Pour almond mixture over fillets and sprinkle with chopped parsley.

Each serving provides: 1½ Fats; 3½ Proteins; ½ Fruit; 70 Optional Calories

Per serving: 281 calories; 24 g protein; 13 g fat; 14 g carbohydrate; 73 mg calcium; 262 mg sodium; 62 mg cholesterol; 2 g dietary fiber

▪ *Sashimi* ▪

Makes 4 servings

In my favorite Japanese sushi bar, the chef dazzles my eye with his lightning hand movements, shaping seaweed, rice, and raw fish into exotic morsels. Sashimi is a little easier to try at home.

½ pound very fresh red snapper fillet, chilled
1 cup each shredded seeded pared cucumbers and grated carrots
2 teaspoons wasabi powder (green horseradish powder)* mixed with 2 teaspoons water

Ginger Dipping Sauce (see recipe below)

1. Chill a serving tray.
2. On a clean cutting board place fillet skin-side down. Using a sharp knife held at an angle, thinly slice fillet into ⅛- to ¼-inch thick slices, wiping knife on clean damp cloth every few slices.
3. Arrange on chilled tray surrounded with cucumbers and carrots; serve with wasabi mixture and Ginger Dipping Sauce.

Each serving (including dipping sauce) provides: 2 Proteins; 1 Vegetable; 5 Optional Calories

Per serving: 108 calories; 16 g protein; 1 g fat; 6 g carbohydrate; 40 mg calcium; 661 mg sodium; 26 mg cholesterol; 1 g dietary fiber

* Wasabi powder is available in Oriental and specialty food stores.

▪ *Ginger Dipping Sauce* ▪

Makes 4 servings, about 2 tablespoons each

¼ cup each canned ready-to-serve low-sodium chicken broth and reduced-sodium soy sauce

1 tablespoon plus 1 teaspoon dry sherry
1 tablespoon slivered pared gingerroot

1. In small saucepan combine broth, soy sauce, and sherry and cook over high heat until mixture comes to a boil; add ginger and cook 1 minute longer. Remove from heat and let cool.

Each serving provides: 5 Optional Calories

Per serving: 20 calories; 1 g protein; 0.1 g fat; 2 g carbohydrate; 4 mg calcium; 604 mg sodium; 0 mg cholesterol; dietary fiber data not available

▪ *Creamy Scallops and Pasta* ▪

Makes 2 servings

2 teaspoons reduced-calorie
  margarine (tub)
2 tablespoons minced shallots
1 small garlic clove, minced
7 ounces bay scallops or sea
  scallops (cut into 1-inch
  pieces)
6 medium asparagus spears,
  diagonally cut into 1-inch
  pieces, blanched

½ cup whole milk
¼ cup part-skim ricotta cheese
2 tablespoons whipped cream
  cheese
⅛ teaspoon white pepper
1 cup cooked angel hair pasta
  (cappelli d'angelo),* hot
1 tablespoon grated Parmesan
  cheese

1. In 10-inch nonstick skillet melt margarine over medium heat; add shallots and garlic and sauté until tender, about 1 minute. Add scallops to skillet and sauté until scallops begin to turn opaque, about 5 minutes; add asparagus and cook, stirring occasionally, for 2 minutes longer. Stir in remaining ingredients except pasta and Parmesan cheese and cook, stirring constantly, until mixture comes just to a boil.
2. To serve, arrange pasta in serving bowl; top with scallop mixture and toss to combine. Top each portion with half the Parmesan cheese.

Each serving provides: ¼ Milk; ½ Fat; 3 Proteins; ½ Vegetable; 1 Bread; 65 Optional Calories

Per serving: 327 calories; 28 g protein; 12 g fat; 26 g carbohydrate; 243 mg calcium; 357 mg sodium; 83 mg cholesterol; 1 g dietary fiber

* Cooked thin spaghetti or linguine may be substituted for the angel hair pasta.

▪ *Shakespeare Sherry Scallops* ▪

Makes 2 servings

"If music be the food of love, play on." This perfect dish is so delicious you won't need music. Dry sherry and lemon and lime juice provide the tang for this made-in-minutes recipe. Try serving it with small red-skinned potatoes and a mixed green salad.

½ pound bay scallops or *sea scallops (cut into 1-inch pieces)*
2 tablespoons dry sherry
1 tablespoon each *chopped chives and freshly squeezed lemon and lime juice*

2 teaspoons margarine, melted
⅛ teaspoon paprika

1. Preheat broiler. In 1-quart flameproof shallow casserole combine all ingredients.
2. Broil 4 inches from heat source until scallops are golden brown, about 3 minutes.

Each serving provides: 1 Fat; 3 Proteins; 15 Optional Calories

Per serving: 162 calories; 19 g protein; 5 g fat; 6 g carbohydrate; 33 mg calcium; 229 mg sodium; 37 mg cholesterol; trace dietary fiber

▪ *Greek Shrimp Sauté* ▪

Makes 2 servings

Feta cheese, garlic, and tomatoes join forces to give fresh shrimp that Aegean touch.

2 teaspoons reduced-calorie margarine (tub)	*¼ cup drained canned Italian tomatoes, chopped*
1 teaspoon olive oil	*1 tablespoon each chopped fresh parsley, chopped fresh dill, and freshly squeezed lemon juice*
½ pound shelled and deveined large shrimp	
¼ cup chopped scallions (green onions)	
2 garlic cloves, minced	*¼ teaspoon oregano leaves*
½ cup dry white table wine	*1½ ounces feta cheese, crumbled*

1. In 10-inch nonstick skillet combine margarine and oil and heat until margarine is melted; add shrimp, scallions, and garlic and sauté over medium-high heat, stirring frequently, until shrimp just turn pink, 2 to 3 minutes.

2. Add remaining ingredients except feta cheese and stir to combine; cook until liquid is reduced by half, 3 to 4 minutes. Add feta cheese and stir to combine; cook until cheese melts, about 1 minute longer.

Each serving provides: 1 Fat; 4 Proteins; ½ Vegetable; 50 Optional Calories

Per serving: 271 calories; 27 g protein; 11 g fat; 6 g carbohydrate; 202 mg calcium; 500 mg sodium; 191 mg cholesterol; 1 g dietary fiber

▪ *Oriental Shrimp Salad* ▪

Makes 2 servings

2 tablespoons teriyaki sauce
1 tablespoon each olive oil,
   rice vinegar, and freshly
   squeezed lemon juice
1 small garlic clove, minced
½ teaspoon minced pared
   gingerroot
¼ pound shelled and deveined
   cooked small shrimp, cut
   lengthwise into halves

1 cup snow peas (Chinese pea
   pods), stem ends and strings
   removed, blanched
¼ cup diced red bell pepper
8 lettuce leaves

1. In medium glass or stainless-steel mixing bowl combine teriyaki sauce, oil, vinegar, lemon juice, garlic, and gingerroot; mix
well. Add shrimp, snow peas, and pepper and toss to coat. Cover
and refrigerate for at least 30 minutes.
2. To serve, line chilled serving platter with lettuce; top with
shrimp salad.

Each serving provides: 1½ Fats; 2 Proteins; 2¼ Vegetables

Per serving: 175 calories; 16 g protein; 8 g fat; 12 g carbohydrate; 83 mg calcium; 824
mg sodium; 111 mg cholesterol; 2 g dietary fiber

▪ *Pollo Brendola* ▪

Makes 4 servings

1 tablespoon plus 1 teaspoon
   olive or vegetable oil,
   divided
¼ cup chopped onion
2 garlic cloves, minced
1 cup canned Italian tomatoes,
   seeded and chopped
¾ cup canned ready-to-serve
   chicken broth
2 tablespoons chopped fresh
   basil
1 tablespoon chopped fresh
   parsley

⅛ teaspoon salt
Dash pepper
4 thin chicken cutlets
   (2 ounces each)
1 baby eggplant (about
   ¼ pound), cut lengthwise
   into 4 equal slices
1½ ounces Fontina cheese,
   shredded
1 tablespoon grated Parmesan
   cheese

1. In 10-inch nonstick skillet heat 1 teaspoon oil; add onion and garlic and sauté over high heat, stirring frequently, until onion is softened, about 1 minute. Add tomatoes, broth, and seasonings and stir well to combine. Reduce heat to low and simmer, stirring occasionally, until flavors blend, 20 to 25 minutes.

2. In 12-inch nonstick skillet heat 1 teaspoon oil; add chicken and cook over high heat, turning once, until lightly browned and cooked through, 2 to 3 minutes on each side. Remove chicken from skillet and set aside.

3. Preheat oven to 450°F. In same skillet heat remaining 2 teaspoons oil; add eggplant slices and cook over high heat, turning once, until lightly browned and cooked through, 1 to 2 minutes on each side.

4. Spoon half of the tomato mixture (about ½ cup) over bottom of 9 × 9-inch baking dish. Arrange chicken in a single layer over sauce; top each portion of chicken with 1 eggplant slice. Spoon remaining sauce over eggplant and sprinkle evenly with cheeses. Bake until cheeses are melted and heated through, 10 to 15 minutes.

Each serving provides: 1 Fat; 2 Proteins; 1 Vegetable; 15 Optional Calories

Per serving: 181 calories; 18 g protein; 9 g fat; 6 g carbohydrate; 128 mg calcium; 499 mg sodium; 46 mg cholesterol; 1 g dietary fiber

▪ *Curried Chicken Bake* ▪

Makes 4 servings

1 tablespoon plus 1 teaspoon   ½ teaspoon curry powder
  margarine   2 pounds chicken thighs and
1½ teaspoons all-purpose flour   drumsticks, skinned
1 teaspoon powdered mustard

1. Preheat oven to 375°F. In small saucepan melt margarine over medium heat; add remaining ingredients except chicken and cook, stirring constantly, until mixture is thick and smooth. **2.** Spray 9 × 9 × 2-inch baking dish with nonstick cooking spray; arrange chicken in a single layer in dish. Using a pastry brush, brush chicken evenly with curry mixture; bake until chicken is browned and cooked through, 35 to 40 minutes, basting with pan juices every 20 minutes.

Each serving provides: 1 Fat; 4 Proteins; 4 Optional Calories

Per serving: 257 calories; 31 g protein; 14 g fat; 1 g carbohydrate; 18 mg calcium; 148 mg sodium; 107 mg cholesterol; 0.1 g dietary fiber

▪ *Spiced Yogurt Chicken* ▪

Makes 4 servings

1 cup chopped onions
½ cup plain low-fat yogurt
¼ cup fresh lemon or lime juice
4 small garlic cloves
⅛ teaspoon each ground turmeric, ground cinnamon, ground cardamom, ground cloves, and ground allspice

Dash salt
15 ounces skinned and boned chicken breasts, cut into 1-inch cubes
2 teaspoons olive or vegetable oil
Garnish: 1 tablespoon chopped fresh cilantro (Chinese parsley)

1. In blender combine onions, yogurt, juice, garlic, and seasonings; process until smooth, scraping down sides of container as necessary.

2. Transfer chicken to medium glass or stainless-steel mixing bowl and add yogurt mixture; toss chicken cubes to coat. Cover bowl and refrigerate for at least 8 hours.

3. Preheat oven to 475°F. Thread equal amount of chicken cubes onto each of 4 skewers. Place skewers onto nonstick baking sheet; brush with any remaining marinade. Brush chicken cubes with oil and roast about 8 to 10 minutes, turning once, until chicken has cooked through. Transfer chicken to serving platter and pour pan juices over chicken; serve sprinkled with cilantro.

Each serving provides: ¼ Milk; ½ Fat; 3 Proteins; ½ Vegetable

Per serving: 176 calories; 27 g protein; 4 g fat; 7 g carbohydrate; 81 mg calcium; 123 mg sodium; 63 mg cholesterol; 1 g dietary fiber

▪ *Spicy Chicken 'n' Cashews* ▪

Makes 2 servings

2 tablespoons each teriyaki
sauce and dry sherry
1 garlic clove, minced
1 teaspoon minced pared
gingerroot
5 ounces chicken cutlets, cut
into 1-inch cubes
1 teaspoon peanut or vegetable
oil
3 mild dried chili peppers
1 ounce unsalted shelled
roasted cashews

1 medium red bell pepper,
seeded and cut into
matchstick pieces
1/4 cup each diagonally sliced
scallions (green onions) and
canned ready-to-serve
chicken broth
1 teaspoon cornstarch
1/2 teaspoon toasted sesame seed

1. In small glass or stainless-steel mixing bowl combine teriyaki sauce, sherry, garlic, and gingerroot; add chicken and turn to coat. Cover and refrigerate at least 30 minutes.

2. In 12-inch nonstick skillet heat oil; add chili peppers and cook over medium-high heat, stirring frequently, until peppers are browned, about 1 minute. Remove and discard peppers.

3. To same skillet add cashews and cook over medium-high heat, stirring frequently, until nuts are lightly browned, about 1 minute. Transfer nuts to plate; set aside.

4. Using a slotted spoon, transfer chicken to same skillet, reserving marinade. Cook chicken over medium-high heat, stirring frequently, until browned on all sides and cooked through, 2 to 3 minutes. Transfer chicken to plate with cashews; set aside.

5. Add bell pepper and scallions to skillet and cook over medium-high heat, stirring frequently, until tender-crisp, 1 to 2 minutes.

6. Add broth and cornstarch to reserved marinade and stir to dissolve cornstarch; add to bell pepper-scallion mixture in skillet, along with chicken and cashews, and cook, stirring constantly, until mixture comes to a boil and thickens, 2 to 3 minutes. Sprinkle with sesame seed just before serving.

Each serving provides: 1/2 Fat; 3 Proteins; 1 1/4 Vegetables; 70 Optional Calories

Per serving: 257 calories; 21 g protein; 11 g fat; 16 g carbohydrate; 46 mg calcium; 868 mg sodium; 41 mg cholesterol; 1 g dietary fiber (this figure does not include sesame seed; nutrition analysis not available)

▪ *Southern Pot Pie* ▪

Makes 2 servings, 1 pie each

2 teaspoons margarine
5 ounces diced cooked turkey
½ cup each diced carrot, celery, and green beans
¼ cup sliced scallions (green onions)
1 tablespoon chopped fresh parsley
1 garlic clove, minced
⅛ teaspoon each pepper and thyme leaves

¼ cup all-purpose flour, divided
1 cup canned ready-to-serve chicken broth
½ cup low-fat buttermilk (1% milk fat)
1 egg
2¼ ounces uncooked yellow cornmeal
¼ teaspoon baking soda

1. Preheat oven to 400°F. In 2-quart saucepan melt margarine; add turkey, carrot, celery, green beans, scallions, parsley, garlic, pepper, and thyme and sauté over medium-high heat, stirring frequently, until vegetables are tender-crisp, 1 to 2 minutes.
2. Sprinkle 1 tablespoon flour over vegetables and stir quickly to combine; stir in broth. Reduce heat to low and cook, stirring frequently, until vegetables are softened and mixture thickens, 5 to 6 minutes.
3. In medium mixing bowl combine buttermilk and egg; set aside.
4. In small mixing bowl combine cornmeal, baking soda, and remaining 3 tablespoons flour; add to buttermilk mixture and stir until smooth.
5. Spray two 1½-cup casseroles with nonstick cooking spray and spoon half of the turkey-vegetable mixture into each; top each with half of the cornmeal mixture and spread evenly over turkey-vegetable mixture. Bake until cornmeal mixture is cooked through and lightly browned, 10 to 12 minutes.

Each serving provides: ¼ Milk; 1 Fat; 3 Proteins; 1¾ Vegetables; 2 Breads; 40 Optional Calories

Per serving: 434 calories; 33 g protein; 12 g fat; 48 g carbohydrate; 154 mg calcium; 828 mg sodium; 163 mg cholesterol; 4 g dietary fiber

▪ *California Club Sandwich* ▪

Makes 1 serving

3 slices reduced-calorie white,
   wheat, **or** rye bread
   (40 calories per slice),
   lightly toasted
2 teaspoons reduced-calorie
   mayonnaise
1 ounce thinly sliced roast
   turkey breast

1 egg, hard-cooked and sliced
¼ cup alfalfa sprouts
2 tomato slices
⅛ avocado (1 ounce), pared
   and sliced
¾ ounce thinly sliced
   Monterey Jack cheese

1. Spread 1 slice of bread with mayonnaise and set aside.
2. Arrange turkey on second slice of bread; top with egg slices and third slice of bread, then top third slice of bread with sprouts, tomato slices, avocado, and cheese.
3. Set reserved bread slice over cheese, mayonnaise-side down. Secure sandwich with two frilled toothpicks and cut diagonally in half.

Each serving provides: 2 Fats; 3 Proteins; 1⅛ Vegetables; 1½ Breads

Per serving: 386 calories; 27 g protein; 18 g fat; 31 g carbohydrate; 255 mg calcium; 538 mg sodium; 254 mg cholesterol; 1 g dietary fiber

▪ *Barbecued Beef* ▪

Makes 2 servings

That American mainstay, barbecued beef, was unknown to me as a child. Now I can cook up a storm for Annabel and her friends and feel like a real American mom.

⅓ cup plus 2 teaspoons
 barbecue sauce
2 tablespoons water
1 teaspoon each honey and
 mustard
¼ pound roast beef, cut into
 thin strips

2 hamburger rolls (2 ounces
 each), cut into halves and
 lightly toasted
2 red onion slices

1. In 8-inch nonstick skillet combine barbecue sauce, water, honey, mustard, and roast beef and stir to combine; cook, stirring occasionally, until beef is heated through and flavors blend, 3 to 4 minutes.
2. To serve, on each of 2 plates place bottom half of each roll; top each half with half of the meat mixture, 1 onion slice, and top half of roll.

Each serving provides: 2 Proteins; ¼ Vegetable; 2 Breads; 60 Optional Calories

Per serving: 331 calories; 22 g protein; 9 g fat; 40 g carbohydrate; 60 mg calcium; 740 mg sodium; 49 mg cholesterol; 1 g dietary fiber

▪ *Hero Melt* ▪

Makes 1 serving

1 teaspoon margarine
1 small garlic clove, minced
2-ounce slice French bread
   (about 3 inches long), cut in
   half horizontally
2 tablespoons each *sliced
   mushrooms and onion*

¼ cup canned ready-to-serve
   beef broth
2 ounces thinly sliced roast
   beef
¾ ounce Monterey Jack cheese
   with jalapeño pepper,*
   shredded

1. In 8-inch nonstick skillet melt margarine over medium-high heat; add garlic and sauté until golden, 1 to 2 minutes. Using pastry brush, brush cut side of each bread half with ¼ teaspoon margarine mixture, leaving remaining mixture in skillet. Arrange bread halves margarine-side up on baking sheet and set aside.
2. Return skillet to medium-high heat; add mushrooms and onion and sauté, stirring occasionally, until lightly browned, 3 to 4 minutes. Set aside.
3. In separate 8-inch nonstick skillet cook broth over medium heat until liquid begins to simmer; add roast beef and cook until heated through, 2 to 3 minutes. Using slotted spoon, remove roast beef from broth, reserving broth; top one slice of bread with the beef slices, then top with cheese. Broil 5 to 6 inches from heat source until cheese is melted and lightly browned, 2 to 3 minutes.
4. While sandwich is broiling, add sautéed mushroom mixture to reserved broth and cook over low heat until heated through.
5. To serve, transfer sandwich to serving plate and top with the mushroom mixture and remaining slice of bread.

Each serving provides: 1 Fat; 3 Proteins; ½ Vegetable; 2 Breads; 10 Optional Calories

Per serving: 408 calories; 28 g protein; 17 g fat; 35 g carbohydrate; 188 mg calcium; 760 mg sodium; 70 mg cholesterol; 2 g dietary fiber

* This peppered cheese adds a hot-and-spicy tang to this hearty open-face sandwich. For a milder flavor, regular Monterey Jack cheese may be substituted.

• *Steak Palermo*

Makes 2 servings

To Italy again, where the fresh mint and balsamic vinegar combine to tantalize your tastebuds.

1 tablespoon balsamic vinegar
2 teaspoons olive oil
1½ teaspoons chopped fresh
mint
¼ teaspoon minced fresh
garlic

Dash salt
¼ teaspoon peppercorns,
crushed
1 T-bone or *porterhouse steak*
(¾ pound)

1. In small bowl combine all ingredients except peppercorns and steak; set aside.
2. Press crushed peppercorns into steak; on rack in broiling pan broil steak 2 inches from heat source, turning once, for about 3 minutes on each side or until done to taste.
3. Remove to warmed platter and brush with mint mixture; serve immediately.

Each serving provides: 1 Fat; 4 Proteins

Per serving: 285 calories; 32 g protein; 16 g fat; 1 g carbohydrate; 11 mg calcium; 141 mg sodium; 91 mg cholesterol; 1 g dietary fiber

▪ *Steak with Oyster Sauce* ▪

Makes 2 servings

A hearty meal that makes me think of Charles Dickens. A nine-teenth-century wayside inn, a roaring fire, the rosy-cheeked barmaid, the genial host . . .

½ pound boneless beef top loin steak

1 tablespoon plus 1 teaspoon reduced-calorie margarine (tub)

1 tablespoon minced shallots

2 tablespoons dry white table wine

1 tablespoon reduced-sodium soy sauce

1 teaspoon each minced fresh parsley and lemon juice

6 medium oysters, shucked

1. On rack in broiling pan broil steak 5 to 6 inches from heat source, until done to taste (4 to 5 minutes on each side for rare; 6 to 7 minutes on each side for medium).

2. While steak is broiling, in 8-inch skillet melt margarine over medium-high heat; add shallots and sauté until golden, about 1 minute. Reduce heat to low; stir in wine, soy sauce, parsley, and lemon juice. Add oysters and let simmer until oysters are firm to the touch, 2 to 3 minutes (*do not overcook*).

3. To serve, arrange steak on serving plate and top with oyster sauce.

Each serving provides: 1 Fat; 4 Proteins; 15 Optional Calories

Per serving: 267 calories; 29 g protein; 13 g fat; 4 g carbohydrate; 38 mg calcium; 503 mg sodium; 96 mg cholesterol; 1 g dietary fiber

▪ *Shepherd's Pie* ▪

Makes 2 servings

An old English favorite. Shepherd's pie is a traditional way of using up roast lamb leftovers, just as cottage pie uses roast beef. Since in our family we seldom have leftovers, I usually make it with fresh lamb. Shepherd's pie freezes beautifully. Make an extra one and freeze it before broiling the potato topping.

2 teaspoons vegetable oil
¼ cup each chopped onion and carrot
¼ pound broiled lean ground lamb
1 tablespoon all-purpose flour
Water
1 tablespoon plus 1 teaspoon dry red table wine

1 packet instant beef broth and seasoning mix
1 tablespoon chopped fresh parsley
1½ ounces potato flakes (instant mashed potatoes)
1 teaspoon butter

1. In 10-inch nonstick skillet heat oil; add onion and carrot and cook over high heat, stirring frequently, until onion is translucent, about 1 minute. Add lamb, reduce heat to medium, and cook about 3 minutes.
2. Sprinkle flour over lamb mixture and stir quickly to combine; cook, stirring constantly, for 1 minute. Add ¼ cup water, the wine, and broth mix and cook over high heat until mixture comes to a boil. Stir in parsley; reduce heat to medium-low and let simmer for 3 minutes.
3. While lamb mixture simmers, prepare potatoes. Using a fork, in small mixing bowl combine potato flakes, ⅔ cup boiling water, and the butter and mix until light and fluffy.
4. Preheat broiler. Transfer lamb mixture to 1-quart flameproof casserole; top with potato mixture and spread over casserole. Broil until potato mixture is golden brown, about 2 minutes.

Each serving provides: 1 Fat; 2 Proteins; ½ Vegetable; 1 Bread; 45 Optional Calories

Per serving: 329 calories; 17 g protein; 18 g fat; 23 g carbohydrate; 33 mg calcium; 564 mg sodium; 60 mg cholesterol; 1 g dietary fiber

▪ *Curried Lamb with Fruits* ▪

Makes 4 servings

John's favorite, re-created by Weight Watchers at his insistence.
The aroma of this curried lamb with fruits and leeks brings him
panting to the table.

1¼ *pounds boned lamb
shoulder, cut into 1-inch
cubes*

1 *tablespoon plus 1 teaspoon
vegetable oil*

1½ *medium bananas
(9 ounces), peeled and diced*

1 *small pear (about 6 ounces),
cored, pared, and diced*

½ *cup chopped, thoroughly
washed leeks*

6 *garlic cloves, minced*

2 *cups canned ready-to-serve
chicken broth*

1 *tablespoon* each *ground
cumin and ground
coriander*

1 *teaspoon* each *chili powder
and ground red pepper*

½ *teaspoon* each *ground
cinnamon and ground
cardamom*

1 *cup plain low-fat yogurt*

2 *cups cooked long-grain rice
(hot)*

1. On rack in broiling pan broil lamb 4 inches from heat source,
turning once, until rare and browned on all sides; set aside.
2. In 12-inch nonstick skillet heat oil over medium heat; add
fruits, leeks, and garlic and sauté, stirring occasionally, until
fruits and leeks are softened and lightly browned, 2 to 3 minutes.
3. Transfer fruit mixture to blender; add broth and seasonings
and process until smooth. Return mixture to skillet, add cooked
lamb, and stir well; bring to a boil. Reduce heat, cover, and let
simmer, stirring occasionally, until lamb is fork-tender, 25 to
30 minutes. Remove from heat and let cool to lukewarm, 10 to
15 minutes. Stir in yogurt, set over low heat, and cook, stirring
frequently, until heated through, 3 to 5 minutes (*do not boil*);
serve over hot rice.

Each serving provides: ½ Milk; 1 Fat; 4 Proteins; ¼ Vegetable; 1 Bread; 1 Fruit; 20
Optional Calories

Per serving: 547 calories; 39 g protein; 19 g fat; 54 g carbohydrate; 190 mg calcium;
643 mg sodium; 109 mg cholesterol; 2 g dietary fiber

▪ *Sausage and Potato Pie* ▪

Makes 2 servings

There's an old English standby called Toad in the Hole in which "bangers" (or sausages) are cooked in an egg batter in a large quantity of beef drippings. This recipe is a little healthier!

1 teaspoon each vegetable oil and margarine
6 ounces thinly sliced pared all-purpose potato
2 tablespoons each minced onion or scallion (green onion) and diced red bell pepper

¾ cup thawed frozen egg substitute
2 ounces cooked veal sausage links, thinly sliced

1. Preheat oven to 425°F. In 10-inch nonstick skillet that has an oven-safe handle, combine oil and margarine and heat until margarine is melted; arrange potato slices in a single layer in bottom of skillet and top with onion and pepper. Cover and cook over medium-high heat, turning once, until potato slices are crisp and browned, 3 to 4 minutes.
2. Add egg substitute to skillet and cook until bottom is set, 1 to 2 minutes.
3. Arrange sausage slices over "eggs." Transfer skillet to oven and bake until "eggs" are set and golden brown, 8 to 10 minutes.

Each serving provides: 1 Fat; 2½ Proteins; ¼ Vegetable; 1 Bread

Per serving: 196 calories; 16 g protein; 6 g fat; 18 g carbohydrate; 44 mg calcium; 361 mg sodium; 29 mg cholesterol; 2 g dietary fiber

▪ *Smoky Sausage 'n' Beans* ▪

Makes 2 servings

Yes, Kelly's been at it again, this time combining white kidney beans with garlic and vegetables for a speedy microwaved sensation.

6 ounces rinsed drained canned white kidney (cannellini) beans, divided
½ cup each diced celery, carrot, and onion
2 teaspoons vegetable oil

2 small garlic cloves, mashed
⅓ cup water
1 ounce smoked beef sausage link, sliced
Dash thyme leaves

1. Using a fork, in small mixing bowl mash 3 ounces white kidney beans and set aside.
2. In 1-quart microwavable casserole combine vegetables, oil, and garlic; cover and microwave on High (100%) for 3 minutes, stirring halfway through cooking.
3. Add mashed and remaining whole beans, the water, sausage, and thyme and stir to combine; cover and microwave on High for 3 minutes. Let stand for 5 minutes.

Each serving provides: 1 Fat; 2 Proteins; 1½ Vegetables

Per serving: 212 calories; 10 g protein; 9 g fat; 25 g carbohydrate: 74 mg calcium; 489 mg sodium (estimated); 9 g cholesterol; 5 g dietary fiber

▪ *Swiss Chard and Fettuccine Sauté* ▪

Makes 2 servings

1 tablespoon each *olive oil*
  and *whipped butter*
2 cups *Swiss chard leaves,**
  trimmed, thoroughly washed,
  drained, and chopped
1 cup *sliced shiitake*
  mushrooms

4 sun-dried tomato halves (not
  packed in oil), cut into strips
1 large garlic clove, minced
½ cup canned ready-to-serve
  low-sodium chicken broth
2 cups cooked fettuccine (hot)

1. In 10-inch nonstick skillet combine oil and butter and heat until butter is melted; add Swiss chard, mushrooms, tomatoes, and garlic and sauté over high heat until Swiss chard is tender, 3 to 4 minutes. Add broth and stir to combine. Reduce heat to low and cook until flavors blend, 3 to 4 minutes.

2. Add fettuccine to skillet and, using 2 forks, toss to combine.

Each serving provides: 1½ Fats; 2½ Vegetables; 2 Breads; 35 Optional Calories

Per serving: 341 calories; 10 g protein; 19 g fat, 47 g carbohydrate; 50 mg calcium; 139 mg sodium; 61 mg cholesterol; 5 g dietary fiber

Variation: Fettuccine-Swiss Chard Toss—Omit butter from recipe and proceed as directed; add 1 tablespoon grated Parmesan cheese along with the fettuccine to skillet. Decrease Optional Calories to 25.

Per serving: 327 calories; 11 g protein; 11 g fat; 48 g carbohydrate; 83 mg calcium; 156 mg sodium; 55 mg cholesterol; 5 g dietary fiber

* Two cups fresh Swiss chard yield about ½ cup cooked Swiss chard.

▪ *Spinach Fettuccine and Vegetables* ▪

Makes 2 servings

Whipped cream cheese gives the pasta a luxurious creaminess and sun-dried tomatoes impart their authentically Italian flavor.

2 teaspoons olive or *vegetable oil*
½ cup each thinly sliced onion, carrot, and mushrooms
1 small shallot, minced
1 teaspoon all-purpose flour
1 cup each canned ready-to-serve low-sodium chicken broth and cauliflower florets

3 tablespoons whipped cream cheese
8 sun-dried tomato halves (not packed in oil), sliced
1½ cups cooked spinach fettuccine (hot)

1. In 10-inch nonstick skillet heat oil; add onion, carrot, mushrooms, and shallot and cook over medium-high heat, stirring frequently, until onion is translucent, about 2 minutes. Sprinkle flour over vegetables and stir quickly to combine; cook, stirring constantly, for 1 minute.
2. Add chicken broth and stir to combine; cook over high heat until mixture comes to a boil. Reduce heat to low; add cauliflower and stir to combine. Cover and let simmer until cauliflower is tender-crisp, about 5 minutes.
3. Stir in cheese and tomatoes and cook, stirring constantly, until cheese melts, about 1 minute.
4. To serve, arrange fettuccine on serving platter and top with vegetable mixture.

Each serving provides: 1 Fat; 4½ Vegetables; 1½ Breads; 75 Optional Calories

Per serving: 307 calories; 11 g protein; 12 g fat; 42 g carbohydrate; 74 mg calcium; 135 mg sodium; 45 mg cholesterol; 7 g dietary fiber

▪ *First-of-Spring Pasta* ▪

Makes 2 servings

½ cup part-skim ricotta cheese
¼ cup skim or nonfat milk
2 teaspoons reduced-calorie
  margarine (tub)
½ cup sliced mushrooms
2 small shallots, minced
1½ cups cooked fettuccine,
  linguine, or tagliatelli (hot)

½ cup each cooked diagonally
  sliced asparagus, carrot,
  and diced zucchini
¾ ounce grated Parmesan
  cheese
¼ teaspoon salt
Dash pepper

1. In blender combine ricotta cheese and milk and process until smooth; set aside.

2. In 12-inch nonstick skillet melt margarine over medium heat; add mushrooms and shallots and sauté briefly (*do not brown*). Pour in ricotta mixture and heat (*do not boil*). Reduce heat and add remaining ingredients; using 2 forks, toss well until pasta and vegetables are thoroughly coated with sauce. Serve immediately.

Each serving provides: ½ Fat; 1½ Proteins; 2 Vegetables; 1½ Breads; 10 Optional Calories

Per serving: 365 calories; 21 g protein; 12 g fat; 45 g carbohydrate; 399 mg calcium; 640 mg sodium; 68 mg cholesterol; 7 g dietary fiber

▪ *Legume and Vegetable Sauté* ▪

Makes 2 servings

A speedy favorite of mine when I get back exhausted from a day's rehearsal.

2 teaspoons olive or vegetable oil	*4 ounces rinsed drained canned pinto beans*
1 cup diced onions	*1 tablespoon chopped fresh parsley*
2 garlic cloves, minced	
2 cups chopped spinach*	*1/8 teaspoon salt*
1/2 cup canned Italian tomatoes, seeded and diced (reserve liquid)	*Dash pepper*

1. In 10-inch nonstick skillet heat oil; add onions and garlic and sauté over medium-high heat, stirring frequently, for 1 minute (*do not brown*). Add spinach and sauté, stirring frequently, until spinach is wilted, 1 to 2 minutes.
2. Add remaining ingredients and stir to combine. Reduce heat to low, cover, and cook, stirring occasionally, until mixture is heated through and flavors blend, 3 to 4 minutes.

Each serving provides: 1 Fat; 1 Protein; 2 Vegetables

Per serving: 196 calories; 10 g protein; 6 g fat; 31 g carbohydrate; 128 mg calcium; 424 mg sodium (estimated); 0 mg cholesterol; 9 g dietary fiber

* Two cups fresh spinach yield about 1/2 cup cooked spinach.

▪ *"Creamy" Garlic Spinach* ▪

Makes 2 servings

This is definitely an irresistible way of preparing spinach. Serve with simply grilled fish or roast beef.

2 teaspoons margarine
2 small garlic cloves, minced
6 cups spinach leaves,*
  trimmed, thoroughly washed,
  and drained

3 tablespoons sour cream
½ teaspoon salt
Dash ground nutmeg

1. In 10-inch nonstick skillet melt margarine; add garlic and cook over medium heat, stirring constantly, for ½ minute (*do not burn*).
2. Add spinach and stir to combine; cook over medium heat, stirring occasionally, until spinach is wilted and tender, about 5 minutes.
3. Pour off any excess liquid from skillet; add sour cream, salt, and nutmeg, and cook over low heat, stirring constantly, until mixture is heated through, about 2 minutes (*do not boil*).

Each serving provides: 1 Fat; 1½ Vegetables; 50 Optional Calories

Per serving: 120 calories; 6 g protein; 9 g fat; 8 g carbohydrate; 200 mg calcium; 736 mg sodium; 9 mg cholesterol; 4 g dietary fiber

* Six cups fresh spinach yield about 1½ cups cooked spinach.

▪ *Lynn's Veggies* ▪

Makes 4 servings, about 1 cup each

My version of ratatouille. A great all-purpose veggie stew that makes the perfect accompaniment to lamb.

1 tablespoon plus 1 teaspoon olive or vegetable oil
2 cups each *cubed pared eggplant and sliced, thoroughly washed leeks*
½ cup each *chopped red and green bell pepper*
1 small garlic clove, mashed
1 tablespoon all-purpose flour
1 packet each *instant beef and chicken broth and seasoning mix*
2 cups canned Italian tomatoes, seeded and chopped (reserve liquid)
2 tablespoons chopped fresh basil
½ teaspoon oregano leaves

1. In 2-quart saucepan add oil and heat; add eggplant and cook over medium heat, stirring constantly, for 5 minutes. Add leeks, bell peppers, and garlic and stir to combine; cover and cook until tender, about 10 minutes.

2. Sprinkle flour and broth mixes over vegetables and stir quickly to combine; cook, stirring constantly, for 1 minute.

3. Add water to reserved tomato liquid to measure 2 cups. Add tomato liquid, tomatoes, basil, and oregano to vegetable mixture and, stirring constantly, bring mixture to a boil. Reduce heat and let simmer until flavors blend, about 15 minutes.

Each serving provides: 1 Fat; 3½ Vegetables; 15 Optional Calories

Per serving: 126 calories; 3 g protein; 5 g fat; 19 g carbohydrate; 94 mg calcium; 289 mg sodium; 0 mg cholesterol; 3 g dietary fiber

▪ *Oriental Eggplant* ▪

Makes 2 servings

*1 teaspoon each peanut or
vegetable oil and Chinese
sesame oil*
*4 cups cubed eggplant (½-inch
cubes)*
½ cup diced onion
*1 teaspoon minced pared
gingerroot*

2 garlic cloves, minced
*½ cup canned ready-to-serve
low-sodium chicken broth*
*1 tablespoon each teriyaki
sauce and seasoned rice
vinegar*
1 teaspoon light corn syrup

1. In 10-inch nonstick skillet heat oils; add eggplant, onion, gingerroot, and garlic and cook over medium-high heat, stirring occasionally, until vegetables are softened, 1 to 2 minutes.
2. In small mixing bowl combine remaining ingredients. Stir into skillet; increase heat to high and continue cooking, stirring occasionally, until eggplant is cooked through, 4 to 5 minutes.

Each serving provides: 1 Fat; 1½ Vegetables; 20 Optional Calories

Per serving: 128 calories; 4 g protein; 5 g fat; 19 g carbohydrate; 79 mg calcium; 369 mg sodium; 0 mg cholesterol; 3 g dietary fiber

▪ *Stir-Fried Broccoli and Almonds* ▪

Makes 2 servings

One of the few vegetables that Benjy has always liked, and Annabel adores. They love the way I prepare it, with almonds and teriyaki sauce.

1 teaspoon peanut or vegetable oil

1 cup each sliced onions and red bell pepper strips

1 ounce slivered almonds

1 small garlic clove, thinly sliced

½ cup canned ready-to-serve low-sodium chicken broth

1 tablespoon teriyaki sauce

2 teaspoons cornstarch

4 cups broccoli florets, blanched

1. In 9-inch nonstick skillet heat oil; add onions, pepper strips, almonds, and garlic and sauté over high heat until onions and pepper strips are tender-crisp, about 1 minute.

2. In 1-cup liquid measure combine broth, teriyaki sauce, and cornstarch, stirring to dissolve cornstarch. Add to almond mixture in skillet and cook, stirring constantly, until mixture comes to a boil.

3. Reduce heat to low; add broccoli, stir to combine, and cook until thoroughly heated, 1 to 2 minutes.

Each serving provides: 1½ Fats; 1 Protein; 6 Vegetables; 20 Optional Calories

Per serving: 249 calories; 14 g protein; 11 g fat; 31 g carbohydrate; 176 mg calcium; 425 mg sodium; 0 mg cholesterol; 3 g dietary fiber (this figure does not include broccoli florets; nutrition analysis not available)

▪ *Spiced Butternut Squash* ▪

Makes 4 servings, 1 squash quarter each

Allspice and cinnamon combine to give delicious butternut squash an autumn warmth.

*1 butternut squash (about
 1½ pounds)**
*2 tablespoons each margarine
 and dark corn syrup*

*⅛ teaspoon each ground
 allspice and salt*
Dash ground cinnamon
½ cup water

1. Cut squash in half lengthwise and discard seeds and membranes; score cut surface of each squash half in a crisscross pattern, being careful not to cut through shell.
2. In 10 × 10 × 2-inch microwavable baking dish arrange halves cut-side up; fill seed cavity of each half with 1 tablespoon margarine and 1 tablespoon corn syrup. Sprinkle halves evenly with allspice, salt, and cinnamon and pour water into baking dish.
3. Cover and microwave on High (100%) for 1 minute. Baste halves with corn syrup mixture and microwave on High until pulp is soft, 10 to 15 minutes longer, basting every 5 minutes.
4. To serve, cut each half lengthwise into halves and top each portion with an equal amount of any remaining pan juices.

Each serving provides: 1½ Fats; 1 Bread; 30 Optional Calories

Per serving: 145 calories; 1 g protein; 6 g fat; 25 g carbohydrate; 77 mg calcium; 149 mg sodium; 0 mg cholesterol; dietary fiber data not available

* A 1½-pound butternut squash will yield about ¾ pound cooked squash.

• *Stuffed Spaghetti Squash* •

Makes 4 servings

There's no end to the variety of ways to serve this golden squash. This version is almost a meal in itself. I sometimes sit a poached egg on top of each serving for a super supper.

*1 spaghetti squash (about
  3 pounds)*
*2 teaspoons each olive or
  vegetable oil and margarine*
*1 cup each sliced onions and
  mushrooms*
1 small garlic clove, minced
4 cups spinach leaves,
  thoroughly washed, drained,
  and torn into pieces*

1 cup cooked long-grain rice
*½ teaspoon each oregano
  leaves, salt, and white
  pepper*
*1 tablespoon plus 1 teaspoon
  grated Romano cheese*

1. Preheat oven to 350°F. Using tines of a fork, pierce squash in several places; place whole squash on baking sheet and bake until tender, about 1 hour.
2. Cut squash in half lengthwise and remove and discard seeds; scoop out pulp, reserving shells. Set aside shells and pulp.
3. In 10-inch nonstick skillet combine oil and margarine and heat until margarine is melted; add onions, mushrooms, and garlic and sauté over medium heat until tender-crisp, about 5 minutes. Add spinach and stir to combine; cook until spinach is wilted and thoroughly cooked, about 5 minutes. Add reserved squash pulp, rice, and seasonings and stir to combine.
4. Spoon half of squash-vegetable mixture into each reserved shell; sprinkle each shell with 2 teaspoons Romano cheese.

Each serving provides: 1 Fat; 3½ Vegetables; ½ Bread; 10 Optional Calories

Per serving: 215 calories; 6 g protein; 6 g fat; 36 g carbohydrate; 148 mg calcium; 400 mg sodium; 2 mg cholesterol; 2 g dietary fiber (this figure does not include spaghetti squash; nutrition analysis not available)

* Four cups fresh spinach yield about 1 cup cooked spinach.

▪ *Beet Sauté* ▪

Makes 2 servings

This colorful side dish, made in minutes, uses beets and shallots to dress up any meal.

2 teaspoons margarine
2 cups sliced pared beets
1 tablespoon minced shallot
½ teaspoon salt
Dash pepper

1 tablespoon white wine
  vinegar
2 teaspoons light corn syrup

1. In 9-inch nonstick skillet melt margarine; add beets, shallot, salt, and pepper and sauté over medium heat until shallot is translucent, 2 to 3 minutes. Stir in remaining ingredients.
2. Reduce heat to low, cover, and cook until flavors blend and beets are tender, 3 to 5 minutes.

Each serving provides: 1 Fat; 2 Vegetables; 20 Optional Calories

Per serving: 118 calories; 2 g protein; 4 g fat; 20 g carbohydrate; 32 mg calcium; 695 mg sodium; 0 mg cholesterol; 1 g dietary fiber

▪ *Bubble and Squeak* ▪

Makes 2 servings

A traditional English way of using up leftover mashed potatoes and cabbage. I like this substitution of brussels sprouts for a deliciously tasty vegetable puree.

1½ cups brussels sprouts
3 ounces pared potato, cut into
  cubes
3 cups water
½ teaspoon salt
2 tablespoons sour cream
1 tablespoon plus 1 teaspoon
  reduced-calorie margarine
  (tub)

2 tablespoons finely chopped
  scallion (green onion)
1 teaspoon all-purpose flour
Dash pepper

1. In 2-quart saucepan combine brussels sprouts and potato; add water and salt and bring to a boil. Cook until vegetables are fork-tender, about 20 minutes; drain well. Set saucepan with vegetables over low heat and shake pan until vegetables are dry.
2. Transfer vegetables to food processor and process just until pureed; transfer puree to bowl and stir in sour cream.
3. In same saucepan melt margarine; add scallion and sauté over medium heat until softened. Sprinkle with flour and stir quickly to combine; cook, stirring constantly, for 1 minute. Add vegetable puree and cook until thoroughly heated (*do not boil*); stir in pepper.

Each serving provides: 1 Fat; 1½ Vegetables; ½ Bread; 40 Optional Calories

Per serving: 132 calories; 4 g protein; 7 g fat; 16 g carbohydrate; 55 mg calcium; 654 mg sodium; 6 mg cholesterol; 5 g dietary fiber

▪ *Southwestern Potato Wedges* ▪

Makes 2 servings

6 ounces baked potato (with
   skin), cut lengthwise into
   wedges
2 teaspoons reduced-calorie
   margarine (tub), melted
Dash pepper
¾ ounce Monterey Jack cheese
   with jalapeño pepper,
   shredded

1 tablespoon finely chopped red
   onion
¼ teaspoon seeded and minced
   hot green chili pepper

1. On baking sheet arrange potato wedges in a single layer, skin-side down. Using pastry brush, brush wedges with margarine, then sprinkle with pepper; broil until browned, about 10 minutes.
2. In small bowl combine cheese, onion, and chili pepper; sprinkle evenly over potato wedges and broil until cheese is melted, 1 to 2 minutes.

Each serving provides: ½ Fat; ½ Protein; 1 Bread

Per serving: 123 calories; 5 g protein; 5 g fat; 15 g carbohydrate; 87 mg calcium; 117 mg sodium; 11 mg cholesterol; 2 g dietary fiber

▪ *Vegetable-Cheese Potato* ▪

Makes 2 servings, 1 potato half each

A favorite Sunday supper dish at Wilks Water was baked potato topped with cheese and broccoli. Add scallions and red bell pepper for a deliciously filling all-in-one meal.

2 teaspoons reduced-calorie margarine (tub)
¼ cup each sliced scallions (green onions) and red bell pepper
½ teaspoon all-purpose flour
½ cup skim or nonfat milk
1 cup small broccoli florets, blanched

1½ ounces Swiss or Gruyère cheese, shredded
1 baking potato (6 ounces), baked and cut in half lengthwise (hot)

1. In 9-inch nonstick skillet melt margarine; add scallions and pepper and sauté over medium heat until tender-crisp, about 2 minutes. Sprinkle flour over vegetables and stir quickly to combine; cook, stirring constantly, for 1 minute.
2. Reduce heat to low and gradually stir in milk; continuing to stir, cook until mixture thickens slightly, about 1 minute. Stir in broccoli and cheese and cook, stirring constantly, until cheese is melted.
3. To serve, onto each of 2 plates set 1 potato half, cut-side up; score pulp in each potato half by making several cuts about ⅛ inch deep in one direction, then several cuts in the opposite direction to form a diamond pattern. Top each potato half with half of the vegetable-cheese mixture; serve immediately.

Each serving provides: ¼ Milk; ½ Fat; 1 Protein; 1½ Vegetables; 1 Bread; 3 Optional Calories

Per serving: 209 calories; 13 g protein; 8 g fat; 23 g carbohydrate; 327 mg calcium; 149 mg sodium; 21 mg cholesterol; 2 g dietary fiber (this figure does not include broccoli florets; nutrition analysis not available)

▪ *Dill Potato Salad* ▪

Makes 2 servings

6 ounces small new red
   potatoes
¼ cup plain low-fat yogurt
1 tablespoon plus 1 teaspoon
   reduced-calorie mayonnaise
½ teaspoon each white
   vinegar and lemon juice

¼ teaspoon salt
Dash white pepper
¼ cup each diced scallions
   (green onions) and celery
2 tablespoons chopped fresh
   dill
Garnish: dill sprig

1. In 1-quart saucepan combine potatoes with enough water to cover; bring water to a boil. Reduce heat and let simmer until potatoes are fork-tender, about 25 minutes; drain well. Quarter potatoes and transfer to salad bowl; set aside.

2. In small bowl combine yogurt, mayonnaise, vinegar, lemon juice, salt, and pepper; add scallions, celery, and chopped dill and mix well. Pour dressing over potatoes and stir gently to combine. Serve warm or cover and refrigerate until chilled; stir again just before serving.

Each serving provides: ¼ Milk; 1 Fat; ½ Vegetable; 1 Bread

Per serving: 122 calories, 4 g protein, 9 g fat, 20 g carbohydrate; 81 mg calcium; 300 mg sodium; 5 mg cholesterol; 2 g dietary fiber

Variation: Potato Salad with Sour Cream Dressing—Substitute 3 tablespoons sour cream for the yogurt. In Serving Information omit Milk and add 50 Optional Calories.

Per serving: 150 calories; 3 g protein; 7 g fat; 19 g carbohydrate; 54 mg calcium; 358 mg sodium; 13 mg cholesterol; 2 g dietary fiber

▪ *Sun-Dried Tomato and Mushroom Salad* ▪

Makes 2 servings, about 1 cup each

As a luncheon party dish, this much-appreciated salad looks as good as it tastes. Sometimes I make it just for myself with an extra serving of cheese for a light pre-theater supper.

2 cups sliced mushrooms
¼ cup sliced red onion
5 sun-dried tomato halves (not packed in oil), sliced
2 tablespoons chopped fresh Italian (flat-leaf) parsley
1 tablespoon each chopped fresh basil and rinsed drained capers
½ small garlic clove, minced

2 tablespoons balsamic or seasoned rice vinegar
1 tablespoon freshly squeezed lemon juice
2 teaspoons olive oil
¼ teaspoon salt
Dash pepper
¾ ounce Fontina cheese, shredded
4 lettuce leaves

1. In medium mixing bowl combine mushrooms, red onion, tomatoes, parsley, basil, capers, and garlic; set aside.
2. In small jar with tight-fitting cover combine vinegar, lemon juice, olive oil, salt, and pepper; cover and shake well. Pour dressing over mushroom mixture and toss to combine. Cover and refrigerate until flavors blend, overnight or at least 30 minutes.
3. To serve, sprinkle cheese over mushroom mixture and toss to combine. Arrange lettuce leaves on serving platter and top with mushroom mixture.

Each serving provides: 1 Fat; ½ Protein; 4 Vegetables

Per serving: 136 calories; 6 g protein; 8 g fat; 12 g carbohydrate; 106 mg calcium; 480 mg sodium; 12 mg cholesterol; 3 g dietary fiber (this figure does not include capers; nutrition analysis not available)

▪ *Beet and Endive Toss* ▪

Makes 2 servings

Another colorful salad for that informal buffet lunch. Or serve on your prettiest salad plates for a charming dinner appetizer.

*2 medium Belgian endives
(about 3 ounces each),
trimmed and cut into thin
strips
½ cup diced peeled cooked
beets
2 tablespoons finely chopped
red onion*

*2 teaspoons olive oil
1½ teaspoons each red wine
or cider vinegar and water
¼ teaspoon Dijon-style
mustard
⅛ teaspoon salt
Dash white pepper*

1. Combine endives, beets, and onion in salad bowl.
2. In jar with tight-fitting cover combine oil, vinegar, water, mustard, salt, and pepper; cover and shake well. Pour over salad and toss to combine. Serve immediately.

Each serving provides: 1 Fat; 1½ Vegetables

Per serving: 71 calories; 1 g protein; 5 g fat; 7 g carbohydrate; 8 mg calcium; 184 mg sodium; 0 mg cholesterol; 3 g dietary fiber

▪ *Green Bean Salad with Yogurt Sauce* ▪

Makes 2 servings

¹/₄ cup plain low-fat yogurt
1 tablespoon chopped fresh
  cilantro
1¹/₂ teaspoons freshly squeezed
  lime juice*
¹/₂ teaspoon granulated sugar
¹/₂ small garlic clove, minced

Dash white pepper
2 cups whole green beans,
  cooked
6 cherry tomatoes, cut into
  quarters
1 tablespoon minced chives

1. In small mixing bowl combine yogurt, cilantro, lime juice, sugar, garlic, and pepper, stirring until thoroughly blended.
2. In salad bowl combine green beans, tomatoes, and chives; add yogurt mixture and toss to coat.

Each serving provides: ¹/₄ Milk; 2¹/₂ Vegetables; 5 Optional Calories

Per serving: 64 calories; 4 g protein; 1 g fat; 13 g carbohydrate; 98 mg calcium; 29 mg sodium; 2 mg cholesterol; 2 g dietary fiber

* If fresh limes are not available, bottled lime juice (no sugar added) may be used.

▪ *Côte D'Azur Salad* ▪

Makes 2 servings

I feel like I'm in the Mediterranean when I prepare this cooked vegetable salad. With the simple addition of two ounces of drained tuna (packed in water), you can turn it into a salad Niçoise.

2 cups cooked cauliflower florets (hot)
6 ounces cooked small new red potatoes, quartered
½ cup blanched whole green beans
2 tablespoons water
1 tablespoon balsamic or red wine vinegar
2 teaspoons olive oil
3 large oil-cured black olives (½ ounce), pitted and minced

1 tablespoon each finely chopped rinsed drained capers and Italian (flat-leaf) parsley
1 garlic clove, minced
½ medium tomato, diced
4 drained canned anchovy fillets, chopped
1 egg, hard-cooked and chopped

1. On serving platter arrange cauliflower, potatoes, and green beans; set aside.
2. Using a wire whisk, in small mixing bowl combine water, vinegar, and oil; add olives, capers, parsley, and garlic and stir to combine. Pour evenly over vegetables.
3. Sprinkle diced tomato, anchovies, and egg over vegetables.

Each serving provides: 1¼ Fats; ½ Protein; 3 Vegetables; 1 Bread; 10 Optional Calories

Per serving: 236 calories; 10 g protein; 11 g fat; 26 g carbohydrate; 88 mg calcium; 686 mg sodium; 111 mg cholesterol; 5 g dietary fiber (this figure does not include capers; nutrition analysis not available)

▪ *Mozzarella Via Veneto* ▪

Makes 2 servings

Lunching in Rome on the Via Veneto with my family in the late 50s I had my first introduction to this mozzarella and tomato salad. Naturally it was made with fresh mozzarella and that's how I make it now. I buy a bag of small mozzarella cheeses in water from the gourmet section of my supermarket.

1 tablespoon each water and red wine vinegar or balsamic vinegar
2 teaspoons olive oil
Dash each salt and pepper
4 red leaf lettuce leaves
½ cup chicory*

1½ ounces mozzarella cheese, cut into 10 equal slices
2 large plum tomatoes, cut lengthwise into 10 equal slices
½ cup sliced pimientos
Garnish: small basil leaves

1. In jar with tight-fitting cover combine water, vinegar, olive oil, salt, and pepper; cover and shake well.
2. Line outside edge of serving platter with lettuce and chicory; alternately arrange cheese and tomato slices in a circle over lettuce and chicory, overlapping slices slightly. Arrange pimiento strips in center of platter.
3. Pour dressing over cheese, tomato, and pimiento strips; garnish salad with basil leaves and serve immediately.

Each serving provides: 1 Fat; 1 Protein; 2½ Vegetables

Per serving: 137 calories; 6 g protein; 10 g fat; 9 g carbohydrate; 172 mg calcium; 183 mg sodium; 17 mg cholesterol; 2 g dietary fiber (this figure does not include pimientos; nutrition analysis not available)

* Four lettuce leaves can be substituted for the chicory.

▪ *Santa Monica Mountain Salad* ▪

Makes 2 servings

In the Santa Monica Mountains of California, where I live, almost every backyard has citrus trees, and avocado orchards abound. A touch of mint adds extra freshness to this lovely appetizer.

*1 small navel orange (about
   6 ounces)*
*1 small nectarine (about
   ¼ pound), pitted and diced*
*¼ avocado (2 ounces), pared
   and diced*
2 cups shredded lettuce leaves
½ cup chopped celery

*2 tablespoons freshly squeezed
   lime juice*
*1 tablespoon chopped fresh
   mint*
2 teaspoons olive oil
⅛ teaspoon salt
Dash pepper

1. Over small bowl to catch juice, remove skin and membranes from orange; reserve juice. Dice orange and set aside.
2. In medium mixing bowl combine orange, nectarine, and avocado; toss to coat; add lettuce and celery and set aside.
3. Add remaining ingredients to reserved orange juice, stirring well to combine. Pour dressing over salad and toss well to coat. Transfer to serving bowl and serve immediately.

Each serving provides: 2 Fats; 2½ Vegetables; 1 Fruit

Per serving: 144 calories; 2 g protein; 8 g fat; 19 g carbohydrate; 80 mg calcium; 173 mg sodium; 0 mg cholesterol; 4 g dietary fiber

▪ *Spinach-Feta Pizzas* ▪

Makes 2 servings, 1 pizza each

This tangy and tasty pizza with its Greco-Roman heritage whisks me back in time to our Paxos trip with tiny baby Benjy. If you feel adventurous and quest the true spirit of the dish, you should try it with a glass of retsina, which is a Greek resinated wine.

2 small pitas (1 ounce each)
1 teaspoon olive or vegetable oil, divided
½ cup well-drained thawed frozen chopped spinach
1 tablespoon each chopped scallion (green onion) and chopped green bell pepper
1 teaspoon chopped fresh dill

½ medium tomato, cut into 4 thin slices
3 ounces feta cheese, crumbled
⅛ teaspoon oregano leaves
Pepper
6 large pitted black olives (1 ounce), each cut into 4 slices

1. On baking sheet arrange pitas and, using a pastry brush, brush top of each with ¼ teaspoon oil; broil 6 inches from heat source until lightly browned, 1 to 2 minutes. Turn pitas over, brush top of each with ¼ teaspoon oil, and broil until lightly browned, 1 to 2 minutes; remove from oven.
2. Turn oven control to 450°F. In small bowl combine spinach, scallion, bell pepper, and dill, mixing well; top each pita with 2 tomato slices, then spread each with half of the spinach mixture. Sprinkle each portion with 1½ ounces feta cheese, half of the oregano, and a dash pepper, and top each with half of the olive slices. Bake until cheese is lightly browned, 5 to 7 minutes. Serve immediately.

Each serving provides: 1 Fat; 2 Proteins; 1⅛ Vegetables; 1 Bread

Per serving: 266 calories; 11 g protein; 15 g fat; 24 g carbohydrate; 297 mg calcium; 805 mg sodium; 38 mg cholesterol; 2 g dietary fiber

▪ *Bacon and Spinach Torte* ▪

Makes 8 servings

This torte tastily and attractively satisfies my love of the savory. A cross between a quiche and a pizza, it has been a winner at a lunchtime gathering of my theater colleagues.

1¾ *cups all-purpose flour*
½ *cup whole wheat flour*
⅓ *cup plus 2 teaspoons whipped butter*
2 *tablespoons plus 2 teaspoons margarine, divided*
Water
2 *cups sliced mushrooms*
½ *cup each chopped onion and red bell pepper*
3 *garlic cloves, minced*
3 *cups thawed well-drained frozen chopped spinach*

3 *ounces diced Canadian-style bacon*
2¼ *ounces mozzarella cheese*
1½ *cups part-skim ricotta cheese*
4 *eggs, beaten, divided*
½ *teaspoon salt*
⅛ *teaspoon each pepper and ground nutmeg*
1 *tablespoon plus 1 teaspoon grated Parmesan cheese*

1. In medium mixing bowl combine flours; with a pastry blender, cut in butter and 2 tablespoons plus 1 teaspoon margarine until mixture resembles coarse meal.
2. Using a fork, stir in ½ cup water; add more water, 1 tablespoon at a time, stirring after each addition and adding just enough water so that mixture clings together and forms a soft dough. Divide dough into 2 pieces, one twice the size of the other, and form each piece into a ball; wrap each ball in wax paper and refrigerate overnight or at least 30 minutes.
3. In 8-inch nonstick skillet melt remaining teaspoon margarine; add mushrooms, onion, bell pepper, and garlic and sauté over high heat, stirring occasionally, until vegetables are tender, 2 to 3 minutes.
4. Transfer to medium mixing bowl; add spinach, bacon, mozzarella cheese, ricotta cheese, all but 2 tablespoons beaten egg, and the seasonings and mix well until thoroughly combined.

5. Preheat oven to 350°F. Between 2 sheets of wax paper roll larger piece of dough into a circle about 12 inches in diameter. Spray 8-inch springform pan with nonstick cooking spray and gently press dough over bottom and up sides of pan; spoon spinach mixture into pan and sprinkle with Parmesan cheese.

6. Roll remaining piece of dough into a circle about 9 inches in diameter. Carefully lift dough circle onto pan; crimp edge of dough to rim of pan. Make several small cuts in center of dough to allow steam to escape. Using a pastry brush, brush reserved egg over dough. Bake until lightly browned, about 1 hour and 15 minutes.

7. To serve, remove sides of springform pan and serve torte on pan's metal base.

Each serving provides: 1 Fat; 2 Proteins; 1½ Vegetables; 1½ Breads; 45 Optional Calories

Per serving: 371 calories; 19 g protein; 18 g fat; 35 g carbohydrate; 296 mg calcium; 571 mg sodium; 144 mg cholesterol; 4 g dietary fiber

▪ *Spaghetti Squash Quiche* ▪

Makes 8 servings

Eliminate the usual pastry crust for this quiche and instead use cooked spaghetti squash, spread over the bottom and sides of a pie plate.

2 cups cooked spaghetti squash
1 cup skim or *nonfat milk*
4 eggs
½ cup evaporated skimmed milk
¼ cup each all-purpose flour and minced onion
2 tablespoons plus 2 teaspoons reduced-calorie margarine (tub)

1 packet instant chicken broth and seasoning mix
¼ teaspoon each double-acting baking powder and dried thyme leaves, crushed
⅛ teaspoon freshly ground pepper

1. Preheat oven to 350°F. Spray 9-inch pie plate with nonstick cooking spray; using the back of a spoon, spread squash over bottom and up sides of plate. Set aside.
2. In blender combine remaining ingredients and process until smooth; pour over squash and bake for 50 minutes to 1 hour (until a knife, inserted in center, comes out dry). Transfer pie plate to wire rack and let stand for 1 hour.
3. Cover and refrigerate overnight.

Each serving provides: ¼ Milk; ½ Fat; ½ Protein; ½ Vegetable; 15 Optional Calories

Per serving: 106 calories; 6 g protein; 5 g fat; 10 g carbohydrate; 114 mg calcium; 250 mg sodium; 107 mg cholesterol; 0.2 g dietary fiber

▪ *Pepper-Mushroom Omelet* ▪

Makes 1 serving

When I taught my children to cook an omelet, I told them that this was "proper cooking." That's what my mother taught me, and I believe it to be true. And so I recall cooking these for Mum at Wilks Water. I called it my "Sunday-by-the-Fire-Supper" treat. We didn't use jalapeño peppers back then, mainly because we didn't know they existed.

2 eggs
2 tablespoons water
¼ teaspoon salt
Dash pepper
1 teaspoon margarine
2 tablespoons **each** *diced green
    bell pepper and scallion
    (green onion)*

½ cup chopped mushrooms
¾ ounce Monterey Jack cheese
    with jalapeño pepper,
    shredded

1. Using a wire whisk, in small bowl beat together eggs, water, salt, and pepper.
2. In 9-inch nonstick skillet melt margarine; add egg mixture to skillet and immediately sprinkle green bell pepper and scallion onto half of the omelet. When egg mixture is partially set, sprinkle mushrooms over mixture and cook until bottom of omelet is lightly browned and firm; using spatula, fold omelet in half.
3. Sprinkle with cheese; remove from heat, cover, and let stand until cheese is partially melted, about 1 minute.

Each serving provides: 1 Fat; 3 Proteins; 1½ Vegetables

Per serving: 281 calories; 19 g protein; 21 g fat; 5 g carbohydrate; 214 mg calcium; 856 mg sodium; 447 mg cholesterol; 1 g dietary fiber

• *O'Redgrave's Irish Soda Bread* •

Makes 24 servings

Because this bread uses baking soda instead of yeast as its rising agent the dough doesn't have to be given special rising time. This makes the bread quick and easy to prepare. Wrapping the hot bread in a clean cloth before it cools gives the crust a deliciously crunchy consistency.

4 cups stone-ground whole wheat flour	*1 teaspoon each baking soda and salt*
2 cups unbleached all-purpose flour, divided	*2 cups low-fat buttermilk (1% milk fat)*

1. Preheat oven to 375°F. In large mixing bowl combine whole wheat flour, 1½ cups all-purpose flour, the baking soda, and salt, mixing well to combine. Make a well in center of flour mixture; pour in milk. Using a large metal spoon, mix well to combine. Using your hands, knead in bowl until well combined.
2. Sprinkle remaining all-purpose flour onto work surface; turn dough out onto floured surface and knead until smooth, 1 to 2 minutes. Shape dough into 7-inch round loaf about 3 inches thick and transfer to nonstick baking sheet.
3. Using a sharp knife, cut a cross about 1 inch deep through surface of dough.
4. Bake for 40 to 45 minutes (until a toothpick, inserted in center, comes out dry). Transfer bread to wire rack and let cool completely. To serve, cut into 24 equal slices.

Each serving provides: 1¼ Breads; 15 Optional Calories

Per serving: 114 calories; 4 g protein; 1 g fat; 23 g carbohydrate; 33 mg calcium; 149 mg sodium; 1 mg cholesterol; 3 g dietary fiber

▪ *Soda Bread* ▪

Makes 20 servings

All over Ireland you'll find people arguing about the authenticity of a soda bread recipe. I lived in Dublin on the East Coast, so here's another version in case you're from the West Coast of Ireland.

3¾ cups all-purpose flour,
   divided
¼ cup granulated sugar
1½ teaspoons double-acting
   baking powder
⅓ cup plus 2 tablespoons
   margarine, softened
1¼ cups dried currants,
   soaked in warm water until
   plumped, then drained

2 teaspoons caraway seed
1¼ cups low-fat buttermilk
   (1% milk fat)
1 egg
1 teaspoon baking soda

1. Spray 9- or 10-inch round baking pan with nonstick baking spray; set aside.
2. In large mixing bowl combine dry ingredients, reserving 1 tablespoon flour; using pastry blender, cut in margarine until mixture resembles coarse meal. Stir in currants and caraway seed.
3. In small mixing bowl combine milk, egg, and baking soda, beating until well mixed; pour into dough and stir to combine.
4. Preheat oven to 350°F. Sprinkle reserved tablespoon flour onto work surface; turn dough out onto floured surface and knead until smooth and elastic. Shape into 8-inch round loaf and place in sprayed pan.
5. Using a sharp knife, cut a cross about ½ inch deep through surface of dough.
6. Bake for about 1 hour (until golden and cake tester, inserted in center, comes out dry). Transfer bread to wire rack to cool. To serve, cut into 20 equal slices.

Each serving provides: 1 Fat; 1 Bread; ½ Fruit; 30 Optional Calories

Per serving: 173 calories; 4 g protein; 5 g fat; 29 g carbohydrate; 51 mg calcium; 143 mg sodium; 11 mg cholesterol; 1 g dietary fiber (this figure does not include caraway seed; nutrition analysis not available)

▪ *Yorkshire Pudding (American Style)*

Makes 4 servings

Made with buttermilk, these popovers get a new twist with the addition of dried rosemary. Eat them with roast beef, as we English do, or try them for breakfast.

¾ cup all-purpose flour	*1 tablespoon plus 1 teaspoon*
⅛ teaspoon salt	*reduced-calorie margarine*
¾ cup low-fat buttermilk	*(tub), melted*
(1% milk fat)	*2 teaspoons dried rosemary*
2 eggs	*leaves, crushed*

1. Preheat oven to 425°F. On sheet of wax paper sift together flour and salt; set aside.
2. In blender process remaining ingredients on medium speed until combined; add flour mixture and process on low speed until smooth.
3. Set four 6-ounce custard cups on baking sheet and place in oven for 5 minutes. Spray each cup with nonstick cooking spray and pour ¼ of batter into each cup. Return to oven and bake for 20 minutes.
4. Turn oven control to 325°F and bake 20 minutes longer. Remove popovers from custard cups and serve immediately (popovers will fall slightly after removing from oven).

Each serving provides: ½ Fat; ½ Protein; 1 Bread; 20 Optional Calories

Per serving: 159 calories; 7 g protein; 5 g fat; 21 g carbohydrate; 77 mg calcium; 190 mg sodium; 108 mg cholesterol; 1 g dietary fiber

▪ *Raisin Scones* ▪

Makes 8 servings, 1 scone each

2 cups less 2 tablespoons all-
  purpose flour, divided
1 tablespoon each double-
  acting baking powder and
  granulated sugar
¼ cup margarine, softened

3 eggs, separated
1 egg, separated
¼ cup skim or nonfat milk
½ teaspoon grated lemon peel
½ cup dark raisins

1. In large mixing bowl combine 1¾ cups flour, the baking powder and sugar; using pastry blender, cut in margarine until mixture resembles coarse meal.

2. Using mixer, in medium mixing bowl beat together 2 eggs, the egg white, milk, and lemon peel just until combined.

3. Make a well in center of flour mixture; pour in egg mixture and, using mixer on low speed, beat until thoroughly combined. Add raisins and stir to combine.

4. Preheat oven to 400°F. Sprinkle 1 tablespoon of the remaining flour on work surface and turn dough out onto floured surface; sprinkle remaining tablespoon flour over dough. Using hands, shape dough into an 8- or 9-inch circle; cut into 8 equal wedges. Transfer wedges to nonstick cookie sheet.

5. In small bowl combine remaining egg and egg yolk and beat to combine. Brush wedges evenly with half of egg mixture. Bake for 5 minutes; brush wedges evenly with remaining egg mixture and bake until golden brown, 8 to 10 minutes longer. Transfer to wire rack and let cool.

Each serving provides: 1½ Fats; ½ Protein; 1¼ Breads; ½ Fruit; 10 Optional Calories

Per serving: 237 calories; 7 g protein; 9 g fat; 33 g carbohydrate; 113 mg calcium; 264 mg sodium; 106 mg cholesterol; 1 g dietary fiber

▪ *Broiled Bananas* ▪

Makes 2 servings

*2 medium bananas (about
  6 ounces each)*
*1 teaspoon each margarine,
  melted, and orange juice (no
  sugar added)*

¼ cup plain low-fat yogurt
*1 tablespoon plus 1 teaspoon
  honey*
Dash ground cinnamon

1. Peel bananas and cut into halves lengthwise, then cut each half in half crosswise; arrange banana pieces in 1½-quart flame-proof casserole.
2. In cup combine margarine and orange juice and, using a pastry brush, brush mixture evenly over bananas. Broil 5 to 6 inches from heat source until bananas are lightly browned and heated through, 3 to 4 minutes.
3. While bananas are broiling, in small bowl combine yogurt and honey, stirring until thoroughly blended; set aside. Transfer bananas and any liquid remaining in pan to 2 dessert dishes. Top each portion with half of the yogurt mixture and sprinkle with cinnamon; serve while bananas are warm.

Each serving provides: ¼ Milk; ½ Fat; 2 Fruits; 40 Optional Calories

Per serving: 181 calories; 3 g protein; 3 g fat; 40 g carbohydrate; 61 mg calcium; 44 mg sodium; 2 mg cholesterol; 2 g dietary fiber

▪ Crème Brûlée ▪

Makes 8 servings

*1 cup evaporated skimmed
  milk*
1 cup whole milk
*3 tablespoons half-and-half
  (blend of milk and cream)*
¼ cup granulated sugar

4 eggs
*1 teaspoon each cornstarch
  and vanilla extract*
*2 tablespoons firmly packed
  brown sugar*
1 teaspoon water

1. In 1-quart nonstick saucepan combine milks, half-and-half, and sugar; cook over medium heat, stirring constantly, until mixture begins to simmer, about 5 minutes. Remove from heat.
2. Using a whisk, in medium mixing bowl lightly beat eggs; add cornstarch and stir until dissolved. Gradually stir in milk mixture. Return milk-egg mixture to saucepan and continue cooking over medium heat, stirring constantly, until mixture coats the back of a spoon, about 3 minutes. Remove from heat; stir in vanilla and set aside.
3. Preheat oven to 350°F. Pour custard mixture through sieve into eight flameproof 6-ounce custard cups. Set cups in 13 × 9 × 2-inch baking dish and pour hot water into dish to a depth of about 1 inch. Cover baking dish with foil and bake for 20 minutes (until custard is set and a knife, inserted in center, comes out clean). Remove cups from water bath and let cool slightly. Refrigerate until well chilled, about 2 hours.
4. Preheat broiler. In small saucepan combine brown sugar and water; cook over medium heat until sugar is completely dissolved and mixture comes to a boil. Drizzle an equal amount of sugar mixture over each custard. Broil until sugar caramelizes, about 3 minutes. Serve immediately.

Each serving provides: ¼ Milk; ½ Protein; 75 Optional Calories

Per serving: 128 calories; 7 g protein; 4 g fat; 16 g carbohydrate; 150 mg calcium; 87 mg sodium; 114 mg cholesterol; 0 g dietary fiber

▪ *English Trifle* ▪

Makes 4 servings

An England without tea or trifle would be a sorry place, so here's a surprisingly light version of my childhood favorite. My husband goes crazy and adds a shot of dry sherry.

2 cups skim or nonfat milk
1 envelope (four ½-cup servings) reduced-calorie vanilla instant pudding mix
4 ladyfingers (1 ounce), cut into cubes
2 tablespoons each reduced-calorie strawberry spread (16 calories per 2 teaspoons), melted, and dry sherry

1 cup strawberries, sliced
½ cup blueberries
¼ cup thawed frozen dairy whipped topping

1. Using milk, prepare pudding according to package directions; set aside.
2. Into each of four 9-ounce dessert dishes arrange ¼ of the ladyfinger cubes. In small bowl combine strawberry spread and sherry; drizzle ¼ of mixture over each portion of ladyfingers.
3. In small mixing bowl combine strawberries and blueberries. Spoon ¼ of berry mixture into each dessert dish, then top each with ¼ of prepared pudding, and 1 tablespoon whipped topping.
4. Cover and refrigerate until chilled, at least 15 minutes.

Each serving provides: 1 Milk; ½ Fruit; 65 Optional Calories

Per serving: 155 calories; 5 g protein; 2 g fat; 28 g carbohydrate; 163 mg calcium; 406 mg sodium; 28 mg cholesterol; 2 g dietary fiber

▪ *Lynn's Lemon Syllabub* ▪

Makes 2 servings

This is my adaptation of an old English dessert usually made with a large quantity of heavy cream and sugar. Now yogurt and ricotta cheese help keep my syllabub on Program.

¼ cup boiling water
1 teaspoon unflavored gelatin
1 cup plain low-fat yogurt
2 tablespoons each part-skim
  ricotta cheese and freshly
  squeezed lemon juice

1 tablespoon each dry sherry
  and grated lemon peel
Granulated low-calorie
  sweetener with aspartame to
  equal 2 teaspoons sugar

1. In medium mixing bowl add water to gelatin and stir until gelatin is dissolved.
2. Using a wire whisk, add remaining ingredients and beat until mixture is the consistency of whipping cream, about 1 minute. Cover and refrigerate until semifirm, 10 to 15 minutes.
3. Using whisk, beat again until mixture is smooth and the consistency of yogurt. Pour into two 10-ounce dessert dishes or glasses. Cover and refrigerate until set, about 1 hour or overnight.

Each serving provides: 1 Milk; ¼ Protein; 5 Optional Calories

Per serving: 116 calories; 9 g protein; 3 g fat; 12 g carbohydrate; 255 mg calcium; 116 mg sodium; 12 mg cholesterol; dietary fiber data not available

▪ *Kiwi Meringues* ▪

Makes 4 servings, 1 meringue each

When I was little, Nanny always made meringues in our linen warming closet! Open the door to get out some clean sheets, and there they'd be, slowly, slowly drying out for a night and a day. I make mine in the oven, then decorate them with dairy whipped topping, kiwi, and raspberries.

2 egg whites
1 tablespoon superfine sugar*
*⅛ teaspoon each cream of
tartar and lemon extract*
*½ cup thawed frozen dairy
whipped topping*

*1 medium kiwi fruit (about
¼ pound), pared and thinly
sliced*
½ cup raspberries

1. Line baking sheet with parchment paper; set aside. In medium mixing bowl, using mixer at medium speed, beat egg whites until foamy; add sugar, cream of tartar, and lemon extract and continue beating until stiff peaks form.

2. Preheat oven to 200°F. Using a pastry bag fitted with a star tip, fill bag with egg white mixture and pipe enough of mixture onto lined baking sheet to form four 5 × 3-inch ovals (if pastry bag is not available, spoon mixture onto baking sheet); fill center of each oval with an equal amount of remaining egg white mixture. Bake until golden and crisp, 45 minutes to 1 hour. Carefully remove meringues from paper to wire rack to cool.

3. To serve, spread 2 tablespoons whipped topping over each meringue and decoratively top each portion with ¼ of the kiwi fruit slices and ¼ of the raspberries; serve immediately.

Each serving provides: ½ Fruit; 50 Optional Calories

Per serving: 70 calories; 2 g protein; 2 g fat; 11 g carbohydrate; 12 mg calcium; 39 mg sodium; 0 mg cholesterol; 2 g dietary fiber

* If superfine sugar is not available, process granulated sugar in blender container until superfine.

▪ Athenian Honey Twists ▪

Makes 6 servings, 3 cookies each

1⅔ cups plus 1 teaspoon all-
purpose flour
½ teaspoon double-acting
baking powder
¼ teaspoon salt
3 eggs, beaten, divided

2 tablespoons each vegetable
oil, honey, and firmly
packed light brown sugar
1 tablespoon toasted sesame
seed
¼ teaspoon ground cinnamon

1. In large mixing bowl combine flour, baking powder, and salt. Measure out and reserve 2 tablespoons egg. Add remaining egg to flour mixture; add the oil and mix well. Turn out onto flat surface and knead until smooth and elastic, 8 to 10 minutes. Let dough sit for 10 to 15 minutes.

2. Preheat oven to 375°F. Roll dough into an 18 × 8-inch rectangle, about ⅛-inch thick; cut into eighteen 8 × 1-inch strips. Spray baking sheet with nonstick cooking spray; twist each strip of dough and arrange twists on sprayed sheet.

3. Brush each twist with an equal amount of reserved 2 tablespoons egg and bake until golden brown, 8 to 10 minutes. Transfer to wire rack and let cool.

4. In small saucepan combine honey, sugar, sesame seed, and cinnamon and cook over medium heat, stirring frequently, until sugar melts and mixture is smooth and syrupy, 3 to 4 minutes. Transfer cookie twists to serving plate and drizzle an equal amount of honey mixture (about ¾ teaspoon) over each.

Each serving provides: 1 Fat; ½ Protein; 1½ Breads; 50 Optional Calories

Per serving: 253 calories; 7 g protein; 8 g fat; 38 g carbohydrate; 56 mg calcium; 159 mg sodium; 106 mg cholesterol; 1 g dietary fiber (this figure does not include sesame seed; nutrition analysis not available)

▪ *Almond Tuiles* ▪

Makes 4 servings, 1 tuile each

2 tablespoons each *granulated* | 3 tablespoons *cake flour*
sugar, margarine, and light | ½ ounce *finely ground toasted*
corn syrup | *almonds*
2 *egg whites*

1. Preheat oven to 350°F. Using mixer at medium-high speed, in large mixing bowl beat together sugar, margarine, and corn syrup until thoroughly combined; add egg whites and beat at medium speed until mixture is foamy. Add flour and continue beating until combined (mixture should have a thin consistency). Fold in almonds; set aside.

2. Spray nonstick baking sheet with nonstick cooking spray. Using half of the almond mixture, spoon batter onto baking sheet, forming 2 cookies and leaving a space of about 9 inches between cookies; using the back of a spoon, spread each cookie into a 6-inch-diameter circle. Bake until edges of cookies are browned, 5 to 7 minutes.

3. While cookies are baking, stand two 6-ounce custard cups bottom-side up and spray each custard cup with nonstick cooking spray.

4. Remove baking sheet from oven and, using a pancake turner, carefully place each cookie onto a custard cup; using your hands, press each cookie around base of custard cup to form cup (if cookie becomes too firm to shape, reheat in oven for 1 minute). Let cookies cool slightly, 5 to 10 minutes, then gently remove from custard cups and place on wire rack to cool.

5. Repeat procedure with remaining batter, making 2 more cookie cups.

Each serving provides: 1¾ Fats; ¼ Protein; ¼ Bread; 70 Optional Calories

Per serving: 152 calories; 3 g protein; 8 g fat; 19 g carbohydrate; 19 mg calcium; 102 mg sodium; 0 mg cholesterol; dietary fiber data not available

▪ *Quick Apple Tart* ▪

Makes 1 serving

So quick I like to make this as a delicious late-afternoon teatime treat. Home after an exhilarating ride on my horse, Minerva, I relax and enjoy an apple tart with a pot of strong English tea.

1 small Golden Delicious apple (about ¼ pound), cored, pared, and thinly sliced
2 teaspoons lemon juice
1 flour tortilla (6-inch diameter)

1 teaspoon confectioners' sugar, sifted, divided
Dash each ground nutmeg and ground cinnamon
½ medium kiwi fruit (about 2 ounces), sliced

1. Preheat oven to 400°F. In small bowl combine apple slices and lemon juice and turn to coat; set aside.
2. On nonstick cookie sheet place tortilla. Decoratively arrange apple slices over tortilla. Sprinkle with ½ teaspoon sugar and the spices. Bake until golden, about 15 minutes.
3. Let cool slightly; arrange kiwi slices over apple slices, sprinkle with remaining sugar, and serve.

Each serving provides: 1 Bread; 1½ Fruits; 20 Optional Calories

Per serving: 167 calories; 3 g protein; 3 g fat; 37 g carbohydrate; 60 mg calcium; 145 mg sodium; 0 mg cholesterol; 4 g dietary fiber

▪ *Sweet Potato-Pecan Pie* ▪

Makes 6 servings

3 eggs, divided
15 ounces peeled cooked sweet
   potatoes, mashed
¼ cup sour cream
2 tablespoons firmly packed
   light brown sugar
1 tablespoon granulated sugar
2 teaspoons margarine, melted
1¼ teaspoons vanilla extract,
   divided

¼ teaspoon each salt and
   ground cinnamon
⅛ teaspoon each ground
   nutmeg and ground allspice
2 tablespoons each firmly
   packed dark brown sugar
   and dark corn syrup
1 refrigerated ready-to-bake
   9-inch pie crust
18 pecan halves (¾ ounce)

1. In medium mixing bowl lightly beat 2 eggs; add sweet potatoes, sour cream, light brown sugar, granulated sugar, margarine, 1 teaspoon vanilla, the salt, cinnamon, nutmeg, and allspice and stir to thoroughly combine. Set aside.

2. In small bowl combine remaining egg, the dark brown sugar, corn syrup, and remaining ¼ teaspoon vanilla, mixing well; set aside.

3. Preheat oven to 350°F. Spray 8-inch pie plate with nonstick cooking spray. Between 2 sheets of wax paper roll pie crust into a 10-inch circle. Fit dough into prepared pie plate; flute or crimp edges. Transfer potato mixture to pie crust; decoratively arrange pecan halves over filling. Spread dark brown sugar mixture over pecan halves, making sure that mixture touches edges of crust; bake for 45 to 50 minutes (until top is puffed and browned and a knife, inserted in center, comes out dry). Serve warm or chilled.

Each serving provides: ½ Fat; ¾ Protein; 1½ Breads; 160 Optional Calories

Per serving: 393 calories; 6 g protein; 18 g fat; 51 g carbohydrate; 53 mg calcium; 365 mg sodium; 110 mg cholesterol; 2 g dietary fiber

Variation: Sweet Potato Pie—Omit pecan halves; proceed as directed. In Serving Information reduce Fat to ¼ and Protein to ½.

Per serving: 369 calories; 6 g protein; 16 g fat; 50 g carbohydrate; 53 mg calcium; 365 mg sodium; 110 mg cholesterol; 2 g dietary fiber

▪ *Three-Layer Marble-Nut Cake* ▪

Makes 12 servings

At Cousin Lucy's when I was little, Frances's Magic Cake was a three-layer marble wonder. Here's my version, with the addition of walnuts, pecans, or almonds.

¾ cup granulated sugar, divided
2 ounces chopped walnuts, pecans, or almonds
1 tablespoon ground cinnamon
2¼ cups cake flour
1 tablespoon double-acting baking powder

½ cup whipped butter
¼ cup plus 2 teaspoons margarine
1½ cups plain low-fat yogurt
2 eggs
2 teaspoons vanilla extract
1 tablespoon plus 1 teaspoon unsweetened cocoa powder

1. Preheat oven to 350°F. Spray 10-inch tube pan with nonstick cooking spray; set aside.
2. In small mixing bowl combine 2 tablespoons sugar, the nuts, and cinnamon; set aside. On sheet of wax paper sift together flour and baking powder; set aside.
3. In large mixing bowl combine remaining sugar, the butter, and margarine and, using mixer on high speed, beat until light and fluffy. Add yogurt, eggs, and vanilla and continue beating until blended. Stir in flour mixture until combined.
4. Spread half of the batter in prepared pan; sprinkle half of the nut mixture over batter. Sift cocoa over remaining batter and fold until combined. Spread cocoa-batter mixture over nut mixture in tube pan; sprinkle with remaining nut mixture.
5. Using a knife, cut through batter several times to swirl. Bake in middle of center oven rack for 40 to 45 minutes (until golden brown and a toothpick, inserted in center, comes out dry). Let cool in pan for 5 minutes. Invert cake onto wire rack and cool completely.

Each serving provides: ¼ Milk; 1½ Fats; ½ Protein; 1 Bread; 95 Optional Calories

Per serving: 262 calories; 5 g protein; 13 g fat; 33 g carbohydrate; 127 mg calcium; 229 mg sodium; 47 mg cholesterol; 0.4 g dietary fiber

▪ *Honey-Banana Health Drink* ▪

Makes 1 serving

1 cup low-fat buttermilk
  (1% milk fat)
½ medium banana (about
  3 ounces), peeled and sliced

2 teaspoons honey
½ teaspoon wheat germ
3 to 4 ice cubes

1. Chill a 12-ounce glass. In blender combine all ingredients except ice; process at high speed until smooth. With motor running add ice cubes, 1 at a time, processing until mixture is thick and frothy.

2. Pour into chilled glass and serve immediately.

Each serving provides: 1 Milk; 1 Fruit; 65 Optional Calories

Per serving: 196 calories; 9 g protein; 3 g fat; 37 g carbohydrate; 289 mg calcium; 259 mg sodium; 10 mg cholesterol; 1 g dietary fiber

▪ *Melba Shake* ▪

Makes 2 servings, about 1¼ cups each

½ cup raspberries
1 medium peach (about
   6 ounces), blanched, peeled,
   pitted, and chopped
½ cup skim or nonfat milk
½ cup low-fat buttermilk
   (1% milk fat)

1 tablespoon plus 1 teaspoon
   granulated sugar
1 teaspoon vanilla extract
6 ice cubes

1. Chill two 12-ounce glasses. In blender combine all ingredients except ice; process until smooth. With motor running add ice cubes, 1 at a time, processing until mixture is thick and frothy. **2.** Pour into chilled glasses and serve immediately.

Each serving provides: ½ Milk; 1 Fruit; 45 Optional Calories

Per serving: 134 calories; 5 g protein; 1 g fat; 27 g carbohydrate; 159 mg calcium; 96 mg sodium; 4 mg cholesterol; 3 g dietary fiber

▪ *English Toffee* ▪

Makes 8 servings, 2 pieces each

Guaranteed to take me back to the London of my childhood. Make a big batch, wrap individually, and take a few in a basket when visiting a friend's house.

½ cup firmly packed dark
brown sugar
2 tablespoons plus 2 teaspoons
margarine

2 tablespoons water
2 teaspoons honey
Dash cream of tartar

1. Spray 6½ × 6½-inch baking dish with nonstick cooking spray; set aside. In 1½-quart nonstick saucepan combine all ingredients. Cook over medium-high heat, stirring constantly with a wire whisk, until sugar is dissolved.

2. Set candy thermometer in pan and cook over high heat until mixture comes to a rolling boil, thermometer reaches 290°F, and a small amount of mixture dropped into very cold water snaps easily (hard crack stage), 5 to 7 minutes (*do not stir*).

3. Pour sugar mixture into prepared baking dish and let harden slightly. Using a knife, score toffee into 16 equal pieces. Let cool completely. Break into scored pieces and wrap each piece individually in wax paper.

Each serving provides: 1 Fat; 65 Optional Calories

Per serving: 91 calories; trace protein; 4 g fat, 15 g carbohydrate; 13 mg calcium; 49 mg sodium; 0 mg cholesterol; 0 g dietary fiber

Epilogue

Dear Reader,

I've often thought what a good thing it is that I am British. With all the problems of low self-esteem and self-destruction I had, I remained far too English to go to a shrink. If I'd had a good analyst, maybe I would never have become an actress. Or written a book.

My life has changed. I know it has helped me, writing this book, and I hope that reading it can help you too. Help you to know that you are not alone. That you can stop the treadmill going around and around.

You *can* do it. This is not the dress rehearsal.

This is your life.

This is living!

Lynn Redgrave

Indexes

INDEX:
My Story/Challenges

INDEX:
Here Comes Food